BERKELEY GUIDEBOOK

BERKELEY GUIDEBOOK

Adventures at the Vortex of Ideas and Audacity

PAMELA GLEASON
with foreward by Adam Hochschild

PATHS LLC

CONTENTS

Map of Berkeley and the Places Profiled in this Guidebook — ix

FOREWARD — 1

INTRODUCTION — 3

THE SACRED LAND OF XUČYUN — 11
The West Berkeley Shellmound — 12

37°52′N — 37
The Campanile Bell Tower — 38

VICTORIAN BLUEPRINTS — 59
Old South Hall — 60

BEAR TERRITORY — 85
Bear Spotting On The UC Berkeley Campus — 86

THE ALMOND COOKIE REVOLUTIONARIES — 99
The Berkeley Marina — 100

LOIS THE PIE QUEEN — 113
Lois The Pie Queen — 114

BERKELIUM, CALIFORNIUM AND THE RED ENEMY — 131
Moe's Books — 132

THE FREE SPEECH MOVEMENT — 153
Sproul Plaza — 154

PEOPLE'S PARK — 173
"A People's History Of Telegraph Avenue" Mural — 174

THE BLACK PANTHER PARTY AND THE THIRD WORLD FRONT — 193
Telegraph Avenue — 194

FIRES AND FAULTS — 221
Tilden Park — 222

BLEEDING BLUE AND GOLD — 241
Memorial Stadium — 242

HOW BERKELEY CAN YOU BE? — 263
Berkeley Bowl — 264

EPILOGUE — 287

ENDNOTES — 299

APPENDIX — 335

About The Author — 337

For Mom and Dad with love and admiration.

MAP OF BERKELEY AND THE PLACES PROFILED IN THIS GUIDEBOOK

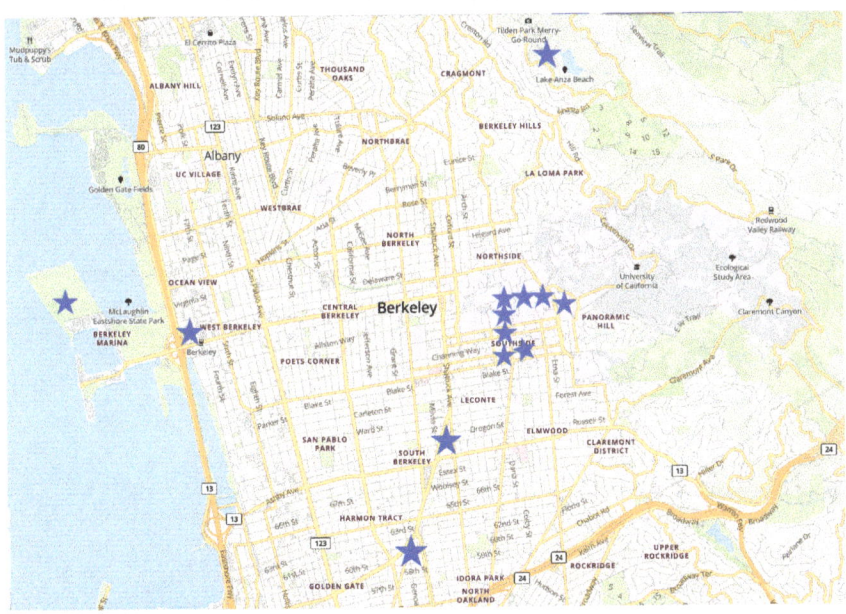

Each blue star on this map of the City of Berkeley represents a location featured in this Berkeley Guidebook. The locations on and around campus are within easy walking distance from each other.
Courtesy of City of Berkeley Open Data.

Foreward

BY ADAM HOCHSCHILD

Despite where it appears on the map, Berkeley is not quite in the United States. With a distinct culture and a history all its own, it has long deserved a guidebook worthy of it, and that's the volume you are holding in your hands. For years, those lucky enough to have taken Pamela Gleason's legendary walking tours of this unique city have wanted its essence preserved in print, and now we have it.

This is not a conventional guidebook, giving restaurants different numbers of stars and classifying hotels by their degree of luxury. That, you can find elsewhere. This is a guide to more important things, going back in history to the days when our beloved city was inhabited by the Ohlone people, and Europeans thought California was an island. (They were not entirely wrong about that: this is not a state like its neighbors.) It's a book that will tell you about Berkeleyans you've heard about, from Robert Oppenheimer to Dorothea Lange, and about those you didn't know, like Lois the Pie Queen.

It will also tell you about the tensions that this stretch of Bayside land has seen: between the Ohlone and early settlers, between Blacks and whites, between people who want to preserve the suburban feel of neighborhoods and those eager to build housing that working people can afford. It will tell you about things that you can see, like the People's Park mural, and those you can't see, like BART tracks slicing South Berkeley in two—which aren't there because activists forced them to be built underground.

It will tell you about other activists who have helped to define Berkeley's remarkable culture, from the great Mario Savio and his fellow crusaders of the Free Speech Movement to the three energetic women who prevented vast tracts of San Francisco Bay from being filled in. These are the sorts of people who have made Berkeley the place it is, and who could have flourished nowhere else.

I've learned from these pages all sorts of Berkeley lore that I previously didn't know: about the full significance of shellmounds, about the fact that in the late 19th century a majority of the Berkeley campus's students were women, and about a key section of seats in Memorial Stadium that show the effect of shifting tectonic plates below ground and are usually reserved for fans of the other team.

Those shifting plates, by the way, could mean that Berkeley as we know it may not be here forever. The city is built atop one of the continent's major earthquake faults, and even the very best construction engineering may not protect us from the big quake that scientists say is coming. And if the Big One doesn't get us, flames might. The last few years have seen Berkeley's skies dark with the smoke of wildfires. Two deadly ones already ravaged parts of town in the 20th century. Its very vulnerability makes this extraordinary city more precious than ever, and lucky to have found exactly the right chronicler in Pamela Gleason.

Introduction

Barrington Hall entrance in 1989.
Courtesy of Wikimedia Commons.

Berkeley is a choose-your-own adventure kind of place. I punched my E ticket the day I moved to Berkeley in 1985. I parked my oil-smoke-spewing Toyota Corolla on Dwight Avenue, not far from the entrance to Barrington Hall, my new home. I'd chosen Barrington because it was the biggest student cooperative in Berkeley. As a transfer student from UC Riverside, I wanted to make lots of friends as quickly as I could. Barrington was also one of the cheapest place to live: $1100 a semester, including meals and five and a half hours of house chores per week. The sign outside said, "Welcome to Barrington, kids! Please keep your hands and arms inside the ride at all times... Do not attempt to exit until the ride has come to a complete stop."

Inside, Barrington wall murals celebrated rebellion. "Fuck The Dead!" was Barrington's unofficial motto, imploring its residents to reject old-fashioned ideas and etiquette. Clothing was optional. One bearded resident wore a flowy white wedding dress and veil, exemplifying Barrington's anything-goes vibe.

Mealtimes were a free-for-all. Cooking was a house chore that required crowd control skills. Before mealtime, hungry Barringtonians drummed their silverware on the Formica tabletops, loud enough to generate complaints from neighbors. When food came out from the industrial-sized kitchen, residents swarmed and grabbed portions in great handfuls.

The Alternative Kitchen, which served only vegetarian and vegan food, was a refuge. A mural on the wall of the Alternative Kitchen depicted the last supper, with the 12 disciples as vegetables: Jesus was a carrot, Judas a beet.

Barrington's infamous "Wine Dinners" featured LSD-laced punch and all-night punk rock shows. Bands like the Dead Kennedys, Black Flag, and Primus turned the dining room into a steaming, swirling mosh pit of flailing arms and legs. Less raucous party-goers clustered in the stairwells, riding out their altered state of mind by clutching onto each other for safety.

Primus wrote the song "Frizzle Fry" on their album *Tales From the Punchbowl* in tribute to Barrington parties. After a couple of deaths from overdoses—including, sadly, a quiet guy from my high school—leaders of the Berkeley Student Cooperative voted to close Barrington in 1989.

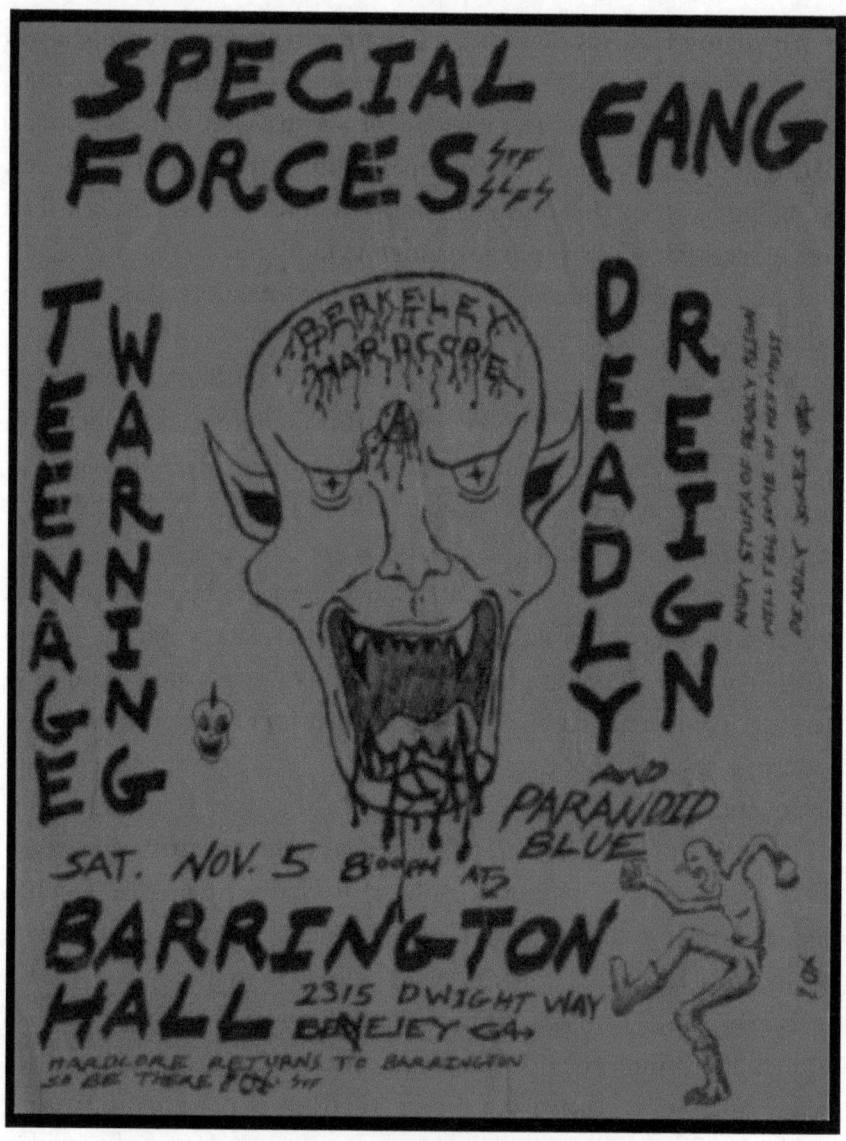

Barrington Hall Wine Dinner poster for November 5, 1983, featuring hardcore punk bands Special Forces Fang, Teenage Warning, Deadly Reign, and Paranoid Blue.
Courtesy of the Cornell Library.

Street-corner drug dealers were on every major street in Berkeley in the 1980s and 1990s. I spent jail time with several of them. One evening, after picking up a barbecued beef brisket dinner at Everett and Jones Barbecue, a police officer caught me making an illegal U-turn on San

Pablo Avenue. After I pulled over, the officer called for backup. Once I was surrounded, the officer read me my Miranda rights and informed me of a warrant out for my arrest. The parking tickets I'd amassed as a student had doubled and tripled with penalty fees.

I climbed into the backseat of the police car for the ride to the Berkeley Jail on Martin Luther King Jr. Way. A tow truck hauled away my car with my barbecue brisket still in the front seat.

After posing for my mugshot and getting inked for fingerprints, I was allowed one phone call. I called my supervisor to let her know that I'd be detained for a couple of days. I hung up feeling pretty certain I'd lost my new job.

My cell block mates found my unpaid parking ticket arrest amusing, but they were careful not to hurt my feelings about it. They welcomed me into the sisterhood of Berkeley's sex workers and drug dealers. With chuckles and smiles, they gossiped about their work colleagues and offered back rubs and advice, like telling me I could claim to be pregnant to get an extra dessert on my meal tray. Most of them worked on or near San Pablo Avenue, where I'd made my illegal U-turn.

That night I slept on a bare metal bunk bed, with no way to block out the reruns of "The Phil Donahue Show" and "Gilligan's Island" blaring from the TVs bolted to the ceiling. The next morning, I rode on the jail bus to the Santa Rita Jail, where they lock up the Bay Area's most serious criminals. On the freeway, I could see the drivers in the cars around me staring at me and my jail sisters. Maybe they were guessing what crimes we had committed.

At the Santa Rita Jail, we walked single-file past a large group of jailed men, who hooted and catcalled us. The guards passed out cheese sandwich lunches, which set off cheerful round of bartering between a dozen or so of my fellow inmates. When I was told to put on an orange jumpsuit, I refused. Then I was ordered onto another jail bus, back to the Berkeley Jail again, put in a dark cramped holding cell.

One by one, the jailers hustled the prisoners out of the holding cell and through a nearby door. When it was my turn, I stumbled through the door, temporarily blinded by the bright lights. Once my eyes adjusted, I could see that I was standing in the prisoner pen in front of a gray-bearded judge in dark robes. There were about 20 people in the courtroom audience, silently staring at me. I immediately recognized one of my work colleagues in the audience. Next to her was a large, bright-colored designer bag, which I later learned was stuffed with several thousand dollars to pay for my bail.

I don't remember if I pleaded guilty or no contest. The judge released me for time served, which erased all of my parking fines. I paid a couple hundred dollars to get my car back from Hustead's Towing lot on Durant Avenue, where it was impounded. For several days, the inside of my car smelled like spoiled meat. Now I'm careful to pay my Berkeley parking tickets on time.

I joined another kind of sisterhood in the late 1990s, when I found a $250-a-month summer sublet in a women's cooperative in South Berkeley, called Harmon House. Harmon House was on Harmon Avenue, the same street where Shyamala Gopalan Harris brought her daughters Kamala and Maya in the late 1960s for Sunday gatherings to study Black writers and listen to "Aretha, Coltrane, Miles," according to Kamala Harris' memoir, *The Truths We Hold: An American Journey*.

At Harmon House, I slept in the attic and took care of an all-black cat named Little Feat. Little Feat's owner left me homeopathic tinctures labeled "Calm Kitty," "Happy Kitty," and "Healthy Kitty," along with the phone number of Little Feat's pet psychic. I shared the house with a ever-changing cast of between five to seven women-identifying housemates, including a circus performer, a full-time anti-war activist, a Lindy Hop dancer, a bellydancer, a professional gardener, a doula, and an AIDS rights activist. There was also a bullet hole in the living room wall, but no one knew the story behind it.

Harmon House, women's cooperative in South Berkeley, hosted an annual erotica-themed party. This is the Love and Libations Party invitation featuring the six party hosts in imagined costumes.
Courtesy of Pam Gleason.

We took turns doing the Harmon House chores, like rinsing and hanging plastic bags to dry for reuse, alongside making the weekly trip for two full grocery carts of food from the Berkeley Bowl. The shopping list had "white death" listed as the code name for sugar, while housemates could pencil in specialty items like bee pollen and kumquats. I remember that these excursions tried my patience because of the time it took to find the right items from Berkeley Bowl's enormous selection of fresh produce and health foods.

Harmon House had its share of wild parties, though not on the scale of Barrington's Wine Dinners. I'd like to forget the erotica-themed party at which we decided to host a kissing booth. Each Harmon House resident signed up for an hour-long kissing shift. A man dressed in nothing but Saran Wrap showed up on my shift. He had terrible breath and after my shift I spent the rest of the party dodging his amorous pursuit. That night I had to kick a dominatrix-styled fairy princess and a cowboy with nothing under his chaps out of my bed so that I could get some sleep.

The $250 per month rent at the Harmon House attracted dreamers and creative types. Nowadays it's hard to find rent in Berkeley for under $2,000 per month, unless you can sleep in the same bedroom with someone else. A colleague told me about a group of eight students sharing a one bedroom apartment. The high cost of living means there aren't many up-and-coming artists, or working class families with young children around any more. Most of Berkeley's teachers and firefighters commute in from elsewhere.

Part of the reason Berkeley is so expensive is that it's at the center of new developments in AI technology. Cerebral Valley has replaced Silicon Valley as the home of the hottest new start-ups. So far, all of the huge new apartment buildings clustered around the downtown area haven't made Berkeley any more affordable.

What's next for Berkeley? I'm sure we'll be surprised all over again. As for myself, the ride just keeps on getting more interesting. I hope you'll enjoy it as much as I do.

The Sacred Land of Xučyun

"Indigenous peoples have the right to the lands, territories and resources which they have traditionally owned, occupied or otherwise used or acquired."

—Article 26, 61/29, United Nations Declaration on the Rights of Indigenous Peoples, September 13, 2007

The West Berkeley Shellmound

Corrina Gould in 2020, on the pavement of Spenger's parking lot at the West Berkeley Shellmound site where her ancestors are buried.
Courtesy of Peter Bittner.

One of North America's largest and most sacred Indigenous burial grounds remains under the pavement in Berkeley, in a three-square-block area where the University Avenue railroad overpass connects to the Interstate 880 Freeway. Recent estimates are that the West Berkeley Shellmound burial ground may be somewhere between 6,000 to 10,000 years old. It's the oldest of the 435 identified shellmound burial grounds encircling the San Francisco Bay. Hundreds of generations of Indigenous families were buried at this site.

Berkeley's Indigenous families chose to lay their loved ones to rest along the waterfront, where the now-culverted Strawberry Creek delta empties into the Bay. Each grave was covered with an arrangement of seashells. Year after year, descendents paid tribute to the graves of their family members and ancestors with more and more shells, layering millions upon millions of shells on the burial grounds. The base of the West Berkeley Shellmound eventually spread over three-square-blocks of land, making it one of the ancient world's largest man-made structures. Its height soared two stories high before Gold Rush settlers and profiteers carted off the above-ground portion for fertilizer.

Nels Nelson took this photograph of what remained of the upper portion of the West Berkeley Shellmound in 1907. Farmers loaded the nitrogen rich burial ground material into horse carts.
Courtesy of the Bancroft Library.

On a couple of blocks of sidewalk pavement, activists traced the outline of the mound's base with white paint to show the West Berkeley Shellmound's original size. Under the pavement, the deepest part of the West Berkeley Shellmound's base is still intact. If the above-ground portion of the West Berkeley Shellmound hadn't been destroyed, it would be visible from space.

UC Berkeley graduate student Nels C. Nelson gave the West Berkeley Shellmound the identification label CA-Ala-307 when he mapped 425 Bay Area shellmounds for his Master's thesis in 1907. By that time, most of West Berkeley Shellmound was already gone, and profiteers turned their attention to the Emeryville Shellmound, which measured some 350 feet in diameter and 40 feet in height before its top portion was removed with a steam shovel. Nelson and others collected bones and sacred objects they'd excavated from the Bay Area's shellmounds and stored them in the basement below the Hearst gymnasium, where a jumble of Indigenous peoples bones and objects were kept haphazardly.

In 1876 entrepreneurs built an amusement park named Shellmound Park on top of the Emeryville Shellmound, a sacred burial site across from Alcatraz Island. The park included a race track, picnic areas, shooting galleries, saloons and pavilions for music and dancing.
Courtesy of the Bancroft Library.

The last Ohlone burial at the West Berkeley Shellmound likely took place around 200 years ago. From 1769 to 1834, Spanish colonizers forced Indigenous people in California to live on mission settlements, obliging them to abandon their languages and customs for their conversion to Catholicism. The late UC Berkeley demographer Sherburne Friend Cook estimated that 37,000 Indigenous adults died during their forced cooperation—almost half of the total who lived in the mission settlements.

Franciscan padres ordered survivors to bury the dead in shallow graves around the mission buildings. After the padres performed the required Catholic burial rites, mourners sometimes placed abalone shells at the mission grave sites, covertly observing their pre-colonial burial traditions.

The Pacific Railroad Act of 1864 transformed the Berkeley waterfront into an industrial zone, with railroad tracks laid directly across the West Berkeley Shellmound. Beginning in the 1890's, the Pacific Guano Company sold cartloads of the nitrate-rich shellmound material for fertilizer and gunpowder.

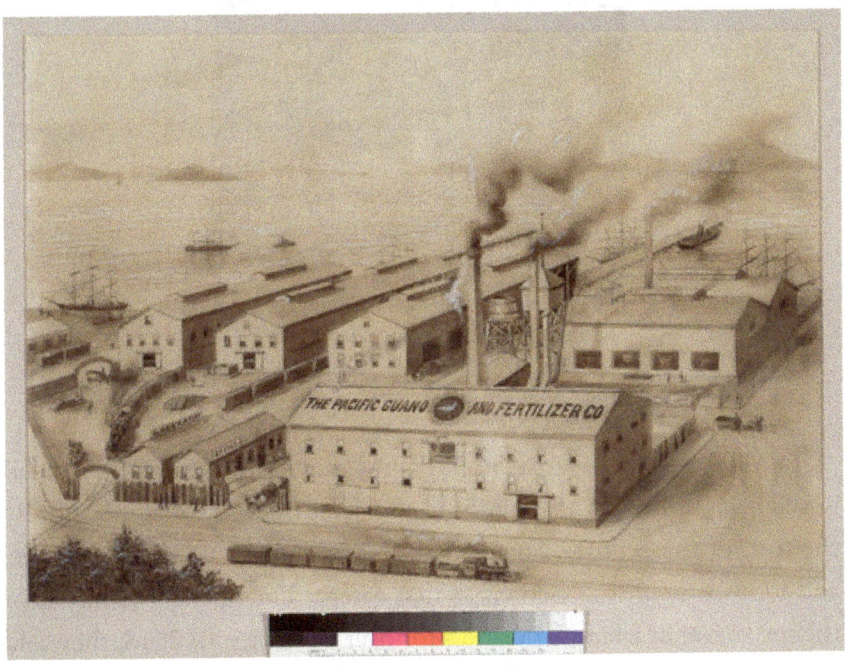

The Pacific Guano Company on Second Street and Hearst Avenue sold fertilizer from the West Berkeley Shellmound. Drawing by George Henry Burgess c. 1897.
Courtesy of the Oakland Public Library.

A report by Archeo-Tec, Inc., published in 2000, later concluded that "the vast majority of debris and artifacts making up the original shellmound were stripped away and removed between 1853 and 1910 and sold as useful products such as garden fertilizer, chicken feed, grading material and road amendments."

Repaved holes in Spenger's parking lot show where archeologists bored into the West Berkeley Shellmound burial site.
Courtesy of the 2014 Archeo-Tec testing report.

In 1890, young Bavarian immigrant Johann Spenger set up a stand to sell beer and clams at the foot of the West Berkeley Shellmound. By the turn of the century, Spenger's Fish Grotto had a regular clientele, and locals touted it as Berkeley's first eatery. The Spenger family kept the restaurant as a family business for over a century. In 2018, they sold Spenger's and its adjoining parking lot to developers.

After several years of court battles to preserve what's left of the West Berkeley Shellmound under Spenger's parking lot, Indigenous activists prevailed. In 2024, Ohlone matriarchs Corrina Gould and Johnella LaRose of the Sogorea Te` Land Trust partnered with the Kataly Foundation and the City of Berkeley to purchase the 2.2 acre

Spenger's parking lot portion of the West Berkeley Shellmound for $27 million. The matriarchs' dream is to create a public park in honor of their ancestors and return the site to its natural beauty by restoring a segment of Strawberry Creek and bringing back its lush habitat. They want the park to feature an educational center to teach school children California's deepest history.

The Sacred Land of Xučyun

Before it was called Berkeley, the most sacred Indigenous land in the San Francisco Bay Area was called Xučyun. Xučyun (HOO-chin), commonly spelled Huchuin, means "homeland" in the Chochenyo Ohlone language. Huchuin's location, with a direct view of the Bay's opening to the Pacific Ocean, is the reason it's so revered.

Sunset over the Golden Gate opening to the Pacific Ocean with Berkeley in the foreground.
Courtesy of Pam Gleason.

The Ohlone believe Huchuin is physically aligned to honor the ancestors and their journey to heaven. It is a place of prayer and celebration, where families gathered for days of dancing and singing in tribute to those who came before them. It's akin to Mecca and Jerusalem in spiritual significance to Northern California's Indigenous people, but thousands of years older. The Ohlone believe that from the beginning of time, Huchuin was blessed with a view that represents the boundless possibilities of the human spirit.

Directly east of Huchuin is the great mountain of Tuyshtak, the highest peak in the San Francisco Bay Area. Tuyshtak means "at the dawn of time." Mount Diablo is its colonial name. Thousands of years of Indigenous storytellers tell the legend of Tuyshtak, where humankind began.

After rising from behind Tuyshtak, the sun arcs overhead and dazzles the Huchuin landscape. The San Francisco Bay's enormous expanse shimmers in the changing hues. Moments of overcast gray sometimes roll through and then the sun instantly reappears, bright and vibrant. At the end of the day's journey, in crescendos of gold, pink, and purple, the sun settles west of the Bay. From Huchuin, the sun's soft farewell illuminates the opening of the Golden Gate and the vast Pacific Ocean beyond. According to Ohlone elders, it's the sky just above the ocean's horizon where the ancestors gather in their eternal celebration, beckoning the living to join them one day.

The land of Huchuin is sacred because it's the only place on land that holds this eternal view—from Tuyshtak's mountain sunrise to the sunset on the ocean's horizon, where the ancestors await. From Huchuin, mankind's story can be traced from birth to heaven, from sunrise to sunset.

Twice a year, in early February and late October, the sun sets directly behind the San Francisco Bay's opening, creating a spectacular "Berkeleyhenge" sunset. Nowadays this alignment perfectly frames the Golden Gate Bridge, which opened in 1937. Before colonization, Huchuin's revered alignment was the reason as many as 300 generations of the Bay Area's Indigenous people chose Huchuin's shoreline for their loved ones' last resting place. At the water's edge, with its direct view of the opening to the Pacific Ocean, generations of families gently arranged their loved ones' remains in beds of seashells, adorning them with sacred amulets, offering prayers and blessings to accompany the spirits' final journey to an eternity of sunsets.

Over thousands of years, the Huchuin shoreline burial place became a man-made mountain of shells, layered deeply in tender affection and prayers. At the same time that Egypt's enslaved toiled on the pyramids of Giza, Huchuin's sacred monument grew taller and dearer, making Huchuin the home of one of the world's largest, longest-enduring, and most heartfelt tributes ever created.

Councilmember Sophie Hahn
City of Berkeley, District 5

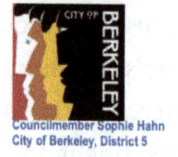

CONSENT CALENDAR
October 11, 2022

To: Honorable Mayor and Members of the City Council
From: Councilmember Hahn (Author)
Mayor Jesse Arreguín (Co-Sponsor)
Subject: Land Acknowledgement Recognizing Berkeley as the Ancestral, Unceded Home of the Ohlone people.

RECOMMENDATION

1. Adopt the Land Acknowledgement Statement Resolution recognizing that Berkeley is the ancestral, unceded home of the Ohlone people.
2. Display the Land Acknowledgement in writing at all in-person or online Regular meetings of the City Council and read the Acknowledgement at the first Regular meeting of each month in which Regular City Council meetings are held.
3. Recommend to all Berkeley Commissions, Committees, Boards, and other elected and appointed City entities to consider inclusion of the Land Acknowledgement in meeting practices and direct the City Manager to convey a copy of this Item and Resolution to all such entities for reference.
4. Direct the City Manager to post the Land Acknowledgement or a prominent link to the Acknowledgement on the home page of the City's website and to create a webpage dedicated to Ohlone history and culture.
5. Now and in the future, consider additional more substantive reparative and restorative actions, including but not limited to those described under the heading "Actions/Alternatives Considered."

SUMMARY
Acknowledging that the City of Berkeley rests upon the ancestral lands of the Chochenyo speaking Lisjan Ohlone people brings attention to their centuries of resistance to colonial violence and reminds our City and community of the need to take concrete restorative actions.

The settlers of California, primarily Europeans seeking religious converts, agricultural land and economic opportunity during the gold rush, committed one of the most egregious genocides in history. Settlers murdered 80 percent of Indigenous people in the state from

---

City of Berkeley Land Acknowledgement Statement Adopted on October 11, 2022 by the City Council and read aloud at the beginning of every City Council meeting.
Courtesy of the City of Berkeley.

The name Huchuin has made a comeback, thanks to land acknowledgement statements which UC Berkeley faculty and administrative leaders routinely read aloud at the beginning of events and conferences.

Dr. LaNada War Jack, Author, Leader of Third World Strike, and Member of the Shoshone Bannock Tribe, acknowledges that Berkeley is Ohlone land in a video played at Cal's opening football game at Memorial Stadium on August 31, 2024.
Courtesy of the American Indian Graduate Program (AIGP).

The purpose of the land acknowledgement statement is to honor thousands of years of Indigenous land stewardship. Indigenous advocates encourage modifying the statements as "living documents" to ensure factual and geographical accuracy. Soon after the first versions of Berkeley's land acknowledgement statements, community members added phrases like "unceded stolen land" and a pledge to "continue to create meaningful actions that uphold the intention of this land acknowledgment." Activists hope that these acknowledgments of the history of the land will go beyond mere words, leading to concrete actions and justice.

What is not yet acknowledged is what a terrible name "Berkeley" is in the first place—especially noteworthy for a university town whose residents and scholars have for generations claimed to be at the vanguard of eradicating systemic and structural racism.

In 2023, Trinity College Dublin faculty scrubbed the name "Berkeley" from one of their libraries because of the overwhelming evidence that its namesake George Berkeley was a racist and slave trafficker. UC Berkeley's faculty and administrative leaders, who routinely read aloud land acknowledgement statements recognizing the unceded land of Huchuin, have not to date indicated if the name "Berkeley" is under review. The university's Building Name Review Committee's mandate clearly states on its chancellor.berkeley.edu website that it will "Consider and advise if other named places that share that of a proposed un-naming (officially or unofficially named) should be included in an un-naming process." If a proposal to consider unnaming Berkeley was submitted, the Building Name Review Committee has not made it public.

Activists want more than unnaming buildings, they want practical reparations. Symbolic gestures are everywhere in Berkeley, but civic leaders agree that the real social justice work has just begun.

"So remember, I said that our ancestors were super smart no matter where they come from?" Corrina Gould, Chair and traditional spokesperson for the Confederated Villages of Lisjan Ohlone, asked a group of 4th graders on a field trip to the Oakland Museum, recorded on video in 2016 for the museum's website.

"Yes!" the chorus of students replied.

"Okay, so the way my ancestors were super smart is that they pretended they were Mexicans and they lived on a ranch in Pleasanton until it was safe for us to come out and talk about being Indian," Gould continued.

"We went through three successions of genocide in a very quick time. It was first the Spaniards, then Mexico right after, then America right after that. The United States government asks you to create all of these documents to prove you are a tribe while you are running from genocide."

Corrina Gould, Chair and Traditional Spokesperson for the Confederated Villages of Lisjan Ohlone.
Courtesy of Peter Bittner.

Gould was one of the first to help educators update California's 4th grade curriculum to include lessons on Indigenous Californians.

Gould's grandparents were part of the Verona Band of the Ohlone. To avoid capture and relocation to Mission San Jose, a few families moved from the shore of the East Bay to a quiet valley along Alameda Creek near the Verona Train Station, close to present day Pleasanton. There, the Verona Band families quietly kept their cultural heritage alive and became collectively known as The Confederated Villages of Lisjan.

Even a short visit back to Huchuin was dangerous, so the exodus from their homeland to the Verona area was permanent.

Ohlone Park Mural on Hearst Avenue near Milvia Street depicting the creation story showing Tuyshtak, Coyote, Eagle and Hummingbird by artist Jean LaMarr.
Courtesy of Pam Gleason.

Mission San Jose was established in 1797. Its main purpose was to convert the Ohlone people who lived along the East Bay shore to Catholicism. Mission San Francisco de Asís, built in 1776, was the first mission to forcibly relocate Bay Area Ohlone. A string of 21 Spanish mission buildings, the first non-Indigenous buildings in California, were connected by El Camino Real—the Royal Road or King's Highway—from San Diego in the south to Sonoma in the north. U.S. Highway 101 of today roughly follows the old El Camino Real route from Los Angeles to San Francisco. The East Bay branch of old El Camino Real follows today's Interstate 580 and San Pablo Road through Berkeley. Hundreds of cast-iron bells commemorate the route and are a painful reminder for California's Indigenous people.

Within a few decades of the establishment of the Spanish missions, an estimated 100,000 Indigenous people—one third of the population in California—died. Measles and other diseases spread rampantly through the mission one-room dormitories, with the death toll made worse by widespread starvation and abuse. Gould and other Indigenous leaders refer to this as the first genocide, though it was largely unintentional. King Carlos III of Spain and his colonial ministers wanted the missions to produce loyal Indigenous citizens who obeyed the tenets of Catholicism. They did not intend for them to die in massive numbers. By contrast, from the beginning of California's statehood, the state's founding fathers passed laws to clear the land of Indigenous people. Some of California's first laws instigated genocide.

When California became the 31st state of the United States in 1850, one of the California Legislature's first acts was to issue investment bonds to fund "Expeditions against the Indians." The California Legislature paid out over $1 million dollars during the first years of the Gold Rush to encourage its extermination campaign. The Act for the Government Protection of the Indians made it legal to arrest Indigenous people for vagrancy. Those arrested could then be enslaved by whomever paid their bail. The state offered to pay all travel expenses to murder Indigenous men, women, and children. Further compensation was awarded with proof of each dead Indigenous person. A body part from a dead man could net as much as $25 (about $1,000 today) from the California treasury. Body parts of women and children earned lesser payouts. A typically cited bounty was $5 per body or scalp, or 25¢ per ear.

Capturing and enslaving children, especially for sale to wealthy households in the Bay Area, was even more lucrative. Indigenous boys could be sold for $200 for outdoor work. Indigenous girls sold for up to $300 for indoor work. Labor as a sex worker or housemaid was highly valued because California's population in 1850 was only 8 percent female. Parents who resisted the capture of their children were killed. "A war of extermination will continue to be waged ... until the Indian race becomes extinct," promised Peter Burnett, California's first Governor, during the State of the State Address on January 6, 1851.

California Indian Bounty Bond Issued in 1852 for $250.
Courtesy of the Bancroft Library.

Devastating public record details like these are abundant in Deborah A. Miranda's book *Bad Indians.* In *Bad Indians,* Miranda describes the harm from the California History curriculum for fourth graders that until recently muted the violence on Indigenous people. Writing a book about what her ancestors endured was, she wrote, "painful, dreaming of destruction, starved children, bones that cry."

As a panelist at the 2022 Bay Area Book Festival, Miranda addressed UC Berkeley's failure to return Indigenous human remains. "A basement full of sadness" is how she described the Hearst Museum storage area underneath the Hearst Gymnasium's swimming pool and tennis courts. Miranda shared that her daughter cried to her over the phone nearly every day after taking a part-time job cataloging the remains. "Why was a baby's white Christening gown with matching tiny white satin shoes preserved so carefully, while her ancestor's bones were strewn around haphazardly?" Miranda said her daughter asked her between sobs. Decades of UC Berkeley students, researchers, and hobbyists have pawed through the bones, sometimes taking them home for display.

This abuse is the reason UC Berkeley is repeatedly cited as the worst offender of The 1990 Native American Graves Protection and Repatriation Act of 1990 (NAGPRA). Two years after NAGPRA became law, on October 12, 1992, the City of Berkeley became the first city in the United States to celebrate Indigenous Peoples' Day in place of Columbus Day, an irony that grows starker over time. Berkeley then and now leads the world in the sheer scale of desecration of Indigenous human remains.

In 2023, Senators and Members of the US Senate Committee on Indian Affairs formally scolded UC Berkeley for its "unacceptable" failure to comply with the NAGPRA mandate to return cultural items and ancestral remains to tribal groups for repatriation. The letter cited a *ProPublica* article which reported that it would take another 70 years at the pace of its current efforts to comply with the law. "It's inexcusable, it's immoral, it's hypocritical, and it has to stop," said Committee Chair Brian Schatz (D-HI).

Alfred L. Kroeber—hand-picked by benefactress Phoebe Hearst to establish the first Anthropology Department west of the Mississippi—led UC Berkeley's collection of Indigenous remains when he became a Professor of Anthropology and the Director of the Hearst Museum of Anthropology in 1909. Kroeber used the Hearst Museum budget to reward grave diggers near and far, incentivizing researchers and hobbyists to send Indigenous human remains to amass the collection. The same year Kroeber settled into his new job at UC Berkeley, Nels C. Nelson, a Berkeley archeologist, completed a map of over 400 Bay Area shellmound burial sites—he called them "shellheaps"—making it much easier for hobbyists to find Ohlone remains.

Kroeber's harm to the Ohlone people went beyond encouraging the desecration of their ancestor's graves. In 1925, Kroeber published *The Handbook of the Indians of California,* the first scholarly book on Indigenous Californians. Kroeber declared in his book that the Ohlone were "extinct for all practical purposes." His negation of the surviving Ohlone tribespeople erased the possibility that they would be recognized by the federal government. Tribes without federal recognition cannot fully govern themselves as sovereign nations nor access federal services through the Bureau of Indian Affairs. For the Ohlone this means their ancestors' remains and sacred artifacts are mired in a red tape-ridden process to prove their provenance.

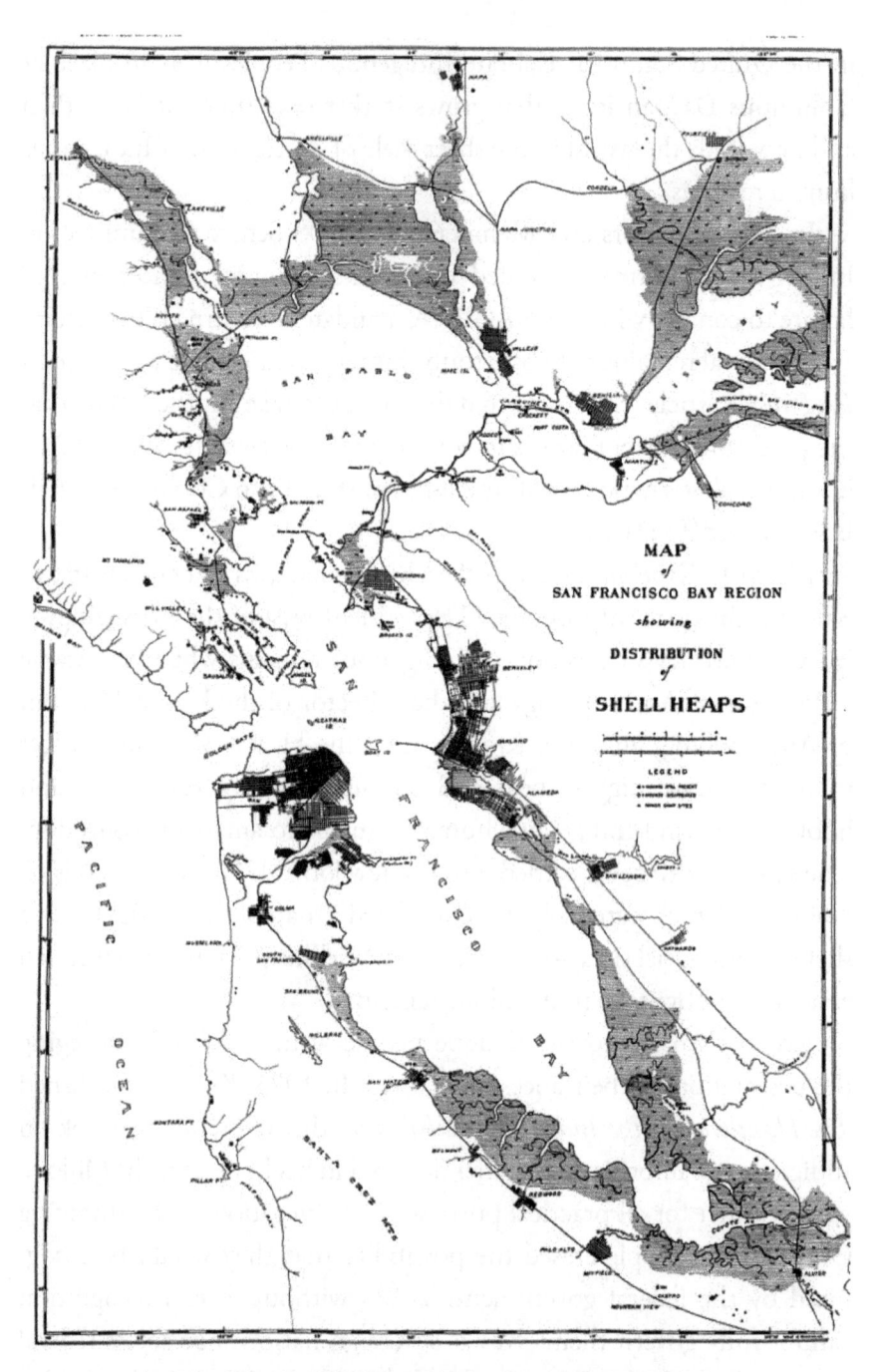

Map of Bay Area Shellmounds c. 1909 by Nels C. Nelson in
"COMPOSITION OF CALIFORNIA SHELLMOUNDS" by the University
of California Publications in American Archaeology and Ethnology.
Courtesy of the Bancroft Library.

The Muwekma Ohlone Tribe of the San Francisco Bay Area's website muwekma.org describes the painstaking, decades-long unresolved legal process for their tribal recognition.

In 1998, the Muwekma Ohlone Tribe submitted "six linear feet" of documentation to the Bureau of Indian Affairs, thereby meeting the mandatory criteria for Federal acknowledgement required under Section 83.7. As a result, the Bureau of Indian Affairs placed the Muwekma Ohlone Tribe on "Ready Status," but waitlisted it behind 21 other tribes under "Active Consideration." The Muwekma Tribal Council calculated that their case would take 24 years to rise to the top of the list of tribes waiting for recognition, so it filed a lawsuit against the Department of the Interior and the Bureau of Indian Affairs. After more than 25 years of legal wrangling, the Muwekma Tribal Council states on its website that it is still hopeful for a yet to be achieved "positive outcome as a result of our multi-year lawsuit against the Department of Interior/BIA."

Beyond his impacts on the Ohlone people, Kroeber's legacy is also tarnished by his treatment of Ishi, believed to be the last living Yahi tribe member in California.

When Ishi was a small boy, armed frontier vigilantes attacked his village and murdered 40 of his tribe members in what became known as the Three Knolls Massacre. In the years that followed, more of the Yahi people were killed, until it was thought there were no survivors left. Ishi—along with his mother, uncle, and one other family member—survived by staying out of sight. After Ishi's last family members died in 1911, Ishi came out of hiding and collapsed in front of an Oroville slaughterhouse, perhaps assuming he would be shot on the spot as an intruder. Instead, he was handcuffed and put into a makeshift jail. Kroeber realized the enormity of discovering California's "last wild man" (as the press had called Ishi) and arranged to transport Ishi from the Orville jail and take him to UC Berkeley as "an object of scientific study."

For nearly five years Ishi lived at the Anthropology Museum as a sort of living exhibit, sensationalized as "the last wild Indian" to the hoards of schoolchildren and visitors who came to see him. In 1916, Ishi died of tuberculosis. Against his last wishes, Ishi's body was autopsied and Kroeber sent Ishi's brain to the Smithsonian.

During his five years as an anthropological exhibit, Ishi was constantly sick, but before that he had never had a cold. Before he died, Ishi's last words were "You stay, I go."
Courtesy of Wikimedia Commons.

Kroeber's name was removed from UC Berkeley's campus in 2021. Amid the national conversations regarding racial justice after the murder of George Floyd, when campus was eerily quiet during the early years of the COVID-19 pandemic, a campus worker wearing a blue surgical mask chiseled off the steel block letters spelling KROEBER HALL from the side of the Anthropology and Art Practice building.

Today, UC Berkeley's Anthropology Department courtyard is one of the locations where Ohlone activists Vincent Medina and partner Louis Trevino have set up their pop-up style restaurant, Café Ohlone by Mak-'amham. Café Ohlone's menu features Indigenous ingredients and dishes and the restaurant's name for the borrowed courtyard space is "oṭṭoy," Chochenyo for a "mending of harms." Medina and Trevino welcome guests to Xučyun by telling Ohlone stories and sharing the land's sacredness through its bounty of earthy tastes.

Vincent Medina and partner Louis Trevino explain how they harvest local greens served at Café Ohlone by Mak-'amham at their Bancroft Avenue location in 2017.
Courtesy of Pam Gleason.

Medina previously spent a decade explaining the history of the San Francisco Bay Area Ohlone people for visitors at Mission Dolores Basilica, which the Spanish forced some of his Ohlone ancestors to build. His new path of retelling the Ohlone story through food earned him *Bay Nature Magazine*'s 2020 Local Hero Award. As guests enjoy Café Ohlone's menu—one that includes acorn bread, forest greens salad, smoked venison meatballs, hazelnut milk chia porridge topped with bay laurel scented blackberry coulis sauce, and wild yerba buena brewed into a mint-like tea—Medina makes one clear request: "Please don't use the past tense when you talk about our people and our culture. Please correct anyone who says the Ohlone are gone. We are here. We need your help to decolonize layers of imposed identity on us."

As Medina and Trevino teach Berkeleyans about their culture at Café Ohlone, the aforementioned Gould uses her platform as spokesperson for the Confederated Villages of Lisjan Ohlone to encourage her extended Ohlone family to dream big.

Since passing her Oakland Museum curriculum onto her daughter and other young Ohlone activists, Gould has focused on restoring the sacred land of Xučyun. Gould and her lifelong friend Johnella LaRose run the Sogorea Te` Land Trust. It's the first women-led urban Indigenous land trust in the country and "maybe even in the world," as the two like to say. Both grandmothers, the Sogorea Te` women call their efforts to restore the land "rematriation" and they call their vision ištune. Their definition of rematriation is the anti-paternalistic restoration of people "to their rightful place in sacred relationship with their ancestral land."

Ištune means dream. The focus of their dream is the rematriation places sacred to the Ohlone people. Their quest to rematriate the West Berkeley Shellmound has become world-renowned.

The website shellmound.org describes the Sogorea Te` ištune: "A 40-foot high mound covered in California poppies is envisioned, with a path spiraling up to the top and a memorial and educational center contained inside the mound." On the website, Gould further describes that "When people go up to the top they could actually see across the bay, like my ancestors would have been able to see from atop the shellmound."

In 2024, Gould and LaRose secured $27 million to purchase the West Berkeley Shellmound with funding from donations for their land tax, called "shuumi." The Katalay Foundation, which supports "the economic, political, and cultural power of Black and Indigenous communities," paid the Sogorea Te' Land Trust a shuumi of $20 million to make the purchase possible. Next, Gould and LaRose's ištune for Sogorea Te` is to build a planetarium-style classroom at the West Berkeley Shellmound, where 4th graders on a field trip would find themselves immersed in a 360° experience of what Xučyun was like for its first several thousand years of human settlement.

Rinihmu Pulte'irkne's Sunset Panel on 3.8 acres of rematriated land in the Oakland Hills near the Joaquin Miller Park Cascade.
Courtesy of artist Cece Carpio with Kahalla, in collaboration with Sogorea Te' Land Trust and the Mitiini Numma Youth Program.

At UC Berkeley, Indigenous advocacy is shedding light on the university's racist colonialist roots. Decolonizing Berkeley is the shorthand name of the class taught by Indigenous affairs expert Nazune Menka, assistant professor at the UC Berkeley School of Law. Menka's syllabus cites source after source proving UC Berkeley's failure to acknowledge or halt the harm to California's Indigenous tribes. Emotional pain is perpetuated through "loss of culture, loss of connection to the land. When you are not only losing a culture that is highly identified with the land and also erasing your ancestors from the land, that's a sense of erasure that is so profound," Menka told *Truthout* reporter Tyler Walicek in 2023.

Phenocia Bauerle, Director of the UC Berkeley Native American Student Development program, also works with university students to address the needs for tribal recognition, repatriation of native remains, and land rights. She supported the creation of a student podcast called "Indigenous United." Early episodes of the podcast explored the historical and legal ramifications of California tribal recognition, as well as the Hearst and Kroeber legacies leading to UC Berkeley's flagrant violation of NAGPRA.

In 2021, Baurele and the Native American Student Development negotiated the use of the Pelican building on campus for use for a few years by the Indigenous community for gatherings, workshops on archival research, Indigenous beading traditions, and language revitalization while the University finds a more permanent place. The name of the building comes from *The Pelican*, a student humor magazine published from 1903 to 1988 that pilloried campus life. "Pelican" is the euphemism that Cal men used at the beginning of the last century to denigrate their brainy women classmates whose noses grew too long from persistently reading books. Pelicans are also the symbol of persistence and community cooperation in Indigenous cultures.

Baurele also runs a residential living program called the Native American Theme Program. Students in the program live together in dormitory suites next to campus and participate in courses, research, and events for the Berkeley community. Monetary reparations began in the fall of 2022 when the University of California Office of the President began offering full scholarships for in-state tuition and fees for all Indigenous University of California undergraduate and graduate students, a $14,000 value. There's a catch though: only students from federally recognized tribes can benefit. Indigenous students whose ancestors lived, celebrated, and were buried in or near the sacred land of Xučyun cannot. First they must win recognition in a court system that to date has denied their existence.

With or without that federal recognition, though, the concept of monetary and land grant reparations has gained momentum. Menka's students are proving to be strong advocates for justice. The Decolonizing Berkeley syllabus cites the 2021 report "The University Land Grab: A Legacy of Profit from Indigenous Land" compiled by UC Berkeley's Centers for Educational Justice and Community Engagement, which connects the profits from the Morrill Land Grant Act and the sale of Californian land to the establishment of UC Berkeley. Decolonizing Berkeley students recognize that land back plans are costly, but many feel that restoring the sacred land of Xučyun—and properly honoring all Indigenous ancestors—is the right thing to do.

Welcome to Huichin Mural at the Shotgun Players theater on Martin Luther King Jr. Way near the Ashby BART station.
Courtesy of artist Geralyn Montano with lettering by Maybe Littlefield. Photo by Pam Gleason.

37°52′N

"Now let me welcome everybody to the wild, wild West. A state that's untouchable like Eliot Ness."

—*Dr. Dre in Tupac Shakur's "California Love" (1995)*

The Campanile Bell Tower

Celebrated Beaux-Arts architect Émile Bénard sketched a giant bell tower as the focus of his award-winning 1899 Berkeley campus design. Bénard situated the bell tower in geographic alignment with the San Francisco Bay's Golden Gate opening, just as the Arc de Triomphe in Paris leads westward as a "voie triomphale" for conquest.

Visitors to the top of the Campanile Bell Tower can observe 360° views of the San Francisco Bay Area.
Courtesy of Wikimedia Commons.

Bell towers are a Victorian symbol of progress and power. Berkeley's Campanile Bell Tower, named for its resemblance to the Campanile di San Marco in Venice, is the third-tallest freestanding bell tower in the world. It is positioned at 37°52' North directly across from the Golden Gate opening. John Galen Howard, who copied many elements of Émile Bénard's designs to build the Berkeley campus, built the Tower.

At 307 feet high, the Campanile Bell Tower reigned as the tallest structure in Berkeley for a little over a century, visible from across the San Francisco Bay. Berkeley's downtown building boom includes a new 317-foot high rise on University Avenue that is expected to help ease the housing crisis with its 599 apartment units. By comparison, the Elizabeth Bell Tower in London (nicknamed Big Ben, the name of its biggest bell) is 315 feet tall. The world's tallest freestanding Bell Tower is the Joseph Chamberlain Memorial Clock Tower at 330 feet. One of the Abraj Al Bait Towers in Mecca has a clock tower that is 1,972 feet, but it has no bells.

The Campanile's observation deck boasts one of the best 360-degree-views of the Bay Area. For a small fee, an elevator takes visitors to the top for breathtaking views of San Francisco, the Golden Gate Bridge, the Bay Bridge, the Port of Oakland, Alcatraz, and Mount Tamalpais. On a clear day, the Farallon Islands are visible just beyond the Golden Gate Bridge.

To the east, visitors on the Campanile's observation deck are treated to a bird's eye view of the 60,000-seat Golden Bears Memorial Football Stadium nestled into Strawberry Canyon. In a clearing near the stadium, the iconic "Big C" is visible, painted into the hillside. At the base of the Berkeley Hills, running from south to north under Piedmont, Gayley, and La Loma Avenues, is the Hayward Fault. To the south, visitors will notice that Telegraph Avenue—named for the area's first transcontinental telegraph lines—leads directly to downtown Oakland.

North of campus is the most affluent area of Berkeley, where buyers are hard pressed to find a house for under $2 million. The steeply graded hill area begins just a couple blocks west of the Hayward fault and rises another 1,000-feet or so to the ridge line.

Northeast of campus is the Berkeley Hills neighborhood called "Nut Hill," famous for its bohemian lifestyle. Locals aren't sure if the name "Nut Hill" comes from the nutty professor types who are from the area, or because of the legendary nut-filled Grecian urns at the Temple of Wings, built in 1911 as an open-air modern dance stage ringed by 34 concrete Corinthian columns. Bernard Maybeck designed the original blueprints for the Temple of Wings, which was partially destroyed in the Berkeley Hills Fire of 1923. From the base of the Campanile, it's about a 30-minute hike into the Berkeley Hills to get a glimpse of the Temple of Wings and the other famous Maybeck-designed houses on "Nut Hill."

The Campanile Bell Tower is next to Memorial Glade and the Bancroft and Doe Libraries.
Courtesy of Pam Gleason.

Completed in 1915, the Campanile has 61 bells—collectively called a carillon—with a piano-style keyboard made of large foot pedals. The "Great Bear Bell," the largest in the carillon, weighs 10,500 pounds. Its radiating vibrations can be deafening to visitors on the observation deck. Most days, except during final exams and semester breaks, a carillonist plays tunes. Classical melodies are the most common, but occasionally one might catch the notes of Beyoncé song or a Beatles favorite. Just before finals, the old Kipling song "They're Hangin' Danny Deever in the Morning" is played to acknowledge the gloomy mood.

The Campanile was once considered an option for graduate student housing. Instead, dinosaur bones from Los Angeles's La Brea Tar Pits sit inside the cool dark expanse. Paleontology students ride the elevator to one of the middle floors, where they can study the dinosaurs or prehistoric dire wolves, camels, horses, sloths, and mastodons also stored there.

Humans aren't the only ones to enjoy the bell tower's views: falcons are the Campanile's rockstar residents. A livestream Cal Falcons Nest Cam with regular Instagram posts provides updates for thousands of followers. Each spring, Cal Falcon fans are treated to the spectacle of the hatchlings breaking out of their eggs and contemplating their first flight. In the quiet times—when the camera is not focused on the bloody dissections of field mice—the live Falcon Cam shows the birds' enviable, awe-inspiring view from the very top of the Campanile.

Falcon drama at the roof-top nesting area on the Campanile Bell Tower is captured year-round on the calfalcons.com livestream..
Courtesy of Wikimedia Commons.

37°52′N

Berkeley sits directly across from the opening of the Golden Gate at 37°52′ North. This coordinate—first mapped by Spain to colonize California—is the reason the California lawmakers chose Berkeley for the first public university in California.

Perhaps of all the ancient treasure maps ever made, the most accurate would have a big X at 37°52′N. After a few hundred years of plundering for gold, ultimately this was the latitudinal coordinate that led to the biggest haul of gold in world history. In the Gold Rush, hundreds of thousands of fortune-seekers from around the world journeyed through the Golden Gate. As San Francisco gold rush commenced, Congress rushed to admit California into the Union as the 31st state. Today, 37°52′N continues to be a beacon for newcomers—for wealth creation, for life-changing opportunities, and for the California good life.

Juan Crespí, a balding Spanish friar with a slight frame and dusty sandals, has the distinction of being the first to find this golden X. Once in Berkeley, Crespí easily spotted the Golden Gate opening, recording and mapping the coordinate for the King's court in Madrid. Spanish ship commanders then sailed to 37°52′N to secure the Port of San Francisco. With the Golden Gate opening secured, all of California, one of the last vast uncolonized wildernesses on the planet, was ruled by Spain.

California first appeared on world maps as a wisp of an island, one of the globe's last uncharted mysteries. Before it was called California, explorers called it "terra nullius," Latin for "land belonging to no one." Mapmakers filled in these blank spaces on the maps with fanciful creatures, like dragons and cyclops.

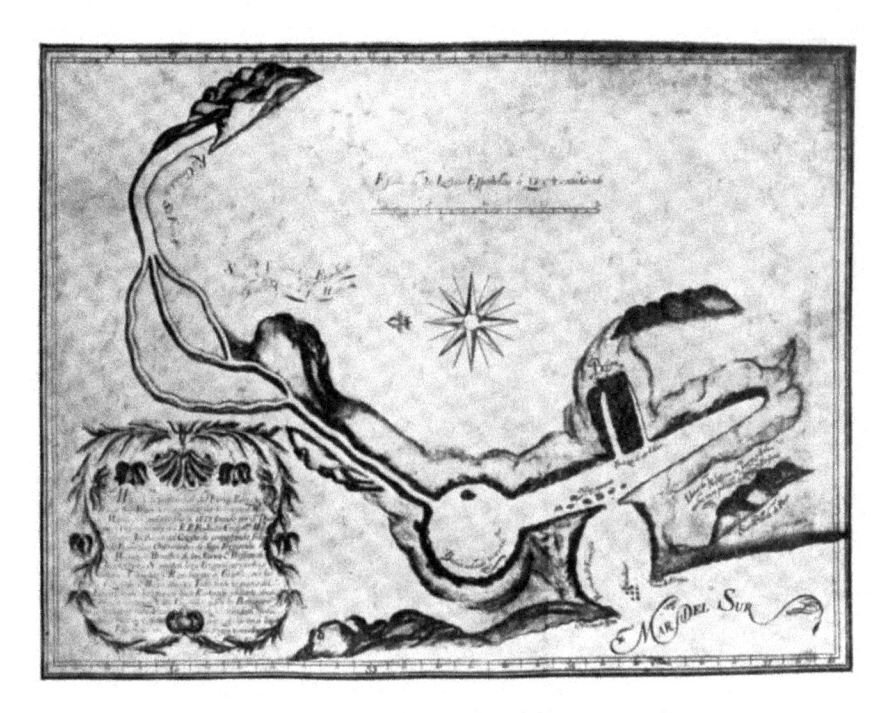

Juan Crespí's map of the San Francisco Bay in 1772.
Courtesy of the Bancroft Library.

In 1510, colonialist explorer Garci Ordóñez Rodriguez de Montalvo wrote *Las Sergas de Esplandian (The Exploits of Esplandian)*, which described a mythical island of riches ruled by Queen Calafía, a Black Muslim monarch with a fierce army of women warriors and attack-griffins. Queen Calafía's island was named California in her honor. In his description of Queen Calafía, Ordóñez Rodriguez de Montalvo wrote:

"Now at the time when those great men of the Pagans sailed with their great fleets, as the history has told you, there reigned in this island of California a Queen, very large in person, the most beautiful of all of them, of blooming years, and in her thoughts desirous of achieving great things, strong of limb and of great courage, more, than any of those who had filled her throne before her."

Mural of Queen Califa in Loreto City Hall, Baja California.
Courtesy of Wikimedia Commons.

Despite the beguiling legend of Queen Calafía, California was still at first of little interest. For Spain, Mexico City at 19°25′N was the focal point for export of American treasure. In the years after the Toxcatl Massacre of 1520—described by missionary Bernardino de Sahagún as a bloodbath where conquistadors hacked Aztecs with swords until "all their entrails would spill out"—the Spanish looted around 200,000 pounds of Aztec gold from Mexico. Tall-masted galleon ships transported this stolen gold from Mexico to Madrid, or to China, after first dodging the gauntlet of Caribbean pirates.

Mapmakers of the time couldn't fathom the true size of North America, let alone California. Giacomo Gastaldi's 1548 map—the world's first "pocket atlas"—imagines that Asia and North America are the same continent and shrinks the Pacific down to the size of the Mediterranean. Gastaldi, the most celebrated European cartographer of his time, depicted the northern reaches of New Spain not going much above 36° North, leaving out Alaska, Canada, and 40 of the "Lower 48" United States. Mongolia was inserted in their place.

Despite these mapping flaws, three famous explorers—Juan Rodrígues Cabrillo (in 1542), Sir Francis Drake (in 1579), and Sebastián Vizcaíno (in 1602)—made it past the Farallon Islands to Drake's Bay, located at 38°N at Point Reyes and just 20 miles north of the Golden Gate. Mysteriously, these explorers' journals and other writings either do not mention or purposely omit finding the enormous bay nearby, even though it would have answered the sailors' most desperate prayers for food and water. A map called Americae Borealis from Scherer's Atlas Novus made in 1699 shows California as an island.

This rendition of the map called Americae Borealis from Scherer's Atlas Novus made in 1699 shows California's most northerly point as Cape Mendocino.
Courtesy of Wikimedia Commons.

Without putting boots on the ground, Cabrillo claimed the coast of California from San Diego up to 42°N, today's California-Oregon border. However, a claim made by sighting land alone would not suffice.

Superpower rules called for flag-planting followed by garrison-building, so finding a port was vital.

For over 200 years after Cabrillo's claim, Manila galleon ships sailed up the coast of California for the trans-Pacific trade. It's nearly incomprehensible from today's vantage point that ship captains unknowingly steered right past the Golden Gate opening each time. Finding the safe harbor of the San Francisco Bay would have made any one of these captains a celebrated hero. But apparently none accomplished the feat.

Captains likely knew that the roiling Pacific Ocean had a penchant for splintering ships that dared to sail too close to California's rocky coastline. The Pacific Ocean violently defies its name with outcroppings of razor-sharp rock, powerful tides, and monster swells. Winter waves can measure up to 60 feet in a place called Mavericks, just south of San Francisco at 37°29′N, site today of one of the world's biggest big wave surfing competitions. Surfers call Mavericks the Mount Everest of surf competitions. A wave like the ones that break at Mavericks can easily sink the kind of multi-mast ships historically used for long distance voyages.

The Farallon Islands, which guard the entrance of the Golden Gate, are especially treacherous for sailors. They're described as spooky and menacing, like giant dragon's teeth emerging from the depths. Sailing on a calm sunny day near the Farallons can turn instantly to violent chaos, with whipping winds and relentless tidal waves. Walls of fog roll in and can blind the way to safety. Frothy sinkholes form at the base of the Farallon's craggy rocks, sucking vessels into a vortex they cannot escape.

Local fishermen call this area the "Red Triangle" because of the all-too-common sight of sea lions chewed into slicks of dark red mixed with sea foam. Lurking in the churning depths, hundreds of great white sharks strike at whatever comes their way.

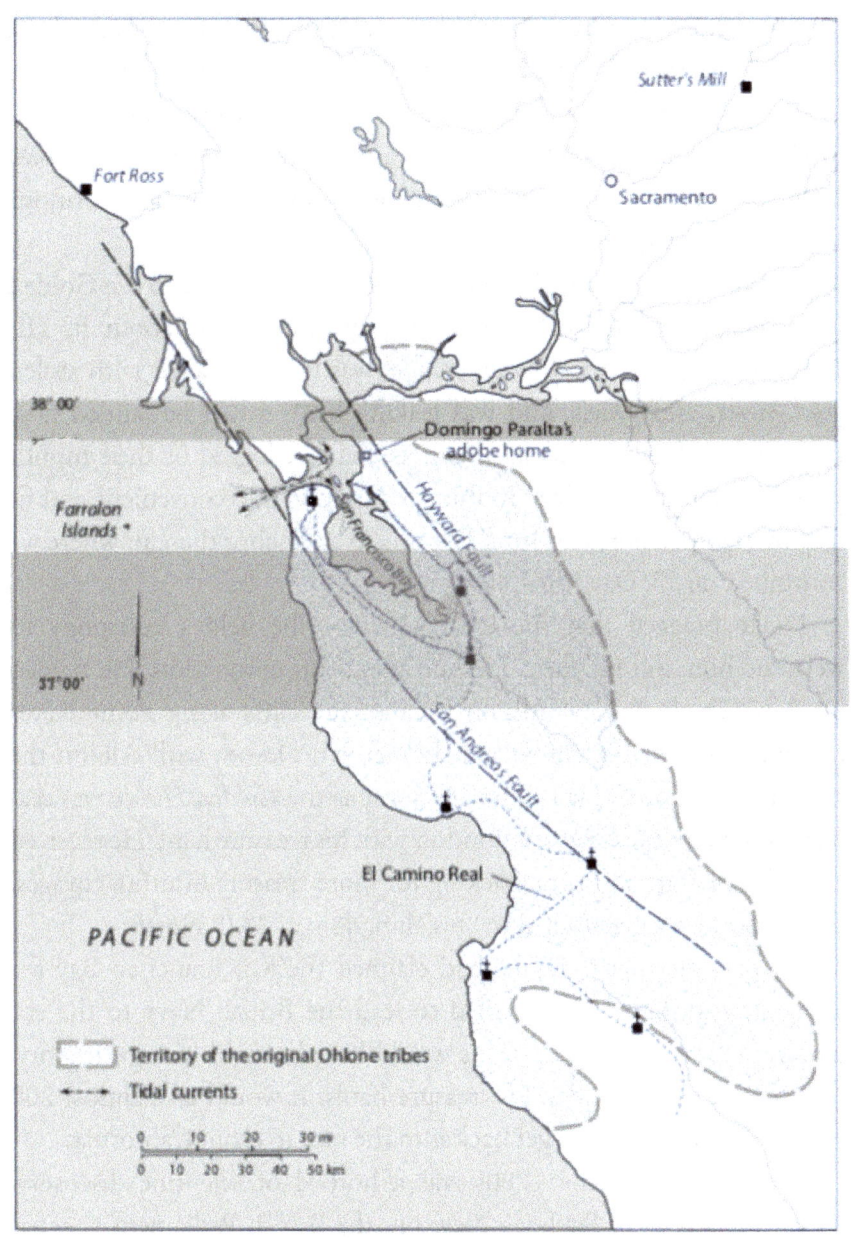

The two gray bars that chart the latitude between 38°N, where Point Reyes is located, and 37°N, where Santa Cruz is located. The Golden Gate is located at 37°49′N.
Courtesy of Bill Nelson.

Though each voyage along the coast of California mapped a little more of the rugged coastline, every explorer still seemed to miss the opening of the Golden Gate. Even Russia's Great Northern Expedition in 1733, which employed as many as 3,000 scientists to map the shores of the Pacific, somehow missed charting the opening to the enormous San Francisco Bay.

The infamous pirate Sir Francis Drake may have found the Golden Gate opening in 1579, but he certainly didn't crow about it. His 121-foot-long ship, the *Golden Hinde*, was heavily loaded with stolen gold, silver, and jewels, and was leaking badly when he landed near Point Reyes. Drake's chaplain Francis Fletcher logged of their month of hull repairs: "in 38 deg. 30 min we fell in with a convenient and fit harborough [harbor] and June 17 came to an anchor therein: where we continued till 23. Day July following."

Drake bragged that the local Miwok tribe held a ceremony to welcome him and his men. He said it was his coronation. He named his new kingdom New Albion because the cliffs along Point Reyes reminded him of the cliffs in his hometown Devon, with Albion the ancient name for Great Britain. As soon as the *Golden Hinde* was seaworthy, Drake sailed back to London with his treasure haul. He received a hero's welcome and royal backing for more treasure hunting voyages, though he never again sailed to "his" kingdom at 38.0° North.

It's possible that if Drake had claimed the San Francisco Bay for Great Britain, he'd be compelled to lead the British Navy to the entrance of the Golden Gate. This would have brought him great glory, but simultaneously ended his treasure hauls. It would take almost 200 years for Great Britain to get back into the race to claim California.

Great Britain in the 1700s was a hotbed of scientific discovery. Under the advice of Sir Isaac Newton, the British Parliament enacted The Longitude Act of 1714, offering prize money to any British commoner who could solve the accurate measurement of longitude. British commoners were fueled on that quest by the same ingredients producing entrepreneurs today: caffeine and financial incentives. By the mid-1700s, London had more than 550 coffee houses where people of all classes and trades intermingled, sharing their latest ideas and knowledge. (Coffeehouses and entrepreneurism go hand and hand in Berkeley too. Peet's Coffee opened in 1966, the start of Berkeley's caffeine craze. Now, Berkeley has over 200 coffeehouses and the highest recorded per capita consumption of coffee of anywhere except San Francisco.)

Without longitude, mapmakers could only guess at the width of continents, with Earth depicted as a slender sphere. North America and the Pacific were mostly missing, omitting around 10,000 miles of planetary's girth. A Virginia Company map made in 1651 actually envisioned the California shore just west of the Appalachian Mountains, somewhere around Kentucky, as a case in point of this phenomenon.

John Overton's map with portrait of Sir Francis Drake, circa 1667 and inscribed "A mapp of Virginia discovered to ye hills, and in it's latt. from 35 deg. & 1/2 neer Florida to 41 deg. bounds of New England"
Courtesy of Wikimedia Commons.

Finally, in 1761, commoner and clockmaker John Harrison solved the measurement of longitude and won the British Parliament's £20,000 longitude prize for his invention of the chronometer. Thousands of missing miles of the fatter-than-previously-thought Earth could finally be mapped.

Captain James Cook was the first explorer to use the new chronometer. Based on a new scientific understanding of nutrition, Cook stocked his ship the *Endeavor* with plant-based foods containing Vitamin C to prevent his sailors from dying of scurvy. These two innovations made it possible for Cook to map the entrance of the Golden Gate on his first voyage in 1768, giving Britain the chance to claim California before Spain or Russia could. The Royal Society of London considered this option as Cook awaited their orders for the *Endeavor's* destination.

Meanwhile, Spain and Russia proceeded with their own West Coast designs. In 1768, King Charles III finalized his plans to colonize the California coast for Spain. Czarina Catherine the Great of Russia, known for her strategic flair, launched the Siberian Expedition that same year. Catherine the Great was interested in claiming North American land from Alaska down to the Farallon Islands, a route Russian trappers had established for the fur trade.

For Cook's first voyage in 1768, the Royal Society of London debated which destination was most scientifically worthy for a multiyear longitudinal expedition. The Royal Society decided to send Cook to the South Pacific instead of the West Coast of North America. It was a victory in the pursuit of science over empire building, swayed by the Royal Society's top priority being to prove the chronometer's longitudinal accuracy.

To assure this priority, the Royal Society gave Cook two sets of instructions at the outset of the voyage. The first set of instructions required Cook to sail the *Endeavor* to Tahiti to track Venus's trajectory as it made its once-every-243-year transit across the Sun. These measurements would prove the accuracy of the chronometer and provide the world's first longitudinal maps of the Pacific Ocean. The world would finally know how gigantic the Pacific is and how much more land remained for exploration. Cook arrived in Tahiti in April 1769, more than a month early. There he charted Venus's trajectory and completed the world's first set of longitudinal maps. Mission accomplished. Then, Cook unsealed the Royal Society of London's secret second instructions.

Smart money suggested that the Royal Society of London's next set of instructions would send Cook to chart the mysterious California coast to claim its interior territory for Britain. Instead, when Captain Cook unfurled the parchment, the secret orders instructed him to proceed south. Cook obeyed, mapping Australia, New Zealand, as well as numerous other territories and islands for good measure. Later, the Royal Society of London rewarded itself for Cook's successful longitudinal mapping by making the Royal Observatory in Greenwich the longitude's prime meridian: zero.

Meanwhile, King Carlos III and his ministers forged ahead with their plans to claim California for Spain. Their secret, not-so-modern, and not-so-speedy mapping technique: send trusted scouts to walk the length of California, carefully counting each step and recording landscape features and distances in small, leather-bound journals.

Considered an "enlightened" king, King Carlos III believed progress and reform could be socially engineered. He believed settlements in California could be imbued with progressive Spanish-style civility and social engineering. He imagined that Indigenous people would be invited into newly created fledgling communities, where they'd learn useful trades and convert to Catholicism. Families would grow and prosper. California would be dotted with Spanish towns, each within a day's walk of another. Ships full of goods would travel back and forth. Catholicism would unite New Spain and Old Spain under God's will. King Carlos III died in the winter of 1778 without knowing he'd inadvertently socially engineered genocide.

To kick start the settlement plan, Spanish families would walk from Mexico to their new community sites in California via a newly christened El Camino Real. Starting in San Diego and Monterey, each settlement in California would become a self-sufficient community, possessing both a garrison and a church.

The first cross-California trek from Mexico to Monterey was the Portolá Expedition. Since Crespí was one of the few members of the Spanish clergy who could both write well and endure hundreds of miles of walking, he became both a scout and scribe for the Portolá Expedition and all that followed. Crespí crisscrossed California five times between 1769 and 1772, keeping careful diaries to record coordinates and describe what he saw. He named one of Southern California's largest rivers *El Río de Nuestra Señora la Reina de los Ángeles de Porciúncula*. The name Los Angeles stuck.

Crespí was one of the Portolá Expedition's scouts who led the first group of 74 bedraggled colonizers to Monterey, but mistakenly walked about a hundred miles too far beyond their Carmel River destination. They ended up somewhere within a few miles of where the San Francisco International SFO Airport is today.

To get their bearings, Crespí and a few other scouts hiked to the top of Montara Mountain, where not only could they see the Pacific Ocean, but also—to their great surprise—they could see the enormous San Francisco Bay. Crespí wrote in his diary that the bay is "a very large and fine harbor, such that not only all the navy of our Most Catholic Majesty but those of all Europe could take shelter in it." Crespí realized that if they could map the opening to San Francisco Bay, California could become a successful center of trade for New Spain.

As Britain and Russia's Pacific explorations gained steam, Crespí's journal made its long journey to Madrid. In Crespí's journal was the secret coordinate and his map—California's first map—of the opening of the San Francisco Bay. Around two and a half years later, a usual amount of time for 18th century round trip correspondence from California, the royal court in Madrid responded with a mandate to chart the latitudinal coordinate for the opening of the San Francisco Bay by spotting it from the "Contra Costa" East Bay Area land. In other words, the royal decree commanded that Crespí walk to Berkeley and find the empire-building secret coordinate, 37°52′N.

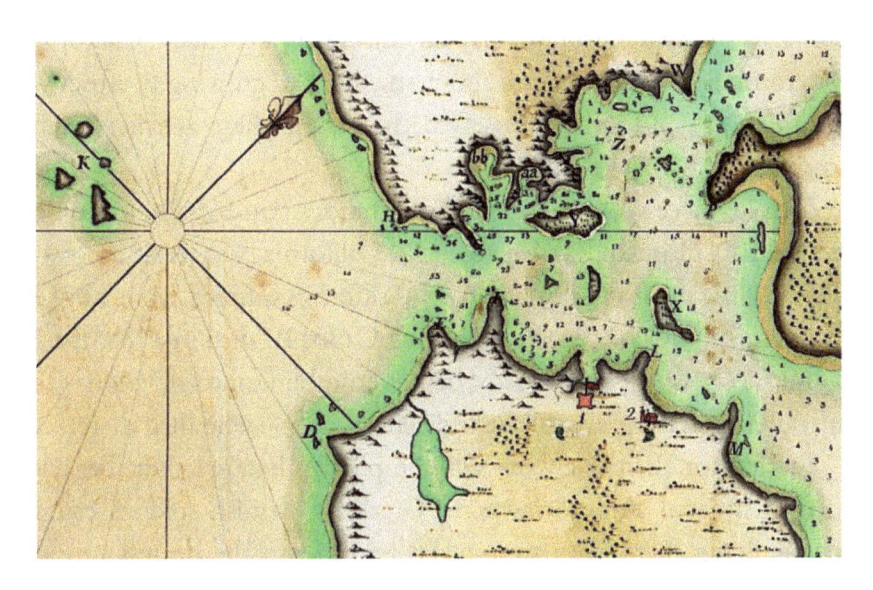

Map of Puerto de San Francisco by José de Cañizares in 1776, the year conscripted Ohlone built the Mission Dolores chapel, the first non-Indigenous construction in San Francisco.
Courtesy of Wikimedia Commons.

Crespí, along with a small band of soldiers led by Spanish army lieutenant Pedro Fages, obeyed the royal decree to find the latitude of the Golden Gate opening. They were the first Europeans to walk the 100-plus mile route from Monterey to Berkeley. Later this route would become Spain's East Bay branch of El Camino Real, roughly the same route as Interstate 880 to Interstate 580.

On the morning of March 27, 1772, a few of Fages's soldiers set out on a bear hunt. They probably knew they were close to their 37°52′N destination. They spotted a bear, which led them north through the rolling hills. The soldiers lost track of the bear, but when they looked up they saw their true prize: due west was the opening of the Golden Gate and a clear view of the Farallon Islands in the Pacific. The bear had led them to Berkeley and 37°52′N.

As instructed, Crespí sent this secret coordinate back to the royal court in Madrid to secure the port of San Francisco and claim the interior of California. In his journal, he noted that a stream was also aligned with 37°52′N. Crespí named the stream Strawberry Creek, making it one of the first European named features in Northern California. (There are Indigenous stories about strawberries growing profusely in the area.) Crespí's journal observed the people there as friendly and hospitable.

Despite successfully mapping the entrance to the San Francisco Bay, the Spanish ultimately failed to make California a successful colony. The Spanish mission settlements in California suffered from hunger, coercion, and disease. By the time King Carlos III died in 1788, the 21 California missions had already begun crumbling into oblivion, each surrounded by the graves of the Indigenous people who died there.

Fearing for their lives, the Ohlone people deserted their Berkeley villages, situated along Strawberry Creek. If Spanish soldiers caught anyone living there, they were taken by force to the nearest mission settlement. From the late 1770s until the 1880s, the human population of Berkeley plummeted.

Meanwhile, cattle multiplied. The Portolá Expedition brought 200 longhorn cattle overland from Mexico, with their numbers in California doubling every six years. Except for the large population of bears, Berkeley was an ideal grazing land because of the open fields full of seed-bearing grasses that Ohlone families cultivated over hundreds of years.

In 1841, the first non-native family settled in Berkeley when Domingo Peralta built a 30-by-18 foot adobe house next to Codornices Creek. The Kingdom of Spain had granted Domingo Peralta's father, Luis María Peralta, nearly the entire Contra Costa East Bay Area as a retirement gift for his lifelong service protecting Spain's missions and presidios in Northern California. Upon his death, Luis María Peralta's 44,800-acre Rancho San Antonio estate was divided between his sons and daughters. (The daughters later sued their brothers under the United States court system.) Domingo Peralta, the third son, inherited the land from Temescal Creek to Cerrito Creek. All of Berkeley belonged to him—but not for long.

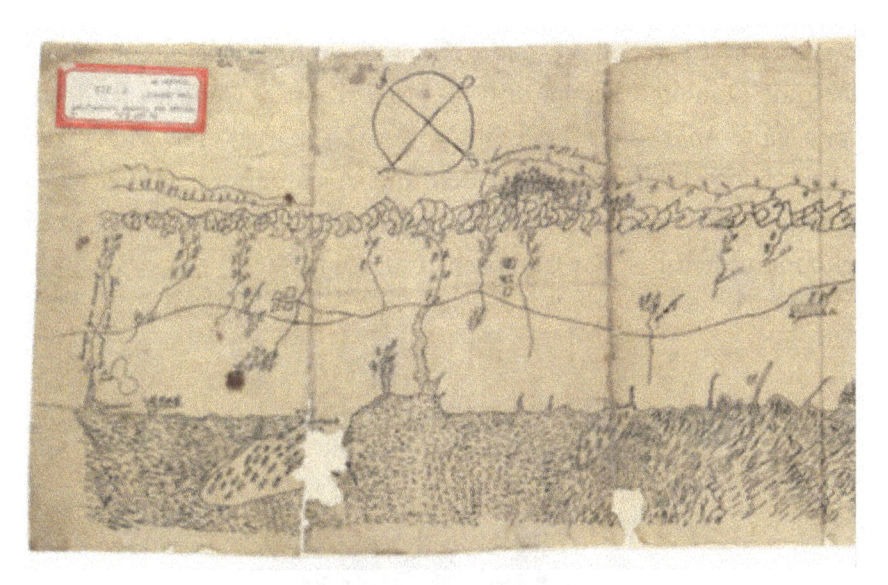

Map of Luis María Peralta's 44,800-acre Rancho San Antonio. The map appears upside down, with the Berkeley and Oakland Hills contours at the top and the East Bay shoreline at the bottom. Vertical lines represent rivers and streams. Berkeley is the far left portion, bordered by the Cerrito Creek, the northernmost creek.
Courtesy of the Bancroft Library.

The Peralta family lost almost all of the 44,800-acres of land after the discovery of gold on January 24, 1848, in a place the local Nisenan people called Cullumah, which means beautiful valley. Cullumah (later spelled Coloma) is at 38°47′, a day's journey from the San Francisco Bay. On February 2, 1848, Mexico relinquished control of California to the United States in the Treaty of Hidalgo. The Mexicans didn't know that gold was discovered in California just nine days before, so they didn't know that they were handing a land of unimaginable riches to the United States. California miners extracted 750,000-pounds during the Gold Rush, more than three times the Spanish plunder from the Aztecs.

By 1849, an estimated 300,000 immigrants poured into San Francisco to try their luck at panning for gold. Most of them stayed well after their luck ran out. Squatters camped out everywhere they thought they could scratch out a living, and fortune hunters turned to land speculation. Even the shallow water off of San Francisco's and Berkeley's coastlines was parceled off, sold, and resold for future development. By the time Domingo Peralta died in 1865, all of his Berkeley land was gone, either sold to pay legal bills or lost to squatters. His widow and 10 surviving children were left destitute. According to the Hacienda Historical Park in Oakland, Domingo Peralta's heirs received a small amount of their East Bay land back in court in 1877.

José Domingo Peralta (1795-1865)
Courtesy of the Bancroft Library.

Well before the Gold Rush, John Frémont was one of the early American advocates for California statehood. As a spy for the U.S. government, Frémont rode through the Peralta's property in Berkeley at least a couple of times in early 1846 while on a reconnaissance mission. Frémont was also in California to foment a rebellion by organizing a militia. In spring of 1846, Frémont appointed himself "Military Commander of U.S. Forces in California" for the fledgling Bear State Republic. Frémont's men, who called themselves the Osos (Bears), took over Sonoma that summer. For three and a half weeks the Osos made Sonoma the capital of the Bear State Republic, until the U.S. military took over.

After the Bear State Republic was dissolved, Frémont made a report to Congress to consider making California a state. In his report, Frémont touted the San Francisco Bay opening as "a golden gate to trade with the Orient" to explain the lucrative trade opportunities that a port would bring, especially with China. His sales pitch—which was at least partially drafted by his politically savvy wife Jessie Benton Frémont—was unnecessary after U.S. coffers began filling with gold in 1848. Nevertheless, the name "Golden Gate" stuck and trade with China flourished. Frémont's declaration to Congress that California would provide "a golden gate to trade with the Orient" proved true. Berkeley's coordinates at 37°52′N located the Golden Gate on European maps, beckoning fortune hunters from around the world ever since.

A postcard illustration of a sunset over the Golden Gate romanticizes the 19th century naval conquest of the San Francisco Bay. The viewpoint is from Berkeley.
Postcard made by Cardinell-Vincent Co in 1913.

Victorian Blueprints

"The cornerstone was laid with a spirit very much like that with which the cornerstones of the old cathedrals must have been laid. The spirit of the new university, instinct with life, was in the air."

— Jack London, reporting on the ceremony to lay the three-ton cornerstone of UC Berkeley's Hearst Memorial Mining Building for the San Francisco Examiner in 1902

Old South Hall

In 1873 when Berkeley was a fledgling university, students studied in one of two buildings: North Hall, devoted to the study of Letters, or South Hall, devoted to the study of Sciences. North Hall was demolished in 1931, so only South Hall remains.

For its first decades, South Hall was where middle-class students learned science—especially the branches of science that would improve agriculture, mechanics, mining, and military might, as stipulated by the mission of Congress's Morrill Land Grant Act of 1862. Land Grant colleges were part of a 19th Century national strategy to make the United States into a world superpower by training young upwardly mobile men for professions using the latest technologies. (Women weren't included in this strategy, but enrolled in droves as soon as they were allowed.)

Old South Hall, built in 1873, is the first of the two original buildings on the Berkeley campus. South Hall was built to house the disciplines of "Science." Old North Hall, razed in 1931, housed the academic disciplines of "Letters."
Courtesy of the Bancroft Library.

Upper class students, who followed their fathers into law, banking, and politics, were mostly men of Letters, so their classes (in history, English, Latin, etc.) were in North Hall. Women students were largely confined to North Hall, with the study of Letters considered more appropriate for them. Today, the College of Letters and Science enrolls the lion's share of UC Berkeley undergraduates. A slight majority of them remain women. South Hall is sometimes nicknamed the "Mary Poppins" building for all of its chimneys. These chimneys kept students from being asphyxiated as they practiced metallurgy, including purifying gold with vials of quicksilver (mercury). Since few safety precautions in scientific experimentation existed until recently, students working on the top floor of South Hall might have succumbed to chemical poisoning, like mercury poisoning, then called mad hatter's disease. Drinking heavily was common for undergraduate men in the early days of the university, and since alcohol and toxins cause the same speech and movement impairments, students conducting experiments in South Hall may have blamed their dizziness on too much partying.

When they weren't attending lectures inside North and South Halls, male students sat together outside the buildings Later, a "Senior Bench" was added. Women had a small basement room under North Hall where they could store their belongings and socialize.
Courtesy of the Bancroft Library.

Today, South Hall looks more or less the same as it did when it was finished in 1873. It's now notably home to the School of Information, which focuses on "Big Data" and artificial intelligence. The School of Information sends some alumni to six-figure jobs at Google, Facebook, and other tech behemoths.

Student campus tour leaders like to point out the small bear statue embedded in the decorative balustrade awning above South Hall's main entrance, since it's the smallest of more than a dozen bear statues on campus. Sometimes the tour leaders will repeat the rumor that Jimmy Hendrix's ghost has been spotted on the lawn area across from South Hall.

The front of Old South Hall is where guests gathered to take student tours of campus for Cal Day on April 13, 2024.
Courtesy of Pam Gleason.

Victorian Blueprints

In 1725, Anglican metaphysics philosopher George Berkeley wrote "A Proposal for the Better Supplying of Churches in Our Foreign Plantations, and for Converting the Savage Americans, to Christianity, By a College to Be Erected in the Summer Islands, Otherwise Called The Isles of Bermuda." George Berkeley (pronounced "BARK-lee") is the namesake for UC Berkeley (pronounced "BURK-lee") founded in 1868. After the land for the first University of California was named in tribute to George Berkeley, the City of Berkeley incorporated in 1878.

Berkeley's fundraising hook was to build a biblically-inspired shining "city upon a hill"—a Christian college that would bring light to the untamed barbaric lands of the Americas. The Berkeley College would be a beacon of hope in a God forsaken world.

There was scarcely a better place to fire up British imaginations than the heavily reefed Islands of Bermuda. Nicknamed "The Devil's Isle" Bermuda was at the center of the Atlantic slave trade and was well-known for its pirates, treacherous surf, and shipwrecked survivors. William Shakespeare called it "the still-vex'd Bermoothes" in *The Tempest*.

Berkeley's gambit was to convince the wealthy that their donations would go to what he deemed as one of the most worthy of Christian causes: saving heathen souls while spreading Anglican values and civility in the Americas, one of the areas of the world that he thought needed it most.

Berkeley envisioned his college on the Island of Bermuda as an institution that would assimilate Indigenous young people by teaching the tenets of Christianity. The Indigenous students would come from newly colonized territories and be taught with the spare-the-rod-and-spoil-the-child discipline of British boarding schools. Indigenous customs, along with left-handedness, speaking out of turn, and other behaviors considered barbarous by Anglican standards, would be snuffed out.

Photo of Hamilton Harbor on the Island of Bermuda in 1869.
Courtesy of the British Royal Collection.

Berkeley was a celebrated philosopher who spent a great deal of time writing fundraising proposals to wealthy admirers. His philosophy could be boiled down to a version of seeing is believing, known as "Berkeley's razor" and commonly represented by the question, "If a tree falls in a forest and no one is around to hear it, does it make a sound?"

Since Berkeley had never set foot in Bermuda, Berkeley's college for theology and the fine arts was built from his imagination. He described an idyllic campus with "summers refreshed with constant cool breezes, the winters as mild as our May, the sky as light and blue as a sapphire, the ever green pastures, the earth eternally crowned with fruits and flowers... The inhabitants have the greatest simplicity of manners, more innocence, honesty, and good nature, than any of our planters, who are many of them descended from whores, vagabonds, and transported criminals, none of which settled in Bermudas."

Berkeley accompanied his proposal with a prolific number of poems and treatises written for the influential and rich, particularly those in King George II's orbit, urging them to fund his university. His

1729 poem, "Verses on the Prospect of Planting Arts and Learning in America," touts Christianity's conquest to save souls in barbaric lands. Berkeley hoped this poem would attract ample funding for him to move permanently to Bermuda to oversee the foundation of his new university.

Ultimately, Berkeley's vision for a university for Indigenous Americans failed. The closest he got to the Bahamas was Newport, Rhode Island, where in 1730 he purchased a plantation and three enslaved people, whom he baptized "Philip, Anthony, and Agnes Berkeley." In 1732, after selling Philip, Anthony, and Agnes to Yale University, Berkeley returned to Oxford and refocused his writings on the miraculous healing properties of pine tar, an Indigenous antiseptic he'd brought back to sell as a cure-all for ailments. In 1734, George Berkeley was consecrated as Bishop of Cloyne Court in Ireland.

Bedroom hallway in Cloyne Court, a Berkeley Student Cooperative that houses 140 students. It's not what George Berkeley imagined for his Berkeley College.
Courtesy of Wikimedia Commons.

Although he never succeeded in raising the money for his envisioned grandiose university, Berkeley's writings were read widely. According to researcher Elizabeth Kiszonas at the University of Arkansas, by 1776, "Verses on the Prospect of Planting Arts and Learning in America" had been printed in its entirety by almost every major newspaper and periodical in colonial America. Each stanza of this poem refers to a stage of the apocalypse from the Book of Revelation, imbuing biblical meaning and urgency to the American westward expansion. The final stanza is about Christianity's last push westward, interpreted by some as the impending victory of civilizing California by converting its Indigenous population:

> *Westward the course of empire takes its way;*
> *The four first acts already past,*
> *A fifth shall close the drama with the day;*
> *Time's noblest offspring is the last.*

— Final stanza of George Berkeley's "Verses on the Prospect of Planting Arts and Learning in America" (1729)

One version of university lore claims that lawyer Frederick H. Billings read aloud Berkeley's "Verses on the Prospect of Planting Arts and Learning in America" at a large rock outcrop overlooking the Bay on April 16, 1860 to dedicate the land to the College of California. This rock outcrop was later named "Founders Rock" for the men who gathered there. Several of the men at this dedication ceremony were ordained ministers, including Reverend Henry Durant. They envisioned the College of California as a Christian seminary. Billings was at the dedication because his brother-in-law Captain Orrin Simmons was squatting on the Peralta family land that they'd chosen for the College of California site.

The 20' x 30' mural Westward the Course of Empire Takes Its Way decorated the west staircase wall in the U.S. Capitol Building in 1862. The title is from George Berkeley's "On the Prospect of Planting Arts and Learning in America." This painting by Emanuel Leutze depicts Americans crossing the continental divide to settle in California. The panel beneath the scene shows the Golden Gate—the idealized destination. It's painted from the viewpoint of the Berkeley shoreline.
Courtesy of Wikimedia Commons.

Billings was the first to set up a law firm in San Francisco at the start of the Gold Rush in 1849, according to his 1890 obituary in *The New York Times*. Billings specialized in California land titles, and his first customers included Senator John Frémont and John Sutter of Sutter's Mill, where gold was first discovered.

In 1854, Simmons won squatters rights to 160 acres of Peralta land through the California Land Act of 1851, which set the prices of 160 acres at $200. By 1857 Simmons owned 700 acres of Berkeley land and in 1864 he sold most of his land for $35,000 to the College Homestead Association, the fundraising arm of the College of California. In 1865, Simmons retired to Oakland, and Billings returned to New York City with a fortune big enough to invest in building railroads and canals.

Founders' Rock at the northeast corner of campus on Hearst Avenue. The small rectangle is the plaque that says "Founders Rock California College April 16, 1860." UC Berkeley geophysicist Horst Rademacher includes this volcanic rock outcrop on his Hayward Fault Walking Tour. Rademacher cites the hypothesis that Founders' Rock was pushed to the surface over millions of years by tectonic movement, and could be 150 million years old, at a time when Jurassic dinosaurs were around.
Courtesy of Omar Rincon.

Of all of the original Founders' Rock men, Henry Durant was the only one to stick around for the founding of the University of California. Durant had come to California as a well-connected Yale seminary graduate in 1853. He spent his first several years in debt, struggling to pay his bills in the sawmill town of Oakland, where he founded the Contra Costa Academy for boys, renamed the College of California in 1855.

Enrollment was dismal for headmaster Durant. Only a few boys attended his classes, held in his Oakland home, previously a fandango dance hall. If funding from the 1862 Morrill Land Grant Act had not come through to purchase Berkeley land, Durant might have returned back East.

Once Governor Haight signed the Organic Act on March 23, 1868, California's Constitution was amended to charter the University of California. The Organic Act took advantage of the federal funding from the Republican Congress's Morrill Land Grant Act of 1862, which was intended to educate farmers, tradesmen, and, according to Congressman Justin Smith Morrill, "those at the bottom of the ladder who want to climb up." The Land Grant Act authorized state legislatures to use the proceeds from the sale of their state's land to fund colleges that would train middle class students and "provide instruction and complete education in all the departments of science, literature, art, industrial and professional pursuits, and general education, and also special courses of instruction for the professions of agriculture, the mechanic arts, mining, military science, civil engineering, law, medicine and commerce."

Durant agreed to continue classes in Oakland, and beginning in 1869 his College of California students became University of California students. Plans to build North and South Halls began, though the name Berkeley had not been universally accepted. In 1873, New York City's Central Park landscape architect Frederick Law Olmstead, who had been chosen to layout the University of California grounds, suggested "whole pages" of names for the University of California site, such as "Bushnellwood, Billingsley, Leawood, Shelterwood, Blythhaven, Villa-hermosa, and La Vistora." Olmstead concluded that Peralta was "natural and proper name," according to research published in 2007 by Joy Fisher.

Fisher also quotes Irishman John Ross Browne's glowing assessment of "town of Berkeley" in a 1866 article for the *Oakland Daily Transcript*, which probably bolstered adoption of the name Berkeley:

> "We learn that there is a movement on foot to survey and lay out a handsome town at Berkeley, embracing within its limits some two thousand five hundred acres of land around the University site.
>
> It is proposed to have it laid out with broad streets, avenues, and railroads; to have the present fences set back at once, along the lines of the avenues, and that each property-owner shall immediately plant rows of ornamental trees along the proposed

sidewalks, so as to present an attractive appearance by the time the new town has made some progress.

The owners of the greater portion of these lands enter heartily into the project, and will no doubt co-operate as soon as they can be consulted.

A concerted movement will then be made by gentlemen of influence and capital to make Berkeley the fashion; to invest it with the attractive features of a University city, like that of Cambridge and Oxford. Several gentlemen of means contemplate building there during the coming season, and they hope to influence wealthy San Franciscans to follow their example. It will be a delightful summer retreat. It is worthy of remark, that of late years it has become . . . the fashion with such of the San Franciscans as can afford it, to send their families out of town during the summer . . .

Berkeley would furnish a charming resort for these out-of-town families, and, at the same time, would be convenient of access from the city. Direct communication with San Francisco would give a great impetus to the new town, and soon establish there a society famed for its culture and refinement."

North and South Hall were completed in 1873, the first buildings on the new Berkeley campus. They had nearly identical structural footprints, but North Hall was made of wood and South Hall made primarily of brick. At the time South Hall was built, it was one of the first buildings in the world to be dedicated to the study of science. South Hall was built with laboratories in mind and state-of-the-art engineering. The number of chimneys would provide ventilation (though certainly inadequate, the dangers from noxious fumes weren't well understood) and its vaulted structure was ahead of its time for taking into account the destructive power of California's earthquakes.

Sketch of the Berkeley campus in 1880 featuring the buildings of Letters (North Hall) and Sciences (South Hall) at the campus center.
Courtesy of Wikimedia Commons.

North Hall was dedicated to the study of letters, the traditional education for the sons of society's top families. When North Hall was condemned for safety reasons in 1917, President Benjamin Ide Wheeler (1899-1919) eulogized it as, "The shrine to those who would loaf and invite their souls."

Unruly students were temporarily tamed by tempestuous President Wheeler, a white-mustached autocrat who wore cavalry boots and galloped about campus on a white charger. Wheeler unintentionally sparked a push for academic freedoms. His highhanded ways provoked a faculty revolt in 1919 that established a strong-willed Academic Senate.

With the completion of North and South Halls, the student population rose to 389, including 222 women. North Hall had a cloak room where women could gather before and after classes.

Women had been admitted starting in 1870, and after graduation many became California's first college-educated school teachers. However, university leaders, all men up until that point, discouraged the women students from being too ambitious. Wheeler was not in favor of women becoming more than housewives. In an article in the *Chronicle of the University of California* titled, "No Man and No Thing Can Stop Me," researcher Geraldine Jonçich Clifford quotes Wheeler's warning the Associated Women Students: "You are not here with the ambition to be school teachers or old maids, but you are here for the preparation for marriage and motherhood. This education should tend to make you more serviceable as wives and mothers."

This postcard shows a horse drawn streetcar that transported both men and women to and from Oakland to the Berkeley campus on Telegraph Avenue. The inscription says, "Street car turning on Euclid Ave. between Ontario and San Antonio Streets, up to 1900."
Courtesy of Berkeley Historical Society.

In 1897, signifying changing times and gender relations, the San Francisco-based heiress Phoebe Apperson Hearst became the University of California's first woman regent. As regent, Hearst used her fortune to secure the future preeminence of Berkeley as the "Athens of the West," replacing her male counterparts' name for Berkeley as the "Yale of the West."

Much of Hearst's philanthropy work was devoted to the education of young women. Her support led to a renaissance of women's participation in education, sports, and the arts. She commissioned the Hearst Gymnasium, with a marble and grecian urn decorated swimming pool; Hearst Hall, a women's reading and recreation gothic-style clubroom with a fifty-foot vaulted ceiling designed by Bernard Maybeck; and funded women's residence halls and fellowships for promising young women not otherwise wealthy enough to attend Berkeley.

Hearst's Midwestern roots gave prudency to the way she wielded her fortune. In addition to supporting women's education, she also supported universal kindergarten, women's suffrage, prohibition, architecture, the study of the great civilizations. The National Congress of Mothers, now known as the Parent Teacher Association, was founded and co-funded by Hearst.

Hearst was sincere in her belief that women should be the moral backbone of society. She believed women's education was the answer to many of society's ills and the counterbalance to the rough and impetuous men's world of fortune hunting and smoke-filled drinking parlors —where her husband, Senator George Hearst, and her son, William Randolph Hearst, thrived.

Both father and son led unscrupulous lives capturing Hollywood's imagination. The TV series and subsequent movie *Deadwood* portrays George Hearst as a power-demented villain who leaves a trail of murdered parlor ladies and miners in his wake.

In the movie *Citizen Kane*, William Randolph Hearst is portrayed as a maniacal tyrant. His mother is depicted as vapid and cold, which infuriated the younger Hearst. Slander was his bread and butter as a real-life tycoon in the newspaper industry, but he believed his mother above reproach.

Phoebe Apperson Hearst wearing a lace decorated gown with son
William Randolph Hearst in a crisp christening gown.
Courtesy of Wikimedia Commons.

Before Hearst's fortune shaped Berkeley into a reputable destination, campus was a raucous place, with drinking, womanizing, and brawling commonplace. Juniors and seniors wore beat up and self-decorated "plugs"—squished and mangled top hats paired with dirty corduroy pants modeled after the infamous rabble-rousing Plug-Uglies Baltimore street gang.

In the 1880s and 1890s, hundreds of freshmen and sophomores marked Charter Day with a mock civil war battle called "Rush" to take over Charter Hill above campus. The freshmen stormed Charter Hill from below with the goal of painting their graduation year onto the hill the evening before March 23, so that the Charter Day merrymakers who arrived the next day could look up to see they had won the battle. Sophomores waited at the top of the hill to repel them by pushing and "rolling" them back down the hill in a melee of bruising fights, broken bones, and bloody noses.

Captives with their hands tied behind their backs are man-handled by the victors of the Charter Hill brawl between new students and continuing students c. 1900. The plug hats of the victors indicate they are likely upperclassmen.
Courtesy of the Bancroft Library.

In 1905, President Wheeler, who'd been lured to campus by Hearst, invited students to work together to create a "Big C" on Charter Hill to end the tradition of the brawl. (Though for awhile afterward, brawls were restarted at the center of campus for old time's sake.)

It's now the Rally Committee's job to coat the cement-girded "Big C" with fresh golden yellow paint. On football game days, if students from rival colleges sneak up the night before a football game to paint the "Big C" their team colors, the Rally Committee rushes to the top of Charter Hill to repaint the "Big C" golden yellow again before game time. Rally Club members are also considering new ways to paint the "Big C"—perhaps in rainbow colors to celebrate Pride Month each June, for example.

As regent, Hearst set her sights on a grand scheme to transform the Berkeley campus into an international "city of learning." She sent Berkeley architect Bernard Maybeck and his wife Annie Maybeck as Berkeley's emissaries to Europe to promote an international architectural competition with "prominent architects, painters, sculptors and landscape gardeners in England and Scotland, France, Germany, Italy, Holland, Belgium, Austria, Hungary and Switzerland." Some 10,000 copies of a prospectus were also sent to Europe to encourage designers to enter the contest, guaranteeing them "absolute freedom to express their ideal of what a great University should embody," with no financial restraints on what the campus designs would cost to build. The grand prize that Phoebe Hearst paid the winning architect was $10,000, the equivalent of over $250,000 today. There were a total of 105 entries, and the top 11 finalists received an all-expenses-paid trip to Berkeley to resketch their designs on site, in synchronicity with the lay of the land.

Celebrated Beaux-Arts Parisian architect Henri Jean Emile Bénard won the international Hearst Competition. His blueprints called for a wide open central campus plaza resembling the concourse of Place de la Concorde, one of the largest public squares in Paris. Bénard's main promenade, in "axe historique" alignment with the Golden Gate, was a continuation of University Avenue. However, some of University leaders objected, preferring an alignment with the original Letters and Sciences buildings, North and South Hall.

Article about Henri Jean Emile Bénard's winning design from the October, 1899 edition of the The Western Journal of Education.
Courtesy of the Berkeley Historical Society.

Phoebe Hearst tried to lure Bénard with another $10,000 to come to Berkeley to begin construction based on his winning design. Bénard was not interested. Rumors circulated that he didn't want to leave Paris because he loved good coffee—which at the time was not easy to find in Berkeley—and because he was deathly afraid of the grizzly bears that occasionally sauntered onto campus.

In any case, Bénard could not be persuaded to come to Berkeley, so fourth-place John Galen Howard readily accepted the prestigious honor of building a world class campus. The final blueprints were an amalgamation of Howard's and Bénard's designs. Howard was a Maybeck protégé, and understood the importance of aligning campus with North and South Hall and the opening of the Golden Gate. By the time the new campus architecture was completed, all of the grizzly bears in Berkeley had been shot or captured, and coffee—though probably watered down and stale—was available. The Hearst Competition succeeded: the prestige and fuss about the University of California blueprints put Berkeley on the world map.

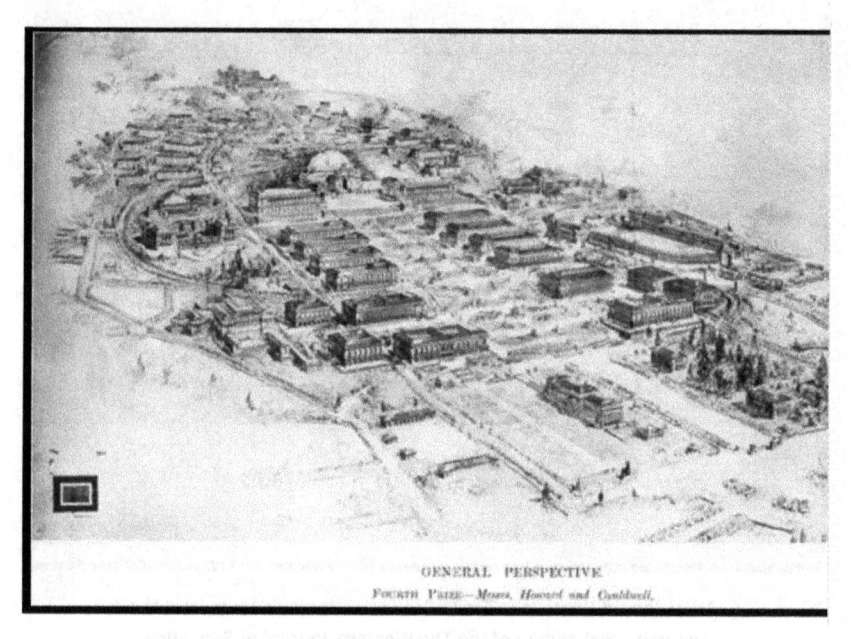

John Galen Howard's fourth-place entry for Phoebe Apperson Hearst's 1899 International Competition to design the University of California campus.
Courtesy of the Bancroft Library.

Hearst also coaxed (or subsidized) her son William's $42,000 gift to build the Greek Theater. A rush of horse-drawn carts took over the upper campus area to complete everything on time for President Teddy Roosevelt's May 1903 commencement address. When it was clear the Greco-Roman colonnade stage structure would not be in place on time, architect Julia Morgan joined Bernard Maybeck to get the job done. Morgan designed a velvet-covered scaffolding to hide the unfinished stage area. Morgan and the often toga-clad Maybeck finished the Greek Theater a few months later, opening with a record-breaking audience of more than 7,000 for a performance of *The Birds*—one of very few Greek plays not featuring men and war, thereby allowing Berkeley's women to play the key roles.

Architect Julia Morgan in front of Notre Dame in Paris. Morgan was the first woman admitted to the prestigious architecture École des Beaux-Arts. After her graduation in 1894 she worked on designs for several well-known Berkeley landmarks, including the Greek Theater, The Berkeley City Club, and the Hearst Memorial Mining Building.
Courtesy of California Polytechnic State University Archives.

Morgan was the first woman to graduate with a bachelor's degree in Civil Engineering from UC Berkeley in 1894 (before the Architecture program started) and also was the first woman to be admitted and graduate from the world famous École national supérieure des Beaux-Arts in Paris.

Morgan's crowning lifetime achievement was the design of Hearst Castle, William Randolph Hearst's dream home where the who's who of the Hollywood's Roaring Twenties elite partied for days. In addition to movie stars like Charlie Chaplin and Greta Garbo, politicians including Winston Churchill stayed at Hearst Castle, which boasted 42 bedrooms, indoor and outdoor swimming pools, tennis courts and an airfield, surrounded by 127 acres of gardens in San Simeon, about halfway between Berkeley and Hollywood.

In *Julia Morgan: Architect of Beauty* by Mark Anthony Wilson quotes William Randolph Hearst short shrifting Morgan's value: "...the best thing about this person is, I pay her almost nothing, as it is a woman."

Berkeley's trailblazing women were undaunted. Ambitious women like Alta Miner Alice Bates were drawn to Berkeley's opportunities for women made possible by Hearst. Bates, the Bay Area's first nurse anesthetist, was the founder of Berkeley's first hospital.

Bates started her practice in 1904 by caring for mothers and their babies at her parent's house on Walnut Street. According to Sutter Health's website about the history of Alta Bates Hospital, Bates secured around $114 to build her first facility, an eight-bed health and nurse training facility, called the Bates Sanatorium. By 1906, Bates Sanatorium graduated its first class of nurses. Over her career, she trained 330 nurses.

In 1908, her hospital expanded to three floors, and by 1928 it was renamed the Alta Bates Hospital, with six stories and 112 beds. She served as hospital director from 1905 to 1949.

Alta Miner Alice Bates started teaching nursing care for women and babies at her parents home in Berkeley in 1904.
Courtesy of Sutter Health's website on history of Alta Bates Hospital.

Some of the very best of Cal's first women graduates taught at Berkeley's earliest public elementary schools. Despite bringing modern standards into the classroom, the demographics of the schools reflected Berkeley's class hierarchy, with wealthy students attending schools close to the University of California campus, and working class students attending schools near the Bay's shoreline. Berkeley's elite students attended the Hillside School and learned math, music, and poetry. One of the world's first kindergartens was established at the Hillside School by eager University of California graduates.

The poor and working class attended the Ocean View school in Berkeley's "drinks and dynamite" district, where the refuse of taverns, tanneries, and the Giant Powder dynamite factory polluted the shoreline and produced foul odors that settled over Berkeley's flatland on breezeless days. Schools for poor children had a curriculum that featured "Manual Arts," including lessons on how to make and use rags for domestic and industrial work.

Among the elite, Hearst's Victorian values and promotion of young women fueled Berkeley's women-led Bohemian culture and continued devotion to creative arts. Isadora Duncan debuted modern dance at the Greek Theater. One of Duncan's childhood friends, Florence Treadwell Boynton, commissioned Maybeck to design her Berkeley Hills home in the style of a Greek Theater stage so she could host performances and teach Duncan's freeform style modern dance to Hillside School girls.

Florence Treadwell Boynton plays a harp at her Temple of the Wings home and dance studio.
Courtesy of Wikimedia Commons.

The Boynton's Greco-Roman colonnade home, called the Temple of Wings, was a steep five-minute hike above the Hillside School, so girls had a good pre-dance warm up from climbing up the hill after school to attend dance classes. Urns of nuts, fruits, and berries rimmed the stage (and living room) floor. Rumors swirled that the Boynton children hated their free-spirited lives—their home had no walls, and sleeping on the stage's roof and eating a steady diet of nuts wasn't as fun as it seemed. Gossips claimed they begged their friends for bites of a sandwich at lunchtime.

Hearst died of the Spanish flu during the pandemic of 1918-1919. Attending her were Ohlone servants, likely from the Verona Band who lived nearby. She'd succeeded in transforming the Berkeley campus and stature, she'd seeded a thriving arts culture, and she left a legacy of empowering women to excel despite society's barriers. One of Hearst's most famous quotes is "Don't ever be afraid to start small." She would probably marvel at the size of Berkeley's campus and student body today. She might agree that the biggest concentration of present and future women leaders are charting their careers on the campus that she built.

Bear Territory

"You know it, you tell the story, you tell the whole damn world this is bear territory!"
— *chant by Cal football fans after a winning game*

Bear Spotting on the UC Berkeley Campus

Life-sized grizzly bear statue in front of Memorial Stadium.
Courtesy of Pam Gleason.

Like the Oski the Bear mascot, most of Cal grizzly bear imitations have been Disneyfied, or are some version of a teddy bear. The most life-like of the bear statues on campus is called "Alerted" by Douglas Van Howd. Located at the main entrance steps leading to Memorial Stadium, it depicts a grizzly bear twisting his head west, as if to see what's coming from the Golden Gate or from the campus that stretches down the hill. Van Howd's grizzly bear has realistically sharp claws, which can snag the clothing of football fans who pose for photos too close to the grizzly. Liberal fans might be disappointed to know that Van Howd is most famous as the official artist for President Ronald Reagan, whom he adored.

The Berkeley Library Stories website has an interactive tour map for the 23 places around campus to spot a bear, including the 10,500 pound "Great Bear Bell" which tolls in the Campanile Bell Tower every hour from 8 a.m. to 10 p.m. The campus would be home to even more bears if Berkeley's public art committee didn't turn down the nearly monthly proposals for new bear statues.

Bear spotting is featured during campus scavenger hunts, orientations, and tours. A tiny sculptured bear hidden in the awning of Old South Hall, one of the two original buildings on campus from 1873, gets the most attention because it's so hard to spot. Cal student tour guides who stop in front of Old South Hall often ask their groups of visitors to locate the inches-tall bear statue.

The smallest Berkeley bear statue sits on the South Hall balcony.
Courtesy of @Littlest_Bear and @CalBearsHistory.

It's hard to imagine what it was like when grizzly bears roamed Berkeley's wide open spaces. Berkeley's original Ohlone people probably knew the bears' habits and stayed clear of them, though early Spanish settlers noted that a few of the Indigenous people they'd met had visible bear claw scars.

Bear Territory

California's state flag.
Courtesy of Wikimedia Commons.

Since the flag of the Bear Revolt debuted in the summer of 1846, the grizzly reigned triumphant as the dominant image on California flags. It has also been closely associated with UC Berkeley for almost as long. The sports teams at UC Berkeley (nicknamed "Cal" by fans) have been called the Golden Bears since the 1895 track team fashioned its own California flag with a golden yellow grizzly bear at the center. "Go Bears!" is the UC Berkeley rallying cry.

The bear was a good choice for UC Berkeley's mascot. For tens of thousands of years, Berkeley was a feasting ground for grizzly bears. Early European explorers found California's coastline teeming with whales, especially three of the largest species on earth: gray whales, humpback whales, and the gargantuan blue whales. Pacific Ocean currents led directly through the Golden Gate to Berkeley's shores before the dredging of modern shipping lanes. This made Berkeley the natural depository for dead whales. Just one washed up whale carcass could provide enough meat to sustain hundreds of bears. The frequent supply of whale carcasses is the reason Berkeley may have supported one of the largest grizzly populations in North America.

Laura Cunningham imagines Berkeley in its natural state in A State of Change: Forgotten Landscapes of California from Heyday Press.
Courtesy of Laura Cunningham.

Large groups ("sleuths") of California grizzly bears were a common sight. French sea captain Duhaut Cilly wrote in 1827 that he'd "often seen herds" of grizzlies roaming around San Francisco. Early Spanish travelers reported they saw as many as 50 grizzlies a day, while some described seeing Ohlone people with disfiguring marks from near-deadly encounters.

In 1772, when the fledgling Spanish settlement of Monterey ran out of its shipped-in rations, soldiers were sent on an expedition to bring back as much grizzly bear meat as they could. The soldiers returned with 9,000 pounds of grizzly meat from a bear killing spree in Los

Osos, a place near present-day San Luis Obispo named for its heavy concentration of bears.

As California's apex predator, grizzlies were an easy shot. A curious grizzly would walk right up to a soldier, which was helpful since many Spanish soldiers did not have good enough aim to reliably shoot other wild game. With muskets and bullets scarce, grizzly meat was the surest source of food for the first Spanish settlers. Each felled bear could provide more than 1,000 pounds of meat.

However, after settlement leaders Juan Bautista de Anza and Gaspar de Portola brought two hundred longhorn cattle overland from Mexico, the Spanish no longer needed to depend on grizzly meat as a food source. The nutrient-rich California bunch grasses made excellent cattle feed, and the longhorns multiplied, doubling their numbers every six years. Grizzly bears, given the species name *Ursus horribilis* (Latin for "horrible bear") in 1815, also saw the free-roaming cattle and sheep as a food source.

When cattle hides became California's first export commodity, ranchers began to offer bounties for killing grizzlies. California ranchers sold shiploads of hides to East Coast suppliers to make leather strap belts for factory machines. Most factories used leather straps until rubber was available at the start of the automobile industry. Traders in Monterey, California assigned a value of a dollar for each hide. Hides were nicknamed "California banknotes" because they served as the state's first trade currency.

For the Spanish and Mexican vaqueros (cowboys) and for quite a few Americano mountain men, killing a bear was the ultimate career achievement and the height of machismo honor. The road at the top of the Berkeley Hills is today known as Grizzly Peak. Before Berkeley's bears became extinct, Grizzly Peak was a good destination for bear hunters.

Some further theorize that the stock market's mascots for bear and bull markets come from this era of bear conquest. A ranchero owner offering a bounty or down payment for the pelts of bears was an investment in protecting livestock. Paying in advance for a bear skin was a speculative purchase that could turn into a gain.

"The Bull Charged Furiously" by cartoonist H.M. Stoops appeared in The San Francisco Call on Jan. 15, 1911.
Courtesy of The San Francisco Call.

California rodeos in the 1800s featured bear and bull fights, regularly held after Sunday mass services as a festive community treat. A prized and fearsome bull would be chosen to fight against a freshly captured bear. A posse of vaqueros tied one of the bear's back legs to one of the bull's, while spectators placed bets on which beast would win. The upward thrust of the bull's horns in contrast with the bear's downward attack of the bull's neck and legs is another explanation of how bear and bull markets were named.

The 1848 invention of the repeating rifle made it easy for hunters to shoot grizzlies by the hundreds. The price of a grizzly pelt jumped from $75 in 1904 to $120 in 1920. By 1924, all of California's wild grizzlies had been shot or had died in captivity. Susan Snyder, co-curator of the UC Berkeley Bancroft Library's grizzly exhibit "Bear in Mind," lamented to a *Berkeleyan* reporter how quickly the extinction occurred. "The grizzly's demise happened so quickly," Snyder said. "In a flash, after the Gold Rush, we went from 15,000 grizzlies to none, all in not more than the life-span of a single bear."

Mascot Monarch Grizzly, G. G. Park.

Monarch in a cage in Golden Gate Park in 1910. He died a year later.
Courtesy of the California State Archives.

In 1889, newspaper magnate William Randolph Hearst challenged reporter Allen Kelly to capture California's last wild grizzly bear—if one still existed—and bring the bear back to San Francisco alive. Hearst knew that Kelly's adventure would sell newspapers. Kelly and four men spent six months camping in Ojai Valley in Southern California baiting bear traps with butchered cattle. Finally, they caught a grizzly bear. Hearst had dubbed one of his papers, the *San Francisco Examiner*, "The Monarch of the Dailies" and he named the 1,100-pound bear Monarch to remind the public of his power in the media.

The Managerie in Golden Gate Park—the forerunner to today's San Francisco Zoo—refused to take Monarch, so Hearst displayed Monarch at Woodward's Garden, a two block amusement park in San Francisco's Mission District. On November 10, 1889, Monarch's first day on display, 20,000 visitors came out to see the captured grizzly bear. The ongoing saga of Monarch was a boon for the *San Francisco Examiner*.

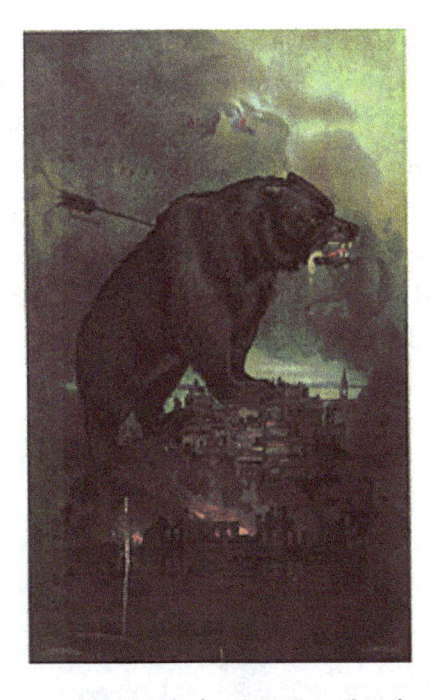

Poster of Monarch after the 1906 earthquake. Monarch is valiantly fighting for survival in the foreground. The destroyed city of San Francisco is burning in the background.
Courtesy of the California State Archives.

Monarch survived the devastating 1906 earthquake and fire, becoming a symbol of San Francisco's resilience and rejuvenation. Thousands of San Franciscans whose homes were destroyed slept in tents in Golden Gate Park for weeks and months after the earthquake. They looked to the bear penned up nearby for strength. A poster shows Monarch with an arrow stuck in his back and foaming at the mouth while valiantly fighting back. The mostly destroyed San Francisco burns in the background. In 1908 it was confirmed that the last known wild Californian grizzly was killed by a rancher in Orange County. Monarch died in 1911 after 22 years in captivity.

Meanwhile, the East Bay's population exploded after the 1906 San Francisco earthquake. Urban attractions and entertainment became big business. Berkeley residents and the 12,000 new Berkeley arrivals from the earthquake no longer needed to go to San Francisco to gawk at caged bears. Idora Park, a six-block amusement park on Telegraph Avenue and just a short trolley ride from the Berkeley campus, had no trouble rivaling the attractions at San Francisco's Golden Gate Park. The Bear Pit at Idora Park, smaller than Monarch's Bear Pit, held as many as four bears. In 1911, the parents of an 11 year old girl received a settlement of $7,500 (around $250,000 today) from the near death injuries their daughter sustained when one of the bears mauled her while she was feeding the bear acorns.

Postcard of bear enclosure at Isadora Park on Telegraph Avenue.
Courtesy of Wikimedia Commons.

In the early 1900s, real life bear cubs served as mascots for Cal home football games. Then Oski the Bear, Cal's current mascot, was introduced in 1941. His name was from a popular student cheer: "Oski Wow-Wow! Whiskey Wee-Wee! Olee! Muckie-eye! Olee! Berkeley-eye! California! Wow!" Oski's Disneyfied costume depicts him as a studious bear with stooped shoulders, wearing a letterman's jacket. Members of the UC Berkeley Rally Club keep the person wearing the Oski costume secret. Two or more students trade off wearing the Oski costume for lengthy events, like football games. Oski's antics are tame—nothing like those of a wild grizzly. He poses for selfies, pumps his fists, and strolls around with his hands clasped behind his back, like a professor deep in thought.

Oski the Bear on the Mario Savio Steps in front of Sproul Hall.
Courtesy of Wikimedia Commons.

Today, California's two remaining species of black bears *(Ursus americana altifrontalis and Ursus americana californiensis)* are the grizzly bear's smaller cousins and are afraid of people. It's illegal to kill California black bears unless they pose imminent danger to people or livestock, both extreme rarities. However, licensed hunters legally kill several hundred black bears each year during California's fall hunting season. Rangers in Yosemite National Park make it a priority to teach bear safety to the park's guests. Bears are omnivores, and if they get a taste of calorie-rich human food, they'll remember the exact spot it came from and return again and again—and will teach their cubs to keep coming to the same location as well. If a park bear continually menaces campsites when it forages for food, it's tranquilized and relocated.

The détente strategy between bears and humans has mostly worked. The California black bear population has risen, nearing as many as 40,000, mostly in the Sierra foothills and mountains. One of those 40,000, a young and not full-grown black bear, became a social media darling overnight when it wandered onto the UC Davis in June 2019. The bear was caught and released without incident.

Every once in a while, the idea of reintroducing grizzly bears into the California wilderness comes up, but so far ranchers have successfully lobbied these ideas down. Montana, Idaho, Wyoming, and Alaska have significant grizzly bear populations, with Alaska's estimated to be as large as 30,000.

The possibility that there will ever be a real bear in Berkeley again is slim, but neighboring Oakland has two sets of grizzly bear brothers: Rubicon and Kenai, the bigger set of brothers, and Tulare and Trukee, who are smaller and lighter in color. The Oakland Zoo keeps a live camera on them during the day while they enjoy their state-of-the-art 2.5 acre habitat in the Oakland Zoo. Alaska's Department of Fish and Game delivered all four together as cubs in 2018, flying them first-class on a FedEx airplane with veterinarian Dr. Joel Parrott, then president of the Oakland Zoo. Before game officers captured the cubs, their mothers were euthanized because they were deemed "public threats." The cubs could not be released back into the wild because it's likely they already had learned their mothers' dangerous behaviors. The four orphans are now living the California life with a pool, a waterfall, and a few good trees to rub up against for the occasional back scratch.

Tulare dips his paws in the water on the first day of autumn in 2024.
Courtesy of the Oakland Zoo Grizzly Cam on August 22, 2024.

The Almond Cookie Revolutionaries

"What's that stinky creek out there
Down behind the slum's back stair
Sludgy puddle, sad and gray?
Why man, that's San Francisco Bay"
— *"70 Miles" by Pete Seeger, 1965*

The Berkeley Marina

Sunsets at the Berkeley Marina are spectacular. Photographers stake out their favorite hilltop spots in Berkeley Marina's 90-acre Cesar Chavez Park to catch the ever-changing palette of colors in the sky and the rippling designs on the surface of the San Francisco Bay. Every sunset is completely unique.

A couple enjoying the sunset as it dips below the Golden Gate at the Berkeley Marina Pier.
Courtesy of Pam Gleason

On top of one hill, the Cesar Chavez Memorial Solar Calendar indicates the hours and the seasons. Surrounding the solar calendar are four large stones imprinted with the four virtues of Cesar Chavez and Dolores Huerta's farm labor movement: courage, hope, determination, and tolerance. Revelers gather at the Chavez Solar Calendar for the quarterly solstice and equinox celebrations.

In 2020, the City of Berkeley amped up its development plans for the Berkeley Waterfront by committing more than $50 million to multi-year improvement projects. Once the development is complete, an all-electric zero-emissions ferry service will begin.

The Berkeley Marina hosts a wide range of recreational activities year-around and offers spectacular bayside views of San Francisco, the Golden Gate Bridge, and Alcatraz Island.
Courtesy of Peter Bittner.

With all of the changes, longtime residents wonder if the Berkeley Marina's traditional Fourth of July celebration with fireworks, music, and children's activities will continue. Soaring public safety costs for firefighters, police, safety and clean up crews threaten other Berkeley Marina traditions, like the guerilla theater productions by the San Francisco Mime Troupe and the Berkeley Kite Festival, that was traditionally held the last weekend of July. According to the *Berkeleyside* news site, the Berkeley Kite Festival held on the hilltops of Cesar Chavez Park could permanently disappear unless a new $45,000 permit fee is reduced. For over three decades, Berkeley Kite Festival enthusiasts launched hundreds of kites of all shapes, colors, and sizes—some the size of small buses— into the near-constant easterly wind that sweeps off the ocean and up the Berkeley flats.

Once a month, the City of Berkeley deposits mounds of compost along Marina Boulevard. This is the result of the city's compost waste program, which turns green waste, including food scraps and yard trimmings, into what gardeners call "black gold." At the Berkeley Marina, green-thumbed residents are encouraged to load up their vehicles with buckets full of compost for their gardens. Occasionally out-of-town commercial trucks take away the compost, but Berkeley residents still seem to have plenty.

Neighbors work together to clean up trash at the bayshore in Berkeley, at the site where Strawberry Creek used to flow freely into the San Francisco Bay.
Courtesy of Pam Gleason.

With miles of pedestrian and bicycle trails, and even free wifi, there's plenty to do at the Berkeley Marina. The Cal Sailing Club and UC Berkeley Cal Adventures offer classes and rentals for kayaking, windsurfing, kitesurfing, canoeing, stand up paddle boarding, and kiteboarding. The water is clean enough for swimming, although swimmers need to be mindful of strong ocean currents and wear wetsuits. The water temperature in the Bay hovers around 55° Fahrenheit, enough to give even the strongest swimmer hypothermia.

The marina has boat slips that can be rented for both short-term and long-term stays. Up to 100 people can live on their boats year around in the Berkeley Marina.

Cesar Chavez Park also features a seventeen acre off-leash dog run and plenty of nature to enjoy. In the spring, the park's hills are dotted with yellow wood sorrel flowers. There's a refuge for burrowing owls on the park's southern shore. These hard-to-spot birds aren't the only wildlife: there are easy-to-spot rascally squirrels and noisy, drama-prone turkeys who also call the park home. If a group of turkeys choose a parked car for their roost, the owner will have to deal with the feisty females. The male turkeys with their full Thanksgiving-style plumage are usually more focused on scratching the ground for morsels.

Few of the visitors to the Berkeley Marina know that decades of garbage—dumped before Save The Bay helped usher in environmental protections—is buried under their feet.

The Almond Cookie Revolutionaries

Esther Gulick enjoyed entertaining in her home at the crest of Grizzly Peak Boulevard, overlooking the expanse of the San Francisco Bay. Her husband Charles Gulick was a popular economics professor at UC Berkeley, and their friends, Kay and Clark Kerr, lived nearby. As the recently elected president of the University of California, Clark Kerr was focused on the expansion of the Berkeley campus, including the new Space Sciences Laboratory. Esther knew President Kerr liked her almond cookies, so when Kay invited her for tea before Christmas in 1960, she brought along a plate of these treats.

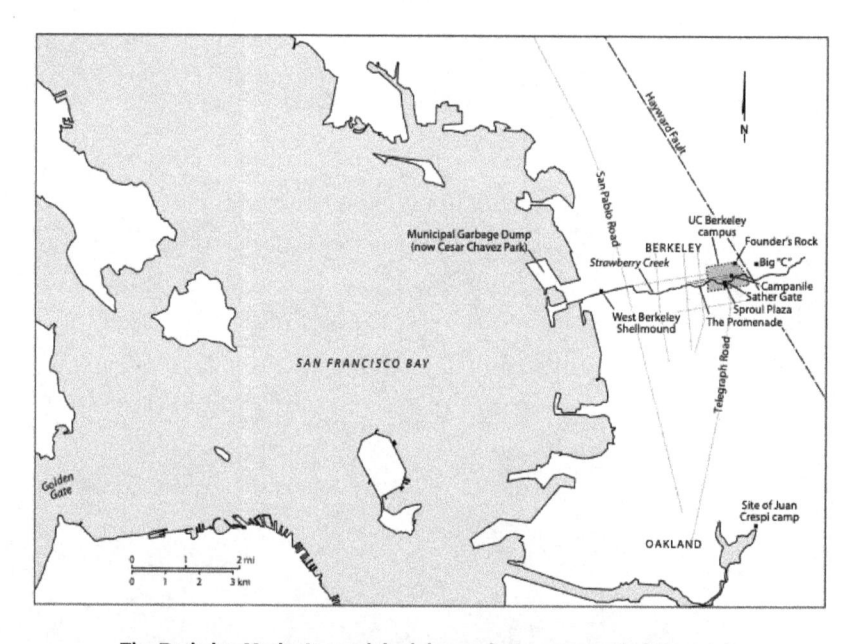

The Berkeley Marina's municipal dump site was converted to a park in the 1990s and named César Chávez Park in 1996.
Courtesy of Bill Nelson.

In addition to Esther Gulick, Kay Kerr invited another faculty wife named Sylvia McLaughlin, whose husband served as the Dean of Berkeley's College of Engineering. While enjoying their tea, the three discussed a map from the Army Corp of Engineers that predicted that by the year 2020 the San Francisco Bay would be fully filled in. The map showed that only a shipping water channel to the Port of Oakland and to Richmond's Chevron Oil Refinery would remain. Already, one-third of the Bay had been filled in by dumped waste, with 80 percent of the original wetlands destroyed. Santa Fe Railroad, which owned the majority of Berkeley's waterfront, formed an influential lobby to sell the Berkeley City Council on the idea of increased commerce from filling in the rest of the Bay. Santa Fe Railroad's plan was to double the size of Berkeley by filling in 2,000 acres of the Bay with debris. A hot topic was the proposal to build the Berkeley International Airport on the newly created landfill.

The Berkeley Gazette published this 1943 plan for the Berkeley International Airport at the Berkeley Marina location.
Courtesy of the Berkeley Historical Society.

From their Berkeley Hills vantage point, Gulick, Kerr, and McLaughlin could see municipal garbage trucks dump load after load of refuse into the Bay at the Berkeley Marina. At night, parts of the municipal dump glowed red from trash fires. They knew that garbage trucks from cities all over the Bay Area were doing the same on their shorelines. "Berkeley's City Council and the business and industrial sector... were anxious to put over 2,000 acres to fill in the Bay so Berkeley could almost double in size... [with] an airport, industrial and commercial buildings, houses, apartments, a hotel or two, a parking lot, and so on," the three women recalled in a 1988 speech for UC Berkeley's College of Natural Resources Albright Lecture that they co-wrote and co-presented.

McLaughlin said she, Kerr, and Gulick "regarded the Bay as one of this country's national treasures... it was unthinkable that most of this beautiful natural resource could be filled." McLaughlin remembers it was Kay Kerr who said, "We've got to do something."

Within a few weeks, they organized a meeting with conservation leaders from the Sierra Club, the Audubon Society, and Save the Redwoods. Their guests agreed it was an important problem to solve, but it was not a priority for their organizations. As they departed, they wished their hosts the best of luck. David Brower, then the Sierra Club's Executive Director said, "Somebody should start a new organization."

And so these three women, who became known as the "Almond Cookie Revolutionaries," did. Gulick recalled in the 1988 Albright lecture that they were "green as grass" when they began the political campaign of their lives. They assembled their Christmas card lists and the addresses of everyone they knew at UC Berkeley and mailed out their first campaign letter, imploring their friends and acquaintances to send a dollar for a "Save The Bay" membership. Ninety percent who received the letter responded. Within a couple of years, Save The Bay had tens of thousands of members.

In the following years, the Save The Bay campaign notched one victory after another, winning in courts and in the State Legislature. Gulick said their "ultimate victory" came on August 7, 1969, when then-California Governor Ronald Reagan signed a bill to create the San

Francisco Bay Conservation and Development Commission. To this day, the SFBCDC is the agency that adjudicates permits to "place fill, to extract materials, or to make any substantial change in use of any water, land, or structure" in or near the San Francisco Bay.

Governor Ronald Reagan signed Save The Bay's bill to create the San Francisco Bay Conservation and Development Commission (SFBCDC) in 1969. SFBCDC became the world's first coastal protection agency.
Courtesy of Wikimedia Commons.

Although the Bay is protected from further infill and industrial development, Save The Bay's work continues. In the 1960s, only six miles of its shoreline was open to the public for recreational purposes. Now the public has access to hundreds of miles of shoreline. In 2016, the Bay Area's Measure AA dedicated $25 million annually to shoreline projects that protect and restore the Bay, and millions more in federal funding is being spent on Bay Area wetland restoration, water quality, and green development projects.

To honor the work of Save The Bay's co-founder Sylvia McLaughlin, the 8.5 mile shoreline from Oakland to Richmond was named McLaughlin Eastshore Park in 2012. Wetland specialists have reseeded native grasses, including fescues, blue wild rye, and California brome. This has, in turn, encouraged the growth of native flowers, such as bluebonnets (lupines), snow-white clusters of yarrow, and bright orange California poppies.

Hydraulic mining dissolved hillsides in the Sierra Nevada foothills. Debris washed into the rivers and flowed to the San Francisco Bay.
Courtesy of the Bancroft Library.

The San Francisco Bay's ecological destruction began with the 1849 Gold Rush. The collective waste of 300,000 migrants who came during the Gold Rush was the first major assault on the the Bay Area's biome. Once the gold that could be panned from the Sierra Nevada tributaries disappeared, capitalists invested in hydraulic mining. For each ounce of gold extracted by hydraulics, tons of debris polluted the Sacramento Delta and from there flowed into the San Francisco Bay. Most of the wetlands, once lush with wildlife, were coated in a thick silt, as was the shoreline. Even today, striped bass caught from the San Francisco Bay have one of the highest rates of mercury contamination in U.S. waters from hydraulic gold mining that happened more than 150 years ago.

The accumulation of millions of tons of debris from hydraulic mining and shoreline dump sites caused Berkeley's white sand beach, just north of Strawberry Creek's ancient shellmound, to disappear. Once-abundant populations of shellfish, salmon, and other fish species that spawned in the Bay's estuaries, tributaries, and marshlands, declined as refuse clogged the waterways. Before the introduction of herbicides, pesticides, and chemical fertilizers in the 1940s, California ranching and farming relied on covering the land with manure and guano, which washed into the waterways along with the refuse from cattle and sheep. Standing water near the shores of the San Francisco Bay began to reek of raw sewage. Garbage from Bay Area settlements and townships was carted and dumped at the water's edge, forming enormous heaps that filled in the shoreline.

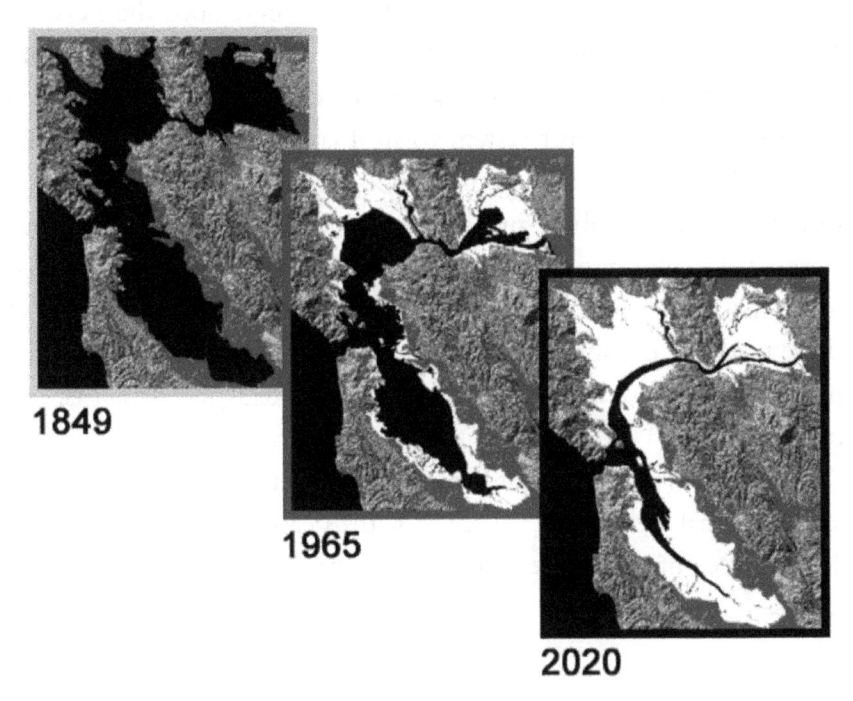

1849

1965

2020

Hydraulic mining and municipal dumping filled the San Francisco Bay with polluted sediment.
Courtesy of the California Department of Fish and Wildlife.

After gold, Californians looked to Bay Area land investment for instant riches. Some turned a quick profit by using landfill to transform marshes into waterfront real estate. The ownership of these lots changed hands often. Just like in San Francisco, underwater portions of Berkeley's shoreline was partitioned to the wealthy and politically connected, who knew that a little political hand greasing meant their soggy plot could return exponential profits.

Investors who purchased Berkeley shoreline land were rewarded when the Southern Pacific Railroad opened a connection through

Berkeley in 1876. Political scheming and shenanigans are the reason railroad tracks were laid in West Berkeley, alongside the San Francisco Bay. It's common knowledge that these tracks are on landfill, which liquefaction turns to jelly in an earthquake.

One titan of waterfront scheming and shenanigans was Oakland's first mayor, Horace Walpole Carpentier, who developed the Berkeley Marina for industry and made his fortune from shady real estate deals. As one of the first lawyers outside of San Francisco, Carpentier used the new California court system to steal land. He became Mayor by stuffing the ballot box with phony ballots, hiring his own gang of thugs to exploit Chinese labor, and claiming ownership of the waterfront. Carpentier's laborers pounded stakes into the shallow water then added fill to make more land. He hired a mapmaker to mark off parcels of shore land and the surrounding water with his name inscribed on the parcels. Then he sold off these parcels to the railroads, industrialists, and ferry operators.

Berkeley's first pier, Jacobs Pier, was constructed in 1853. The Berkeley Municipal Pier, which is aligned with Alcatraz Island, was built in 1929 to accommodate the Golden Gate Ferry Company's automobile ferries.

Jacobs Pier, Berkeley's first pier, was constructed in 1853.
Photo courtesy of the Bancroft Library.

To get from San Francisco to Berkeley before the building of the Bay Bridge, motorists drove to the end of University Avenue, then to the end of the 3.5-mile-long pier to load onto the ferry. Since the pier reached almost all of the way to Treasure Island, the ferry ride to San Francisco was pretty quick—but the wait to board wasn't always.

On Cal Football game days, traffic from Memorial Stadium to the Berkeley Municipal Pier could be backed up for hours. After construction on the Bay Bridge was completed in 1936, the Golden Gate Ferry Company only operated for two more years. In 1938, the Berkeley Municipal Pier was rededicated for fishing and recreation. In 2015, the dilapidated pier closed for repairs as engineers worked to reconfigure the structure to accommodate the new ferry service.

In the past decade, the City of Berkeley has embarked on a renewal plan for the Berkeley Marina, including the $8 million Marina Streets project. Since the landfill below the Berkeley Marina constantly shifts, it's a challenge to keep the roads, utility lines, and structures in good condition. Newly paved roads and new boat docks retrofitted with aluminum gangways serve as signs that the City continues to invest in developing the Berkeley Marina. Occasionally a methane burp will surface from the long-buried 1.6 million tons of garbage beneath the grassy surface, although it's been decades since you could create a small explosion with a lighter. An aging network of around 12,000 feet of PVC piping under the east side of Cesar Chavez Park channels methane to a flare station, where it is burned and cooled before being released into the air from a small tower next to the off-leash dog run area. In 2024, engineers fixed a methane leak. They use drones to detect repositories of hazardous radioactive waste, harmful DDT and dieldrin pesticides dumped by the Stauffer Chemical Company from 1960 to 1971.

The family-oriented Ecology Center at the Berkeley Marina hosts a number of activities, like teaching school children ecology and ocean, bay, and wetland conservation. Instructors there are carrying on the Almond Cookie Revolutionaries' legacy into the present. "Bellies for Jellies" encourages kids and adults to lay down on their stomachs on the Berkeley Marina dock and hang their heads over the side to peer into the depths below to count all of the species they can see. Lucky belly botanists will spot a jellyfish or starfish.

The Almond Cookie Revolutionaries' legacy also lives on through the Save The Bay organization they created, which teaches K-12 modules in Bay Area history, geology, ecology, biodiversity, and watershed science that meet California's Common Core and Next Generation Science Standards. Students work along the shoreline, picking up trash, weeding out invasive plants, and planting seedlings to help restore the ecological health of the Bay. California State Park rangers have to date restored 1,833 acres of McLaughlin Eastshore State Park. Work continues to connect McLaughlin Park and Berkeley shoreline to the Bay Trail. When completed, the Bay Trail will include 500 miles of shoreline trails, connecting all nine counties surrounding the San Francisco Bay, including 47 bay-side cities and the seven major bridges that cross over the Bay.

Lois The Pie Queen

"Jesus, I know Lois is with you, and I know she's going to want to cook for you, and when she asks, 'Lord, what would you like?'—Could I suggest the pork chops?"

—*Michael Ringbom, longtime cook for Lois The Pie Queen who helped Lois Davis make apple, cherry, and pecan pies*

Lois The Pie Queen

Lois The Pie Queen t-shirt design.
Courtesy of Chris Davis.

As a high school student in the 1940s, Lois Davis became famous for the pies she and her mom Mathilda, along with her sisters Earnestine and Bernice, baked for church gatherings and fundraisers. As an adult, Lois turned this success into a business and opened Lois The Pie Queen on Sacramento Street in Berkeley. She chose Berkeley for her restaurant so her young children, Chris and Tramaine, could attend the the Bay Area's best schools.

Sacramento Street was Berkeley's center of Black commerce. Its businesses were listed in the Green Book, a guidebook for Black travelers who sought out African-American businesses for the combined reasons of pride, community, and safety.

Lois The Pie Queen was an instant hit, and Black families traveled from all over the Bay Area for fried chicken, waffles, and pie—followed by a stop at Reid's Records two doors down to browse the latest hits. In 1973, the restaurant relocated to 851 60th Street in Oakland, on the corner Adeline, just south of the Berkeley border. Berkeley's first Black mayor, Gus Newport, in office from 1979 to 1986, touted the restaurant as his political headquarters and held meetings there.

Lois played a pioneering role in the Bay Area music industry by supporting young artists. Daughter Tramaine Hawkins became a gospel sensation and national treasure. Her son, Chris Davis, a Berkeley High star athlete, immersed himself in the music industry while helping his mom run the restaurant. Photos of famous musicians cover a full wall in the restaurant. Chris remembers the early days when Digital Underground's Humpty Hump, Shock G, Chopmaster J, hip hop DJ Kenny-K, and their protégé Tupac Shakur hung out at Lois The Pie Queen before they were famous.

Celebrities with local roots, from Kamala Harris to Zendaya, stop by when they're in town, along with a past and present who's who of sports legends. Tony Green, a hometown hero who created the curriculum for the country's first African American Studies Advanced Placement high school class, sometimes brings his students in to learn about local history. Regulars know that it's Lois The Pie Queen—with a capital "T" for "The"—in honor of Lois and her family legacy.

Popular menu items include the Reggie Jackson Dinner, named after the former A's star's regular order of fried pork chops, eggs, grits, and biscuits, and Lemon Ice-box Pie, a dreamy recipe created by daughter Tramaine Hawkins.

On Sunday afternoons, when there is usually a line out the door, Lois's son Chris makes sure guests are attended to with refills of hot coffee. Chris has run the restaurant since Lois passed away in 1993. He's got his mom's smile, soft voice, and gentle demeanor, lavishing attention on his regulars—especially ladies wearing gorgeous Sunday church hats, a tradition his mom loved and admired. Lois's grandson Corey Jackson represents the new generation, but he's just as devoted to the original recipes and old-style service as the rest of the family.

Baseball legend Reggie Jackson and Lois Davis in 1974. Jackson was a lifelong patron of Lois The Pie Queen. His favorite meal of fried pork chops and fixings is still on the menu as the Reggie Jackson Special.
Courtesy of Chris Davis.

Lois The Pie Queen

Lois Davis was Berkeley's first famous female restaurateur and one of the Bay Area's most successful restaurant owners. Her clientele included the lifelong devoted patronage of baseball legend Reggie Jackson. Her life is an American success story.

Lois Davis kept in constant motion as she served her customers at Lois The Pie Queen.
Courtesy of Chris Davis.

Berkeley's anti-Black racism mirrors California's history. Congress admitted California as the 31st state on September 9, 1850, and nine days later, on September 18, 1850 Congress passed the Fugitive Slave Act, requiring by federal order that slaves in free states be returned to their owners as a compromise to keep the Southern slave-owning states from seceding. This made it unsafe for Black Americans to travel to California, since slave catchers were incentivized by cash—$10 per captured enslaved person, and $5 per captured Black person, even if there was proof they were legally free. By way of context, $5 was the going rate for an acre of land in 1850.

Two Black laborers, Hannah Burns and Peter Burns, are the first recorded Black residents of Berkeley. Hannah Burns and Peter Burns lived on the 827-acre farm of their former enslaver, Napoleon Bonaparte Byrne, whose house called "The Cedars" was built on today's location of Berkeley's Congregation Beth El synagogue. The Byrne property included the Codornices Creek and its creek valley at the base of the Berkeley Hills, the current location of the Berkeley Rose Garden and Codornices Park.

The 1860 California census shows Peter Burns and Hannah Burns, the first two entries on page 51, indicated with 'B' for Black. They resided with Napoleon Bonaparte Byrne, a slave owner from Missouri who bought farmland in the portion of the Oakland Township that would later be called Berkeley.
Courtesy of Ancestry.com.

Hannah Burns was just eight years old when she arrived in Berkeley in 1859 after a six-month wagon journey from the Missouri plantation where the Byrnes and their enslaved laborers lived. The census at the time lists her profession as "Nurse" and her job was likely to help with the four Byrne children, whose ages ranged from a newborn to eight. Peter Burns was 32 when he arrived. He was the driver of the Byrne family wagon. It's unclear if Hannah Burns and Peter Burns are related.

Letters from Mary Tanner Byrne's correspondence with friends and family are in the Bancroft Library, providing clues about the lives of Hannah Burns and Peter Burns. Most of the letters' contents either cover Mary Tanner Byrne's busy social calendar and frequent trips to San Francisco or anecdotes about her children, four more of whom were born after she arrived in Berkeley. In one letter she enthuses about the $7 blue and pink colored bonnets she bought for herself and one of her daughters. Mary Tanner Byrne wrote that Peter Burns became well-known for the elegant coattail suit he wore atop the Byrne family carriage, writing that she adored riding on Berkeley's only road, San Pablo Road, calling it "one of the handsomest roads in the state." On weekends, wealthy men would trot their most expensive horses down the road from Oakland to San Pablo and back.

San Pablo Road in 1912. Under Spanish rule it was El Camino de la Contra Costa. It's now also State Route 123.
Courtesy of the Bancroft Library.

Mary Tanner Byrne's husband Napoleon Bonaparte Byrne was a staunch pro-slavery Confederate who often complained that too many of his neighbors were "Damn Yankees!" He considered running for the California State Legislature as a Southern Democrat, following the example of fellow pro-slavery southerner Edmund Randolph, a neighbor whose property was located further down San Pablo Road.

Randolph named nearby Richmond, California after his hometown of Richmond, Virginia—the capital city of the Confederacy—and spent his later career politicking for Nicaragua and other Central American countries to join the Confederacy as slave states.

Later, when Napoleon Bonaparte Byrne purchased farm land near along the San Joaquin River, he had 500 Chinese workers build dikes and farm the flood-prone land. The Berkeley Historical Plaque Project mentions that Hannah Burns continued to work as a domestic worker after the Byrnes family relocated, with Peter Burns becoming a whitewasher in Oakland, applying lime coatings to barns and other structures. Through the rest of their lives they probably only met a few other Black people living in the San Francisco Bay Area. The 1860 census recorded only 4,086 Black residents living in California. California's Black population would continue to be sparse until the first Great Migration from the South.

During the first Great Migration, a period that stretched from 1916 to 1940, an estimated 2 million Black people left the South because of poor employment prospects and violent oppression. California's Black population increased to around 22,000 by 1940, a small fraction of those who moved to northern metropolitan areas during the first Great Migration.

The second Great Migration, occurring from 1940 to 1970, brought over 300,000 to California. In 1939, just before this second huge wave, Lois Ruth Cleveland—who would become known to all as Lois The Pie Queen—came with her family on the two-day train trip from Oklahoma City to the Oakland train depot, then onto their new home in Richmond, California. There, the Cleveland family settled into a refurbished wood frame house just a short walk from where the Henry J. Kaiser Company would build the Richmond Shipyards in 1941 and 1942.

The Cleveland family's arrival in Richmond, California, in 1939 coincided with the beginning of a population surge in which the San Francisco Bay Area gained half a million new residents, a 35 percent increase between 1939 and 1945. By 1944, the Richmond Shipyards

District was the largest shipbuilding facility in the world, and within its first five years, 900,000 workers would build 747 ships.

Historian Marilynn Johnson called the booming war-time population a "Second Gold Rush"—also the name of her 1993 book on the topic—because the change in demographics in the San Francisco Bay Area was as dramatic as the Gold Rush 100 years prior. Berkeley resident and pioneering photojournalist Dorothea Lange chronicled this change, taking photos of workers changing shifts at the shipyards. Some of these, including the photo nicknamed "Black Rosie The Riveter," would become among her most famous. Lange described the scene as, "All ages, races, types, skills and backgrounds. A deluge of humanity."

The USS General C. G. Morton (AP-138), a cargo ship, returns to the San Francisco Bay where it was built and launched from the Richmond Shipyards in 1943. On July 17, 1944, the munitions aboard the SS E. A. Bryan exploded in Port Chicago, around 25 miles northeast of Berkeley. The majority of the 320 killed and the 390 injured in the explosion were Black Americans.
Courtesy of the National Park Service.

Lois's grandfather, Jefferson John Cleveland, was born a year after President Lincoln's January 1, 1863 Emancipation Proclamation. He was the first in his family to be born into freedom after the family's multi-generational enslavement on a Georgia plantation. At 20, he married his sweetheart Nettie. Together they bought a farm in Oklahoma's Indian territory large enough to support several generations of Clevelands. They built five houses on the farm to accommodate their children, grandchildren, and great grandchildren.

Lois was the oldest Cleveland grandchild and a fast learner. On their Oklahoma farm she learned to cook, sing, and read the Bible from two generations of formidable Black women—her grandmother Nettie from Georgia, her mother Mathilda from Louisiana, her aunt Maggie from Alabama, and her aunt Anna from Texas. Lois learned their favorite recipes by heart. The whole family loved her skillet-fried hoecakes, named as such because biscuits could be baked in the fire on the iron surface of a flat hoe.

At age 10, Lois's parents Jefferson John Cleveland, Jr. and Mathilda Cleveland visited a nearby town to hear a traveling preacher. The preacher's passion and his ability to let the power of Jesus take over his body seemed a miracle and electrified them. National Association for the Advancement of Colored People (NAACP) founder W. E. B. DuBois called this form of worship "the frenzy" and wrote about its cultural context for Black Americans. For Pentecostal Christians and for the Black members of the Church of God in Christ, founded in 1907 in Memphis, Tennessee, speaking in tongues was an ecstatic revelation from the Holy Spirit. But to Grandfather Cleveland, this was a heretical brand of Christianity for which he wouldn't stand, leading to Lois's parents to move her and her sisters—Bernice (age eight) and Ernestine (age six)—to the Oklahoma oil boomtown of Ponca City. There, Lois's father took the name E. E. (Elmer Elijah) Cleveland and began his own ministry, the Church of God in Christ in Ponca City. Lois would never have the chance to cook with her grandmother and aunts again, but she didn't forget their recipes.

Reverend E. E. Cleveland's ministry opened a whole new world of contacts and possibilities for the young Cleveland family. From 1933 to 1938, President Franklin D. Roosevelt's "New Deal" created employment opportunities and class mobility to families across the United States, particularly in coastal industrial areas which were booming with shipyards and factories. W. E. B. Du Bois was skeptical that New Deal opportunities would be good for Black Americans. A common refrain was that Roosevelt's "New Deal" was more like an "Old Deal" for Black Americans. Ibram X. Kendi's research in his 2016 book *Stamped From The Beginning* confirmed these suspicions, with Kendi writing, "Blacks' primary vocations were excluded from the laws' new job benefits, like minimum wage, social security, unemployment insurance, and unionizing rights."

Reverend E. E. Cleveland and his wife Mathilda committed their lives to preaching. They felt their calling was in California, where the shipping and munitions industry began offering Black men—and eventually Black women—wages unheard of in the South. They moved from their one-room Ponca City home in Oklahoma to a three-bedroom home not far from Richmond, California's railroad tracks and munition factories.

Once settled, Reverend E. E. Cleveland's congregation grew rapidly. He offered his ministry around the clock to serve the shipyard workers, with Mathilda Cleveland staying home to cook and renovate the house with her young daughters. Upon completion, the Cleveland house had eight rooms, including a sun porch. Lois and her sisters were convinced their mom had built the grandest Black family home in all of Richmond.

Mathilda enlisted her daughters to start a catering business to feed the hundreds of laborers who worked at the shipyards and surrounding factories that had mushroomed along the East Bay shoreline. The sisters earned what they could by regularly making hundreds of sandwiches late into the night to feed the Richmond laborers who worked around the clock, seven days a week. Laborers often shared "hot beds," beds that could be rented out to three or more men during each 24-hour cycle. The Cleveland women also made pies—apple, sweet potato, and mixed berry—for their father's church fundraisers.

Gospel music was the first Black music genre to be played on California radio stations, and Reverend E. E. Cleveland—who earned the nickname "Dad Cleveland" by his parishioners—gave live sermons featured on "Lucky 13" *KDIA Radio 1310*. "He did that program for 35 years and was one of the first radio preachers in the state," remembered Lois's sister Ernestine. Lois was considered a teen prodigy, and her talent won the role of lead singer in her father's church choir. Her solos in church and on the radio earned her the nickname of "Songbird of the East Bay."

In 1949, Lois married Duvall Davis. Together they'd saved enough money to buy a small coffee shop on Sacramento Street in Berkeley. They named it Lois The Pie Queen, Lois's lesser-known nickname gained from so many years of baking pies. The shop was tiny, with just enough room for six tables and a countertop. Starting at 3 or 4 a.m. the couple prepared hearty breakfasts of eggs, chicken fried steak, biscuits, pancakes, pork chops, hash browns, and lots of hot coffee so they could offer free refills. After the breakfast shift, Lois baked the pies and biscuits, and made the meals for lunch and dinner. Lois kept her toddler Christopher and new baby Tremaine close to her while she worked. Being a mother never stopped Lois. When she went into labor with Tremaine during a Sunday church service, she insisted on finishing her solo hymn before leaving for the hospital.

The Sacramento Street location was perfect for Lois The Pie Queen. In 1949, Dad Cleveland became pastor of the Ephesian Church of God in Christ on nearby Alcatraz Avenue in Berkeley. Berkeley had a reputation for its good public schools. Lois wanted her children to stay there to have the best education possible. The story of Ruth Acty, Berkeley's first Black school teacher, was well known and an inspiration for Black families in the San Francisco Bay Area.

Acty was first appointed to teach Kindergarten at Longfellow Elementary School in 1943, where 30 percent of the students were Black. (Longfellow is now a Middle School located near the present-day

Berkeley Bowl.) Acty's classes at UC Berkeley qualified her to teach older children, but she was assigned to teach Kindergarten because, at the time, it was thought that young children hadn't yet learned to be prejudiced. Also, since Kindergarten was optional, objecting white parents could keep their children from attending Acty's class.

Ruth Acty's Kindergarteners at Longfellow Elementary School learn Chinese calligraphy from a visiting dignitary c. 1943.
Courtesy of the Berkeley Unified School District.

Acty's breakthrough assignment came after a five-year campaign to persuade the Berkeley Board of Education to hire Black teachers. That campaign was led by Frances Mary Albrier, a nurse and activist who'd moved to Berkeley with her family from Alabama in 1920. Albrier was just one of 17 UC Berkeley Black students at the time. She later sought a career in nursing, but was turned away from jobs she was qualified to do. Instead, Albrier ran for office elected to the Alameda County Democratic Central Committee and founded the East Bay Women's Welfare Club. Just as Albrier inspired Acty, Albrier was inspired by

Vivian Logan Rogers, UC Berkeley's first African American graduate in 1909.

In addition to the advantage of sending the Davis children to Berkeley schools, Lois The Pie Queen's location on Sacramento Street was ideal because it was at the heart of Black commerce in Berkeley. Sacramento Street businesses were advertised in The Green Book—a segregation-era guide that pointed Black travelers towards businesses that would serve them. Sacramento Street in Berkeley was a destination for the Black community from all around the San Francisco Bay Area.

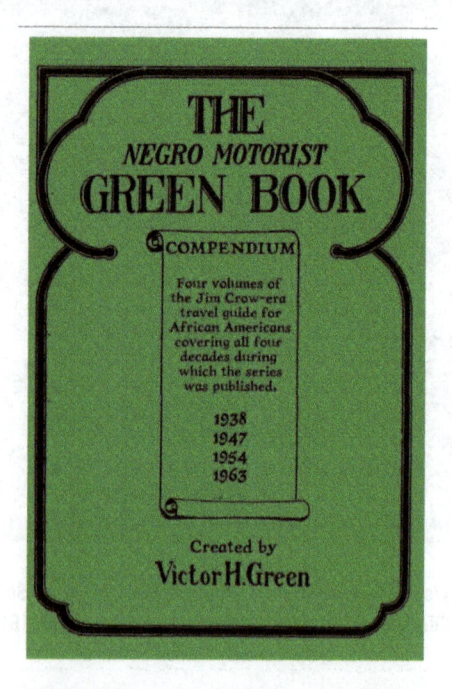

Black businesses in Berkeley's Sacramento Street were listed in the The Green Book created by Victor H. Green for Black travelers.
Courtesy of the Schomburg Center for Research in Black Culture.

Two doors down from Lois's shop was Reid's Records, considered the best Black record store in California for its rich selection of gospel, jazz, and blues. Betty Reid Soskin, another member of Berkeley's entrepreneurial aristocracy, founded Reid's Records in 1945 with her first husband Mel, who worked the swing shift at the Kaiser shipyards.

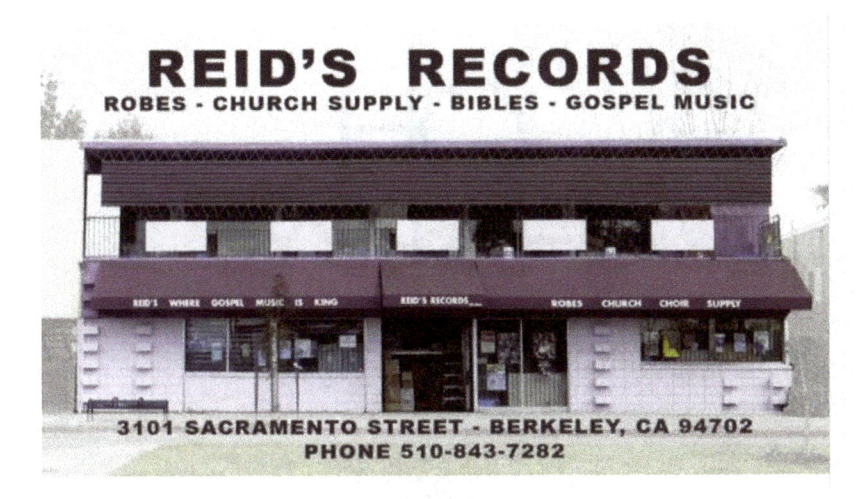

Advertisement for Reid's Records, founded in 1945 by Mel and Betty Reid. Reid's closed in 2019. In 2023 a fire destroyed the building.
Courtesy of the Berkeley Historical Society.

Both the Davis family and the Reid family shared a love of music. In 1968, teenage daughter Tremaine Davis—who would become the world famous Grammy Award winning gospel singer Tremaine Hawkins—led the Northern California State Youth Choir in the song "Oh Happy Day" with the Hawkins family. According to her son Chris, Lois Davis paid for the record's first recording sessions at the Ephesian Church in Berkeley with her earnings from Lois The Pie Queen.

"Oh Happy Day" was an immediate hit. Both Martin Luther King, Jr., and Bobby "Lil Bobby" Hutton, a member of Oakland's Black Panther Party, had just been killed. The local Black community was in deep mourning, and the Cleveland, Davis, and Hawkins families joined together to respond with pies, songs, and prayers.

Dad Cleveland presided over Hutton's memorial at the Ephesian Church, attended by a sentry of Black Panthers. The Panthers, in their uniforms of black berets and leather jackets, paid their respects by lining up silently in formation on the sidewalk outside the church, entering after all of the other mourners had taken their seats in the pews.

Record cover for "Oh Happy Day" featuring Tremaine Hawkins and recorded at the Berkeley Ephesian Church in 1968.
Courtesy of Wikimedia Commons.

Patrons of Lois The Pie Queen have come from all over. Tupac Shakur's parents were Black Panthers and frequented Lois The Pie Queen. Reggie Jackson, Hall of Fame right fielder for the Oakland Athletics, was a regular who told anyone within earshot that Lois's fried pork chops were the best in the world. (Lois named the fried pork chops the Reggie Jackson Special.) Athletes from the San Francisco Giants, the Oakland Raiders, the San Francisco 49ers, the Oakland A's, and the Golden State Warriors have been regulars over the years. Entertainers, musicians, and politicians followed. Gus Newport, mayor of Berkeley from 1979 to 1986, held political meetings and office hours at Lois The Pie Queen.

Today the walls of Lois the Pie Queen are covered in photos of famous patrons. Queen Latifah stops by when she's in town. Kamala Harris, who grew up in Berkeley, visits on occasion. Former President Barack Obama promised to drop in next time he's in the Bay Area. On "Pi Day"—a world celebration for math enthusiasts—it's almost impossible to get a table.

Owner Chris Davis (in the black Lois The Pie Queen t-shirt) with Barbara Lee and friends sharing memories and slices of pie at Lois The Pie Queen.
Courtesy of Chris Davis.

After Lois Davis's death in 1993, son Chris and his children have kept the quality of the food and the ambience up to Lois's Southern hospitality standards. Rising about the happy hum of homestyle dining, satisfied customers show their delight with the kind of praise Lois Davis would appreciate most: a deep belly laugh, a favorite gospel reframe sung out loud, a head bowed in grateful prayer, or an exuberant "Hallelujah!"

Berkelium, Californium and the Red Enemy

*"Mankind invented the atomic bomb,
but no mouse would ever construct a mousetrap."*
—*Albert Einstein*

Moe's Books

Moe Moskowitz had a beatnik's soul. According to his daughter Doris, who now runs her father's bookstore, he'd been kicked out of the Young Communist League because he had "too many opinions" and was dismissed from Cooper Union for having "a low attitude," before finding brotherhood in a circle of anarchists in the East Village. His outlandish antics laced with Yiddish expletives were a hit in New York's avant-garde experimental theater scene. He was the kind of person who would make J. Edgar Hoover's blood boil.

"In God and Moe We Trust" is imprinted on Moe's Bucks, a currency for book lovers to sell their used books to buy more used books.
Courtesy of Doris Moskowitz.

In 1955, Moskowitz came to California, the same year Allen Ginsberg first read his poem "Howl" at San Francisco's Six Gallery, which would become the epicenter of the beatnik movement. After marrying electric heater heiress Barbara (Barb) Ann Hicks, Moskowitz moved to Berkeley. With his new wife's financial backing and business prowess, Moskowitz opened Moe's Books at 2476 Telegraph Avenue in 1959.

Moskowitz's stunts exposed Berkeley's fascist leanings and made him a local celebrity. In 1961, he fought a battle with the City of Berkeley to keep a newspaper kiosk outside of his bookstore that the *The Berkeley Review* dubbed "The Battle of the Kiosk."

In 1968, Moskowitz was arrested in his bookstore for having pornographic materials because some of his comic books, including his best seller *Snatch*, had nude and suggestive images. According to the *San Francisco Chronicle*, Moskowitz wryly argued that the sexual comic material was "clean stuff. No leather stockings, or whips." When Berkeley passed its no-smoking ordinance in 1986, Moskowitz was continuously cited for smoking his signature three-per-day Cuesta-Rey and Macanudo cigars.

According to business partner Bob Baldock, Moskowitz regularly received threats. One letter he received stated, "Moe, you commie-loving creep, keep it up and we'll blast you and all your bookesh faggy elk." Moskowitz's response was to put up a sign next to the letter in the front window that said, "Do what you will, I'm powerless to stop you, but for Christ's sake...spare the elk."

"Some People's Park" is what Doris Moskowitz said her father called nearby People's Park. He was cynical about the aims of Berkeley's protest leaders, who he thought were more interested in provoking a clash than preserving a community space. Still, he kept Moe's Books open during the riots for protesters to duck inside to get away from the tear gas or escape the fuzz through the backdoor exit. Moskowitz and rival Telegraph bookseller Fred Cody, owner of Cody's Books, founded the Berkeley Free Clinic, a "street medicine" clinic for injured protesters.

Moskowitz's outsized personality and his fair trade practices—issuing Moe's Bucks currency so customers could buy new books by selling their old ones—made Moe's Books a favorite destination. The *San Francisco Chronicle* declared, "India has the Taj Mahal. Berkeley has Moe's." With four floors and around 200,000 new and used books, it attracts visitors from all over the world.

Author Malcolm Margolin presided over Moe's memorial service in 1997. Moe's life was celebrated with mirth and whimsy. Margolin was pleased to see several nude women in the audience—paying their respects with exactly the kind of irreverence Moe loved. A compilation of poems and tributes to Moskowitz, *On the Finest Shore*, starts with a stadium-style chant "MOE-MOE-MOE-MOE"— and ends with "What's the best bookstore in the West? Who keeps his place like a well-loved nest?"

Moe Moskowitz (1921-1997) opened Moe's in 1959. In the 1950's, Berkeley was home to the famous Beatnik writers Allen Ginsburg, Jack Kerouac, Gary Snyder, and Robert Duncan.
Courtesy of Doris Moskowitz.

Berkelium, Californium and the Red Enemy

Nuclear physics and Berkeley first became synonymous nearly a hundred years ago. In 1929, just one year into Ernest Lawrence's position as associate professor at UC Berkeley, he announced, "I'm going to be famous!" as he hurried across the Berkeley campus, unable to contain his excitement. Lawrence could not wait to tell his LeConte Hall colleagues his idea for an atomic particle-splitting "proton merry-go-round." according to Michael Hiltzik in his 2015 book *Big Science: Ernest Lawrence at the Invention that Launched the Military Industrial Complex.*

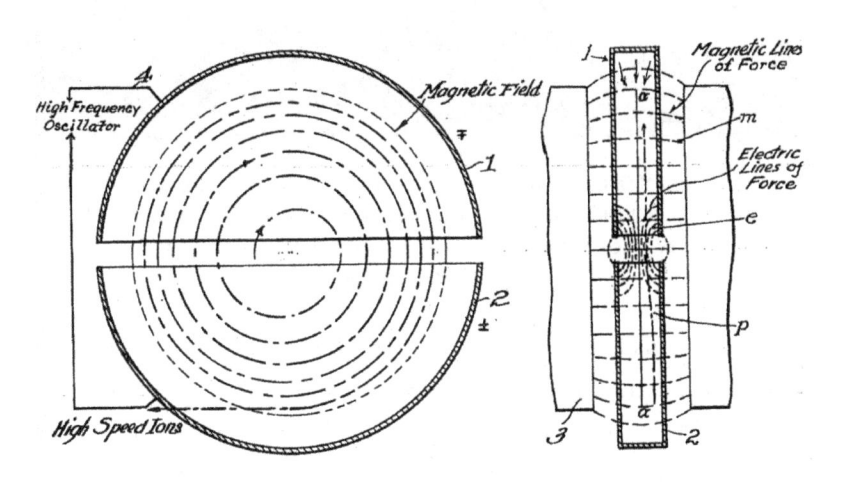

Ernest O. Lawrence's diagram of the first prototype of a cyclotron for U.S. Patent 1,948,384.
Courtesy of Wikimedia Commons.

Lawrence was browsing through a magazine called *Archiv fuer Elektrotechnik* in the Bancroft Library when a design by Norwegian physicist Rolf Widerøe fired up his imagination. Lawrence's "Aha!" moment was to create a linear atomic particle accelerator by using two electrode magnetic poles to create a spiral motion. The acceleration rate would speed up by increasing the kinetic energy with each spin.

The cylindrical design solved the "race to a million volts" problem—the vast and logistically impossible amounts of electricity needed to blast particles using linear designs. Lawrence nicknamed his atom-smashing invention a "cyclotron."

Ernest O. Lawrence stands inside the cyclotron reactor at the building site above campus. This location is now known as Lawrence Berkeley National Laboratory or the Hill Campus.
Courtesy of Lawrence Berkeley National Laboratory.

Lawrence was a showman who knew when to turn on the charm. Actor Josh Hartnett captured Lawrence's midwestern folksiness in the Oscar-winning film *Oppenheimer*, the 2023 film based on the Pulitzer Prize winning book *American Prometheus: The Triumph and Tragedy of J. Robert Oppenheimer* by Kai Bird and Martin J. Sherwin.

His affable personality made him a natural fundraiser. When University of California President Robert Gordon Sproul nominated him for San Francisco's prestigious Bohemian Club, described in *Imperial San Francisco* as an "exclusive brotherhood composed of some of the nation's most powerful and conservative industrialists, bankers, and weapons makers," Lawrence easily mixed with the Club's elite, securing substantial financial backing for UC Berkeley's Physics Department.

Lawrence's prototype cyclotron, that he'd built from shards of glass, metal, wires, and orange sealing wax, looked a bit like a round-shaped homemade whiskey flask. Iterations of the cyclotron kept getting larger, until Lawrence's final version was 184 inches in diameter attached to a 220-ton magnet. Its fifteen-foot-thick cement encasement filled the specially made Cyclotron Building, a round, domed structure four stories high with connecting laboratories and offices. "With a forty-nine hundred ton cyclotron it may be possible to change any element into another at will... that would give us complete mastery over the physical world," Lawrence told *The National Farm and Home Hour*, a radio news broadcast for rural Americans.

Champagne party announcement on a physics classroom chalkboard in honor of Ernest O. Lawrence's 1939 Nobel Prize. Element 103 was named Lawrencium in 1961 in tribute to him.
Courtesy of the UC Berkeley Physics Department.

Despite the cyclotron's electrical efficiency, Berkeley residents' house lights flickered whenever the cyclotron pulled its maximum voltage from the electricity grid. Occasionally the entire city lost electricity in a full blackout. However, unless Berkeleyans worked with Lawrence on his experiments in the Radiation Lab, they had no idea that the outages were caused by the huge blasts of electricity used to test the world's first particle accelerators. This was just the beginning of the bond of secrecy that surrounded what Lawrence's team called the "RAD Lab."

In 1939, Lawrence became UC Berkeley's first Nobel Laureate "for the invention and development of the cyclotron and for results obtained with it, especially with regard to artificial radioactive elements." Using the RAD Lab's discoveries, Lawrence and his colleagues filled in the periodic table of elements starting in 1937 with Technetium, the world's first man-made synthesized element. After a few more names based on Greek, Latin, or countries, they discovered atomic number 97 and named it Berkelium in 1949. In 1940, they discovered Californium, atomic number 98.

Bakary Kebba Minteh, wearing a Berkelium (Bk 97) hoodie, on the steps of UC Berkeley's Physics Building.
Courtesy of Pam Gleason.

The cyclotron made its first popular appearances as an important plot device for the Superman daily comic strips. In the April 13, 1945, comic strip Professor Duste—looking uncannily like Professor Ernest Lawrence, with slicked back hair and thin wire frame glasses—says to Superman and another professor, "If you just step over to the physics lab with me, gentlemen, I've a little device that should end this talk of invulnerability once and for all!"

Superman comic strip about the cyclotron in a series of strips by writer Alvin Schwartz and artist Wayne Boring.
Courtesy of Brian Cronin from his book Comic Book Legends Revealed.

As they stand next to the spaceship-like cyclotron in the next day's comic strip, Professor Duste says, "Gentleman, the strange object before you is the cyclotron—popularly known as an 'atom-smasher.' Are you still prepared to face this test Mr. Superman?"

Superman steps into the atomic chamber, and the suspense builds over the next several strips. Claiming that if Superman can survive the cyclotron his term paper about Superman's powers will be a proven success, a college student named Gilmore pulls the lever that releases a bombardment of atoms.

Gilmore's student status is reinforced by the big block "C" on his sweatshirt, a possible wink to the Cal "Big C" on Charter Hill, located just below Lawrence Road and Cyclotron Road.

At the end of the two-week series featuring the cyclotron, Superman emerges from the chamber unharmed. Professor Duste dashes Gilmore's hopes for a better term paper grade by concluding that the cyclotron must have malfunctioned.

Nearly twenty years later, the character Cyclotron appears in 1983 as an atomic scientist who battled Atom by exposing him to lethal levels of radiation. This gave Atom his superpowers to shrink or enlarge his body and objects from subatomic size to giant size.

An even more Berkeley-centric comic strip called *Nukees* starred a "ten ton nuclear killing machine" robot ant, powered by a nuclear reactor in its abdomen.

"Wanton destruction" is how Berkeley Professor Darren Bleuel, the curly blue-haired nuclear physicist who created *Nukees* in 1997, describes his cartoon robot ant's occupation on the comic's website at nukees.com.

The nuclear-power ant was constructed by a character named Danny, a rogue researcher in Etcheverry Hall, and described by Bluel as "a motivated, yet confusing theorist whose mind works on a plane with which no one is quite comfortable. Works without questioning, and questions without thinking. Doesn't talk much about his past, possibly by choice, possibly by court order."

The giant robot ant, able to easily scale the Campanile Bell Tower, was constructed in a cavernous space called the Nuclear Reactor Room, in Etcheverry Hall, constructed in 1964 to house a two story nuclear reactor pool in its basement room.

Nukees by Darren Bleuel imagines a giant radioactive ant living in Etcheverry Hall's basement.
Courtesy of Darren Bleuel.

Though radiation sparked the public's imagination, the dangers were real. In 1941, in room 307 of Gilman Hall, Glenn T. Seaborg and his collaborators discovered plutonium-239, crucial for the development of the atom bomb. In 1976 and 1981, technicians removed uranium contamination from room 307 and adjacent rooms in Gilman Hall. The UN Scientific Committee on the Effects of Atomic Radiation (UNSCEAR) estimates that 5,000 children in the effected areas of the former Soviet Union (Belarus, Ukraine and Russia) contracted thyroid cancer from exposure to Plutonium-239 in the 1986 Chernobyl nuclear accident.

Because of Seaborg's discovery of plutonium-239, Lawrence was forced to refocus his mission away from discovering new man-made elements within just a couple years of winning the Nobel prize in physics. The U.S. military redirected him and his RAD Lab team to produce explosive plutonium fissile from dime-sized pellets of uranium.

By 1942, the new RAD Lab buildings were the start of a massive investment for the military's top secret Manhattan Project. The new building site, with its sweeping views of the San Francisco Bay and perfect perch on top of the Berkeley Hills overlooking campus, made it seem like the plan for the world's first nuclear bomb was hidden in plain sight.

Robert Oppenheimer, who would become known as the "father of the atomic bomb," joined the RAD Lab while a professor at the

California Institute of Technology. He was lured to UC Berkeley with a full professorship position in 1936.

Oppenheimer was a chemistry major at Harvard, but with Lawrence's discoveries, the fields of chemistry, physics, and engineering were now intersecting. This "Big Science" approach, with teams of scientists across an array of disciplines and backed with ample resources, was later coined the "Military Industrial Complex" for the its out-sized influence on the acceleration of science and engineering technology for military use. The Manhattan Project paved the way for multi-million dollar federal and corporate funding at university research facilities.

Albert Einstein said Robert Oppenheimer could solve his security clearance issues easily. "The problem was simple: All Oppenheimer needed to do was to go to Washington, tell the officials that they were fools, and go home." Einstein was too leftist to contribute to the Manhattan Project.
Courtesy of Wikimedia Commons.

By the end of the 1930s, the Berkeley Hills were full of scientists from Europe whose children attended the Hillside Elementary School together. The children's last names were a veritable who's who of the era's scientific geniuses. Some had come as the result of Operation Paperclip, whereby the U.S. intelligence apparatus secured safe passage to the United States for 1,600 scientists to flee Nazi persecution. Oppenheimer pledged three percent of his Berkeley salary to bring Jewish German physicists to the United States. The Hillside school children knew that every time the lights flickered on and off, it was because

Berkeley's electric grid was failing from the pull of electricity needed by the RAD Lab. Many of their fathers worked on the cyclotron atomic testing machinery.

The RAD Lab employed not only physicists, but biologists, physicians, engineers, chemists, and data technicians from all over the world, with the nearby campus cafeteria abuzz with futuristic ideas. One widely held idea was that radiation's biggest benefit to humanity would be medical breakthroughs, and in particular, the ultimate cure for cancer. Lawrence's brother, physician John H. Lawrence, used radioactive phosphorus from the cyclotron for the first experimental radiation treatments for leukemia. Oppenheimer and other Berkeley scientists eagerly gave tours to visiting scientists interested in exploring these ideas. This openness became a national security risk in 1942, when the RAD Lab under the leadership of Lawrence and Oppenheimer began experimentation using the cyclotron to separate fissionable uranium-235 from uranium-238 to harness its explosive energy.

Lawrence Berkeley National Laboratory started construction for the Manhattan Project in 1942.
Courtesy of UC Berkeley's Physics Department.

According to Katherine A. S. Sibley in *Red Spies in America: Stolen Secrets and the Dawn of the Cold War*, a youthful U.S. War Department counterintelligence spy named Lt. Col. John Lansdale pretended to be a Berkeley law school student to determine if the RAD Lab's researchers were sharing too much information. By eavesdropping on lunch conversations in the cafeteria "to infiltrate Berkeley and snoop on the physicists there," Lansdale concluded that "atomic research on campus was common knowledge."

Lansdale was right: Soviet spies targeted the UC Berkeley RAD Lab and Oppenheimer in particular. In 1946, the Military Intelligence Service's team of mostly women cryptanalysts in Arlington, Virginia decoded messages for the Venona project that confirmed espionage in Berkeley was the Soviet's top priority.

Oppenheimer had many friends who were so-called "card carrying communists." His move to Berkeley in 1936 coincided with a time in U.S. history when the communist party was linked with labor rights and fairer economic practices. Oppenheimer's younger brother, Frank —who later founded the Exploratorium in San Francisco—and Frank's wife Jackie were avowed Communist Party members. Oppenheimer began an affair with Jean Tatlock, a graduate student at UC Berkeley who wrote for the *Western Worker*, the Communist Party of America's periodical for the West Coast. Haakon Chevalier, a UC Berkeley professor of French Literature who would later be the reason for Oppenheimer's revoked security clearance, was one of his closest friends. According to Gregg Herken, a senior historian at the Smithsonian Institution and author of *Brotherhood of the Bomb: The Tangled Lives and Loyalties of Robert Oppenheimer, Ernest Lawrence, and Edward Teller,* Chevalier's letters to Oppenheimer prove that both were part of a secret group of communist faculty members.

Oppenheimer met his future wife Kitty in 1939 and they married in 1940. Kitty was an active member of the Communist Party of America until the death of her first husband, Joseph Dallet Jr., a Chicago-based Communist Party union organizer. In 1937, Dallet joined the Lincoln Brigade, a volunteer American military coalition that served on the side of Spain's elected Republicans against Franco's fascist takeover. Kitty intended to accompany Dallet to Spain, but was sidelined for a few months after an emergency operation to remove her ovarian cysts. During her recovery, Kitty learned Dallet was killed in battle. *Letters from Spain by Joe Dallet, American Volunteer, To His Wife* were published the following year.

Once married, the Oppenheimers settled in their house on One Eagle Road, just north of the UC Berkeley campus, and just a short walk from Chevalier's house, where Kitty dropped off her young children when she and her husband traveled out of town. In addition to their own Vodka-infused parties, the couple attended parties on both sides of the Bay, including fundraisers in San Francisco for Lincoln Brigade survivors, where attendees—many of whom were unabashed communists—had fond views of the Soviet Union, the only world power that came to the aid of the democratically elected Republicans during the Spanish Civil War. After the ravages of the Depression and World War II, thought leaders touted communism as a possible antidote to the failures of capitalism and the brutality of fascism. Stalin's mass executions weren't known to the world until Nikita Khruschev came to power in 1956.

Starting in 1941, the FBI kept close surveillance on Oppenheimer: they opened his mail, bugged his home and office, and tracked his whereabouts. Shortly after the new RAD Lab was built at its new site overlooking the Berkeley campus, the FBI uncovered the Soviet's successful spying infiltration. Despite this knowledge, Oppenheimer's position remained protected. The progress of the Manhattan Project and nuclear weaponry were too important. Lt. Col. Lansdale, who had been the first to spy on the RAD Lab for the FBI, testified later in the 1954 Oppenheimer Security Hearing that "I reached the conclusion that he [Oppenheimer] was loyal and ought to be cleared."

Despite Lansdale's support, eventually Oppenheimer's security clearance was permanently revoked. In 1949, at the peak of the Red Scare, Oppenheimer testified before Joseph McCarthy's House Un-American Activities Committee (HUAC) that several of his graduate students at the Berkeley RAD Lab were communists. During the HUAC hearings, Oppenheimer purposefully omitted his close relationship with Chevalier and his knowledge of Chevalier's communist contacts in order to protect him.

During the secretly held 1954 Oppenheimer Security Hearing, Oppenheimer was shocked to hear the years-old tapes that revealed he had been protecting Chevalier from investigation. Publicity of this revelation could have permanently destroyed Oppenheimer's reputation and career. Herken, the historian whose research unearthed Chevalier's letters to Oppenheimer, cites an exchange of letters in 1964 that indicate Chevalier took Oppenheimer's communist activities to his grave. In one letter, Chevalier confirmed with a friend that he would not write candidly about Oppenheimer's political activities in his memoir. "I decided that I shouldn't, even though the fact is of considerable historical importance." Chevalier kept secret Oppenheimer's political leanings because he understood that socialism and communism had become widely vilified in the United States, and did not want his Berkeley friend and neighbor to be disgraced. Instead, Oppenheimer remained a hero to most Americans.

Isidor Isaac Rabi, who won the Nobel Prize in Physics in 1944, watched the first test of the atomic bomb alongside Oppenheimer on July 16, 1945. Rabi, who'd won the betting pool for his estimate that the Trinity bomb would be the equivalent of 18 kilotons of TNT, glimpsed Oppenheimer's pride after the blast "his walk was like High Noon... this kind of strut. He had done it."

Later, for a news conference marking the twentieth anniversary of the Trinity bomb in 1965, Oppenheimer affirmed that he did not regret his role in history. Conceding that sometimes his conscience bothered him, he said to the *CBS News with Walter Cronkite* reporter, "I think when you play a meaningful part in bringing about the death of 100,000 people and the injury of a comparable number, you naturally don't think of that as—with ease." His real regret was that the atomic bomb was not available to use against Nazi Germany.

In 2022, filmmakers shot footage at UC Berkeley for the movie *Oppenheimer*. Its 2023 release, alongside the release of Barbie, sparked a cultural phenomena called "Barbenheimer," stoked by clever memes proliferating across social media platforms. Students began sporting all-gender Barbie Pink fashion items in hex color code #e0218a.

Are Barbie and Oppenheimer on their way to the Physics Building?
Courtesy of @shadowknightdk (Twitter).

In December 2022, U.S. Secretary of Energy Jennifer Granholm—a former adjunct professor at Berkeley after serving as Michigan's governor from 2003-2011—reversed the decision vacating Oppenheimer's security clearance. "In 1954, the Atomic Energy Commission revoked Dr. Oppenheimer's security clearance through a flawed process that violated the Commission's own regulations," Granholm wrote. "As time has passed, more evidence has come to light of the bias and unfairness of the process that Oppenheimer was subjected to while the evidence of his loyalty and love of country have only been further affirmed." Even in the city affectionately known as the People's Republic of Berkeley, as emblazoned on shirts and bumper stickers for sale on Telegraph Avenue, Oppenheimer's communist connections and the price he paid for them are still not common knowledge.

Days before Granholm's exoneration of Oppenheimer, she made another historic announcement that celebrated the work of a new generation of scientists at the Lawrence Berkeley Lab: the achievement of fusion ignition, a clean energy solution that's expected to be a game-changer for combating climate change. Granholm announced it as "a landmark achievement for the researchers and staff at the National Ignition Facility who have dedicated their careers to seeing fusion ignition become a reality, and this milestone will undoubtedly spark even more discovery."

Though Lawrence Berkeley Lab scientists are no longer experimenting with radioactive material, theoretical nuclear physicists continue to work on national security priorities—like how to diffuse a "dirty" bomb, a terrorist weapon that spreads radiation to everything in its sphere.

UC Berkeley and Lawrence Berkeley Lab scientists lead the world nanotechnology innovations. Moore's Law, Berkeley chemistry graduate Gordon Moore's 1965 prediction that the size of data transistors would continue to get exponentially smaller, has proven true. With nanotechnology-sized data stored on particles too small to see, Moore's law has held for decades. At the Molecular Foundry, Lawrence Berkeley Lab's nanofabrication facility, scientists are creating "structures that control light, electron, or energy flow... on ultrafast time scales" according to its website foundry.lbl.gov.

UC Berkeley's interdisciplinary approach pioneered by Lawrence, Oppenheimer, and others, is considered the breakthrough that paved the way for "Big Science" and "Big Data." Students vie for courses in data science because computational analytics are needed in every industry. In South Hall, UC Berkeley's oldest building, degrees in Library Science have been replaced by degrees in Information Science, and graduates work on complex software algorithms for tech giants instead of with books for libraries.

The RAD Lab's interdisciplinary "Big Science" and "Big Data" approach and large-scale project management legacy provided a foundational model for the career of Robert McNamara, an economics major at UC Berkeley, who earned status with his peers by rowing varsity crew, joining the Phi Gamma Delta fraternity on Channing Way, and gaining entry into Phi Beta Kappa and the Order of the Golden Bear, UC Berkeley's most elite societies for undergraduates.

McNamara, who started out his career as an expert on applying "Big Data" principles to accounting, was hired to apply his "scientific management" analytics at Ford Motor Company. The success of this approach skyrocketed McNamara to the top of the company, becoming the first person outside the Ford family to be promoted company's president, with compensation of $3 million a year (worth about $32 million today), making him one of the top paid corporate executives in the world at the time. When John F. Kennedy was elected President in 1960, he offered McNamara the position of Secretary of Defense, a position that paid only $25,000 a year, but McNamara eagerly exchanged his astronomical salary for a chance to apply his "Big Data" theories to U.S. foreign policy.

With all of the computing resources of the Pentagon at his disposal, McNamara used quantitative modeling techniques to calculate the number of troops, bombs, and military strikes it would take to subdue the Viet Cong, led by elected communist leader Ho Chi Minh. McNamara's calculations at the Pentagon persuaded President Kennedy to sign the Limited Nuclear Test Ban Treaty. McNamara coined the term "assured destruction," which he defined as a nuclear retaliation effort that would destroy twenty to twenty-five percent of the Soviet Union's population and fifty percent of its industrial output. President Johnson, who kept McNamara on after Kennedy's assassination, described McNamara's work ethic this way: "He's like a jackhammer. No human being can take what he takes. He drives too hard. He's too perfect."

By the end of 1965, McNamara's job as Secretary of Defense had made him a wreck. McNamara's confidence in himself and the outcome of the Vietnam War plunged, and by 1967 his colleagues worried he was having a nervous breakdown. The top secret *Report of the Office of the Secretary of Defense Vietnam Task Force,* later known as the Pentagon Papers, was released internally in January 1969. McNamara agreed with its findings: the U.S. had waged an unwinnable war in Vietnam, yet kept committing more resources and relying on body count numbers to justify the war's escalation.

McNamara described the Vietnam War as a tragedy that offered many lessons during the spring semester of 1996, when McNamara was a guest lecturer at UC Berkeley. After Errol Morris released *The Fog of War: Eleven Lessons from the Life of Robert S. McNamara* in 2003, McNamara publicized his own sets of lessons. One lesson: "We failed to recognize that in international affairs, as in other aspects of life, there may be problems for which there are no immediate solutions... At times, we may have to live with an imperfect, untidy world." In other words, six decades after first studying the computation models that were used to ramp up the RAD Lab's bomb-making capacity, McNamara told Berkeley students that the analytics he used to project a victory in Vietnam weren't actually grounded in reality.

Berkeley professors are increasingly aware of the ethically wobbly justifications for using science to justify political outcomes. In an effort to prevent future lapses, the Berkeley Ethics and Regulation Group for Innovative Technologies (BERGIT) promotes discussions across disciplines to integrate ethics and science through policy discussions. UC Berkeley science and engineering students are required to take ethics courses to graduate. Professors like Nobel Laureate Jennifer Doudna, an expert in RNA and CRISPR gene altering technology, are careful to explain the care they take to not cross ethical lines.

In Berkeley, "Big Science" and politics have been intertwined from the start. On tall sign posts at Berkeley's borders signs greet all who enter: "Berkeley CITY LIMIT" and, below that, "Nuclear Free Zone." Most passersby assume these signs are symbolic, but after the Nuclear Free Berkeley Act passed in 1986, it created very real changes for the nuclear engineering department at Etcheverry Hall. Its prized nuclear reactor was decommissioned for good, and the giant structures required for nuclear experimentation were relocated at Lawrence Livermore National Laboratory, a forty-five-minute drive southeast of Berkeley.

The Berkeley City Council passed "The Nuclear Free Berkeley Act" (Ord. 5784-NS § 1, 1986) on November 4, 1986, at the height of the arms race between the USSR and the United States.

The Nuclear Free Berkeley Act stipulated:

1. To oppose the arms race by prohibiting work for nuclear weapons;
2. To begin a peace conversion plan;
3. To establish a citizen's right to know about nuclear weapons work;
4. To minimize City contracts with and investments in the nuclear weapons industry;
5. To prohibit nuclear reactors;
6. To prohibit food irradiation plants;
7. To require labeling of irradiated food sold in Berkeley; and,
8. To oppose the nuclear fuel cycle as a whole.

With proliferation of malicious AI as the newest existential threat, the City of Berkeley's Nuclear Free Act seems quaint and out-of-date.

A Nuclear Free Zone sign marks the border of the City of Berkeley.
Courtesy of Wikimedia Commons.

The Free Speech Movement

"The University does not deserve a response of loyalty and allegiance from you. There is only one proper response to Berkeley from undergraduates: that you ORGANIZE AND SPLIT THIS CAMPUS WIDE OPEN!"

— September 10, 1964 SLATE announcement

Sproul Plaza

Sproul Plaza is UC Berkeley's main thoroughfare and hub of activity. The best time to visit is Wednesday from noon to 1:00 p.m., when student organizations set up tables to promote their work, attract new members, and fundraise by selling cupcakes or In-and-Out burgers. Occasionally student groups will bring service dogs or llamas for the students to pet to help relieve stress. Dance troops, a cappella groups, musicians, and DJs provide entertainment.

Sproul Plaza on Homecoming Day on October 18, 2019, Cal's last public festival before the pandemic began in March, 2020. After a year of online coursework so students could work safely from home, Sproul Plaza is full again.
Courtesy of Pam Gleason.

Noon is also when the most likely time to experience the legacy of the Free Speech Movement. Political speakers stand at the top of the Sproul Hall steps, near the plaque honoring free-speech advocate Mario Savio. During a protest, several speakers will line up to talk. Traditionally when the Campanile Bell Tower strikes 1:00 p.m., the crowd disperses. But during big protests, the speakers will call on the audience to march down Telegraph Avenue toward downtown Oakland.

The number of helicopters overhead signals the importance of the protest. One or two helicopters means a peaceful demonstration will make the local evening news. Three or four helicopters means it's likely to make the national news. In uneventful years, April 22 Earth Day protests against the use of fossil fuels, with a few thousand participants led by local high schoolers, are the biggest events. In recent years, students protesting the violence in Gaza is almost a daily occurrence.

If a protest turns violent, all of the news outlets show up. The extra publicity is why outsiders stage their protests on Sproul Plaza. Berkeley students often resent it when outsiders take over Sproul Plaza, and most will stay away unless it's a cause they believe in. But most will also say that they hope that at least one huge protest happens while they're enrolled, as a right of passage before graduation.

The Martin Luther King Jr. Student Union Building is across from Sproul Hall. Inside is the César Chávez Student Center, the Berkeley Art Studio, the Basic Needs Center, and various food kiosks. The Amazon Fulfillment Center takes the space that was once used for the student bookstore. A reuse clothing exchange and a meditation space is on the basement level where the ASUC bowling alley used to be. Skateboarders and parkour athletes practice their moves in Lower Sproul Plaza. The Cal Band gathers in Lower Sproul Plaza before performances. Bandmates gather in circles by instrument types, with woodwind, brass, and percussion musicians tuning up in separate groups. The tuba musicians, the fan favorites, practice precise moves to punctuate their marching flare.

The Golden Bear Café, a mini-mart for hungry students, is located on Sproul Plaza's west side. The café's architecture is reminiscent of 1960s sci-fi television series, like *The Jetsons* or *Lost in Space*. Students can use their student IDs to purchase food items. At the end of the semester, students with leftover credit on their meal plan buy ice cream pints by the dozens, adding belly cramps to the list of woes during final exams.

Student groups set up tables on Sproul Plaza. Promotions are clever, with costumes, QR codes, and sweet treats as enticing conversation starters. Representatives of the Period Project informed others about reproductive health with lighthearted smiles on April 13, 2024.
Courtesy of Pam Gleason.

The Free Speech Movement

Berkeley's Free Speech Movement was sparked by a dispute over a 26-foot-long strip of brick. Located at the south entrance to campus, where Telegraph Avenue dead ends on Bancroft Way, this cobbled walkway was the starting focal point of a pitched battle between students and the university's administration in the fall of 1964. A volatile mix of change and new ideas had already been set in motion when Berkeley students began the fall quarter that year of 1964.

The first wave of Baby Boomers turned 18 in 1964. Public school officials raced to keep up with the huge numbers of baby boomer children as they pushed K-12 schoolroom capacities to their limit. Colleges across the country braced for a huge spike of freshmen. UC Berkeley's administration had been preparing for years for the huge influx of students, who would increase their enrollment higher than almost any other university in the world.

Clark Kerr, unanimously chosen to be president of the UC system in 1957, was the architect of California's higher education needs as its population surged. Kerr was featured on *Time Magazine's* cover on October 17, 1960. Inside, an article titled "Education: Master Planner" summed up the challenge: "Few states are growing faster than California: whether by birth or by migration, the population increases by one a minute. Each year California's growth matches the size of San Diego. Each day it needs one new school."

Kerr, an economist by training, wrote scholarly papers and books around the theme of a "multiversity"—a multipurpose university as the center connecting the spokes of civic institutions and ideals, serving and uniting people for the betterment of everyone. "What the railroads did for the second half of the last century, and the automobile for the first half of this century, may be done for the second half of this century by the knowledge industry: that is, to serve as the focal point for national growth," Kerr proclaimed in his 1963 book, *The Uses of the University*, considered a classic among academics.

Clark Kerr, nicknamed "the Machiavellian Quaker" by UC Berkeley administrators, was on the cover of Time on October 17, 1960.
Courtesy of Time Magazine.

In preparation for the huge numbers of the aforementioned Baby Boomer students, Kerr oversaw the expansion of UC Berkeley's campus, using state-sanctioned eminent domain to seize the land of homes and businesses to expand campus south of Strawberry Creek and Sather Gate. In addition, the university seized several blocks of housing on the south side of campus to create 12 high-rise dormitories to house the incoming wave of entering freshmen. One of these dormitory blocks remained a vacant lot, and later became People's Park.

Sproul Plaza and the Student Union served as centerpieces of this eminent-domain expansion. Sproul Plaza was designed to be a Pompeian Forum-styled gathering place, the center of social and civic activity for the entire community, and a noontime gathering place for lunch and leisure. As expected, thousands of freshmen converged on Sproul Plaza to meet each other for the first time in September 1964.

Simultaneously, administrators introduced a new IBM punch card registration system. It was Berkeley's first computerized course registration, designed specifically to handle the thousands of incoming students and record-breaking attendance numbers. Students stood in line to fill out their IBM punch cards, gathering in bunches to discuss upcoming social events, the start of the Cal football season, and to try to make sense of the civil rights political upheaval.

For political leafleters, this was a boon. The summer of 1964 had been momentous. While Martin Luther King Jr.'s "I Have a Dream" speech celebrated its one-year anniversary, race riots sparked by police brutality in Philadelphia, Rochester, and New York City rocked the country. The civil rights tactics of students from Historically Black Colleges and Universities (HBCUs) spread from the Greensboro Sit-in to Freedom Rides to promote Black voter registration in the South. The HBCUs reached out to university students across the country to join them in their demands for civil rights. Berkeley students who joined the Freedom Rides returned from the South with horrific stories of racial abuse.

IBM employee demonstrates how a computerized punch card system works. UC Berkeley administrators launched the punch card system for fall registration in 1964, causing long lines of students. The words "DO NOT FOLD, SPINDLE, OR MUTILATE" printed on each punch card became a protest slogan for the Free Speech Movement.
Courtesy of Wikimedia Commons.

In Mississippi, three young activists from the Congress of Racial Equality (CORE), one Black and two white, were abducted and missing. This tragedy proved a final impetus to push through the Civil Rights Act on July 2, 1964, finally ending Jim Crow laws. On August 4, 1964, the tortured bodies of the three activists were found dead in shallow graves. The Ku Klux Klan, in collusion with local police, had murdered the three for their efforts to register Black voters.

At the time of the murders, a few UC Berkeley students worked in Mississippi for the HBCU-run Freedom Summer voter registration project. Ku Klux Klan terrorists attacked Mario Savio and two others working to register Black voters in Jackson, Mississippi. Savio and the other UC Berkeley students returned after Freedom Summer determined to implement the civil rights leadership and organization skills they'd learned in the South from the Black students and Martin Luther King, Jr. Once on campus again, Savio devoted himself to recruiting and organizing Cal students on behalf of the Student Nonviolent Coordinating Committee (SNCC). When the fall semester began, they recruited students by tabling at the new entrance of campus, the 26-foot-long brick walkway at the end of Telegraph Avenue.

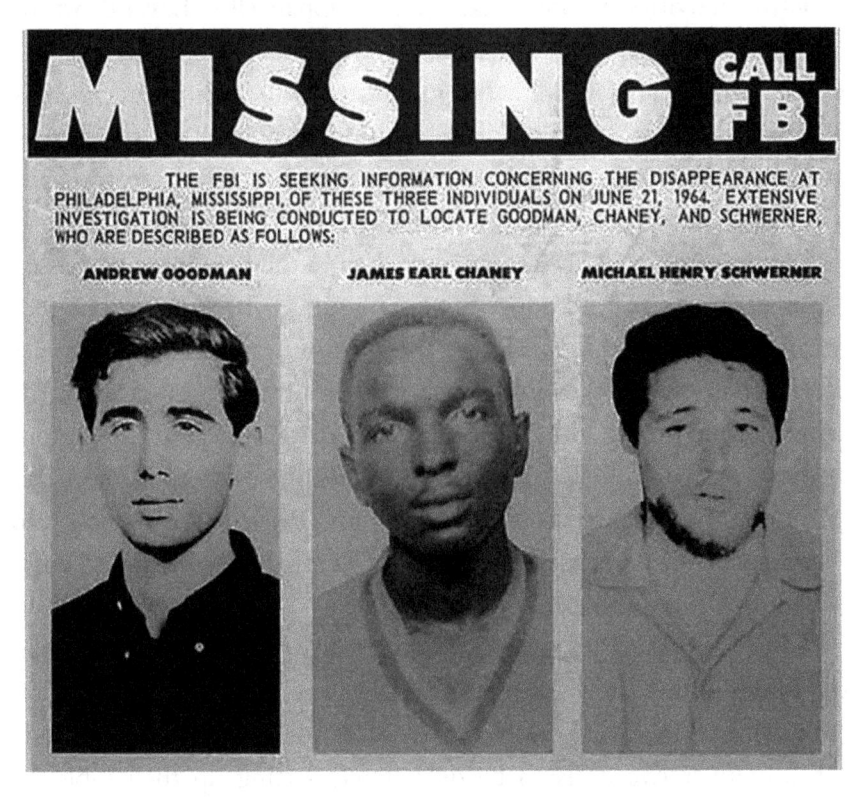

FBI poster for the missing college students who were in Mississippi to register Black voters. Their bodies were found in August, 1964, the month before the start of The Free Speech Movement.
Courtesy of the FBI.

Perhaps sensing that the crowds of new students and the political activities at the Telegraph entrance could be an inflammatory mix, top administrators decided that political tabling, leafleting, and gatherings on the 26-foot strip of UC Berkeley property would no longer be tolerated. SLATE, a leftist political group named for issuing a slate of candidates they recommended UC Berkeley students to elect every year, issued a manifesto for action on September 10, 1964: "The University does not deserve a response of loyalty and allegiance from you. There is only one proper response to Berkeley from undergraduates: that you ORGANIZE AND SPLIT THIS CAMPUS WIDE OPEN!"

Vice Chancellor Alex Sherriffs, tasked with reporting communist or leftist activities, wrote a statement to Chancellor Edward Strong expressing his dismay. His statement warned that the SLATE students were calling for a revolution. "It is most distasteful reading, but I believe you should read it. It is a call for revolution. It is deceitful, slanderous, and incredibly hostile towards you, and it takes on the Regents by name, and the whole University of California."

On September 14, 1964, one week before the beginning of classes, Dean of Students Katherine Towle announced by letter to student organizations that the policies of the Administration concerning use of University facilities would "be strictly enforced" in all areas of the University including "the 26-foot strip of brick walkway at the campus entrance on Bancroft Way and Telegraph Avenue between the concrete posts and the indented copper plaques on Bancroft way which read 'Property of the Regents, University of California. Permission to enter or pass over is revocable at any time.'"

Savio and other Cal student leaders who'd spent their summer in the South immediately argued that this was in violation of their First Amendment right to free speech. The student leaders decided to mock this administrative decision by deliberately setting up their tables at Sather Gate and on the steps of Sproul Hall, in clear defiance of the new campus policy.

Cal student leaders began meeting daily, sometimes through the night, to plan and organize on behalf of civil rights, just as they'd learned from the HBCU student leaders, who had taught them the strategies and tactics based on the tenets of Mahatma Gandhi's nonviolent resistance movement.

Students for a Democratic Society (SDS) set up their tables in front of Sather Gate despite being warned by the dean of students that political material was not allowed on campus.
Courtesy of the veterans of the Free Speech Movement (FSM), who preserved thousands of documents, photos, and first-hand accounts of the student efforts for the Free Speech Movement Archives, located online at fsm-a.org.

The tactics adopted from the Black students included dressing and acting professionally at all times, learning how to peacefully resist violent behavior from the police and others who sought to quiet their voices, and engaging with top civic leaders to find common ground and solutions in the pursuit of protecting civil rights for everyone.

Within just a couple of days, they formed the United Front, representing 18 student groups spanning ideological backgrounds—including Youth for Goldwater, Campus Women for Peace, the University Young Democrats, the University Young Republicans, and the College Young Republicans—and signed their group names to a petition declaring "tables at Bancroft and Telegraph may be used to distribute literature advocating action on current issues." SLATE signed at the top of the list.

The United Front held an all-night vigil on the steps of Sproul Hall on Sunday, September 27, readying themselves for seven days a week of civil disobedience during the second week of classes.

The prohibition of political materials on campus had been a long-standing policy at Berkeley. The thinking was that a university should be neutral and students should be protected from the influence of political dogma. Political agitators, including the formidable San Francisco longshoremen unionists and the "Wobblies"—the nickname for the International Workers of the World—set up their soap boxes right outside Sather Gate, the campus entrance before Sproul Plaza's construction was complete. During the Depression, soapboxers and labor rights organizers became more active, which led then-President Robert Gordon Sproul to ban all political and religious meetings on campus.

Still, so-called "Hyde Park" areas—named after Speaker's Corner in Hyde Park, London—were tolerated. In 1959, when Sproul Plaza was completed, Sather Gate was no longer the south entrance of campus, though it remained one of UC Berkeley's main "Hyde Park" areas along with the 26-foot cobbled brick entrance at Bancroft and Telegraph. Dean Towle's announcement on September 14, 1964 revoked the toleration of political speech in these areas, and throughout campus.

The main tactic the United Front student groups used to test the administration's resolve was to set up tables in highly visible, unsanctioned on campus locations—in front of the "Hyde Park" area in front of Sather Gate, on the steps of Sproul Hall, and in other prime spots, like Ludwig's Fountain, named for a loyal dog that would wait there while his owner attended classes.

On Wednesday, September 30, five students overseeing tabling efforts were cited with notifications that they would need to appear before the student conduct committee to face possible expulsion. Three hundred others asked to be added to the citation list in solidarity with the five. Students arrived at Sproul Hall by the hundreds for the disciplinary meeting. Student leaders Mario Savio, Sandor Fuchs, and Arthur Goldberg shouted from Sproul's second-floor balcony, encouraging more students to join them in the halls and outside the deans' offices.

The administrators decided that only the original five would be allowed into the disciplinary meeting, along with three additional student leaders, including Mario Savio. He carried with him a petition signed by 500 students that stated, "We the undersigned have jointly manned tables at Sather Gate, realizing that we were in violation of University edicts to the contrary. We realize we may be subject to expulsion."

With the meeting finally underway, the eight students received an indefinite suspension. Just before midnight, with hundreds of students still protesting in the hallways outside of his office, Chancellor Edward Strong issued a statement that concluded, "I regret that these eight students by their willful misconduct in deliberately violating rules of the University have made it necessary for me to suspend them indefinitely from the University."

The next day, on October 1, tensions intensified when administrators asked Berkeley Police to remove anyone still tabling on campus. The police arrested Jack Weinberg, a tall and outspoken graduate student who was manning a table for the civil rights organization Congress On Racial Equality (CORE). Students spontaneously surrounded the police car and refused to move. Around 2,000 students gathered in protest around the police car for 32 hours while student leaders negotiated with administrators for free speech rights. One by one, students who wanted to address the crowd took off their shoes before climbing on top of the police car, so that the vehicle would not be harmed while they used its roof as an ad-hoc stage.

The Berkeley Police arrested Jack Weinberg for tabling on campus for the civil rights group Congress On Racial Equality (CORE).
Courtesy of Calisphere.

Mario Savio spoke to students about civil rights from the roof of a Berkeley Police car on October 1, 1964.
Courtesy of the Oakland Museum.

Throughout October, the ACLU and other national civil rights groups expressed their support for the Free Speech Movement, as it began to be called. The students held noontime victory rallies on the steps of Sproul Hall, emboldened and proud of their new-found power. They also collected donations to pay for the $334.30 in damage to the flattened roof of the police car. Student groups met around the clock to decide what should be done. State and national politicians leaned on Chancellor Strong to control his students. When polled, 95 percent of California citizens said they did not support the students' demands.

Finally, as the winter holidays and final exams week approached, the Free Speech Movement leaders organized a sit-in at Sproul Plaza.

The purpose was to show their frustration with Chancellor Strong and other university leaders for not following through with their promises from the October 1-2 police car sit-in; they also hoped to force the administration back to the bargaining table.

On December 2, thousands of students participated in an overnight demonstration on the steps of Sproul Hall and in its corridors. Joan Baez serenaded the students on the steps of Sproul Hall, then joined the throngs inside. The students entertained themselves by practicing how to go limp when confronted by the police arrive. They held a Hanukkah celebration and sang "Free Speech Carols" to Christmas music.

```
                IT BELONGS TO THE UNIVERSITY      copyright 1964
words:Joe La Penta                                Cireco Music co.,
Music: Twelve Days of Christmas                   BMI

On the first of semester the dean said to me,
"It belongs to The University."
On the second of semester the dean said to me,
"No bumper stickers, it belongs to The University"
3rd:"Don't ask for members"
4th:"Don't collect money"
5th:"NO CIV-IL RIGHTS!"
6th:"No organizing"
7th:"No       : mounting action"
8th:"No demonstrations"
9th:"You'll be suspended"
10th:"We'll call out troopers"
11th:"Maybe we'll bargain"
12th:"Our word is law!"
```

UC Berkeley students sang protest songs to the tune of Christmas carols at the December 2, 1964 overnight takeover of Sproul Hall. The next morning's arrests of nearly 800 people remains one of the world's largest mass arrests of peaceful protestors.
Courtesy of Free Speech Movement Archives.

That same day in front of an audience of several thousand, Savio gave the speech of his life that still lives on as legendary in the popular imagination. On the Sproul Hall steps he declared, "We're human beings! ... There's a time when the operation of the machine becomes so odious—makes you so sick at heart—that you can't take part. You can't even passively take part. And you've got to put your bodies upon the gears and upon the wheels, upon the levers, upon all the apparatus, and you've got to make it stop. And you've got to indicate to the people who run it, to the people who own it, that unless you're free, the machine will be prevented from working at all."

Meanwhile, the Alameda County Police prepared for a mass arrest. In the early morning hours, the police surrounded Sproul Hall and dragged the young activists out one by one for the twenty-five mile ride to Santa Rita Jail. Nearly 800 protestors were booked, one of the largest number of arrests in a peaceful protest. This mass arrest established Berkeley as the lightning rod of student activism. Students at campuses across the United States and the world ignited in protests. Savio was jailed for 120 days, and told the San Francisco Chronicle he "would do it again."

Joan Baez (wearing a cross necklace) sang and played her guitar for the overnight protestors inside of Sproul Hall on December 2-3, 1964.
Courtesy of Wikimedia Commons.

Students passively resisted arrest on the morning of Dec 3, 1964 by not standing up and instead letting their bodies go limp. This made it difficult for police to drag them out of Sproul Hall and into the buses waiting to take them to Santa Rita Jail. 800 were arrested.
Courtesy of Wikimedia Commons.

The Free Speech Movement, which started on the first day of classes—on September 11, 1964—ended less than two months later. On December 8, the Faculty Senate voted to grant free speech rights on campus. A new acting chancellor, Martin Meyersen, started his term on January 3, 1965, and established new rules that allowed free speech on campus. Meyersen also designated the steps of Sproul Hall as a discussion area, where political groups could set up their tables and pass out their literature.

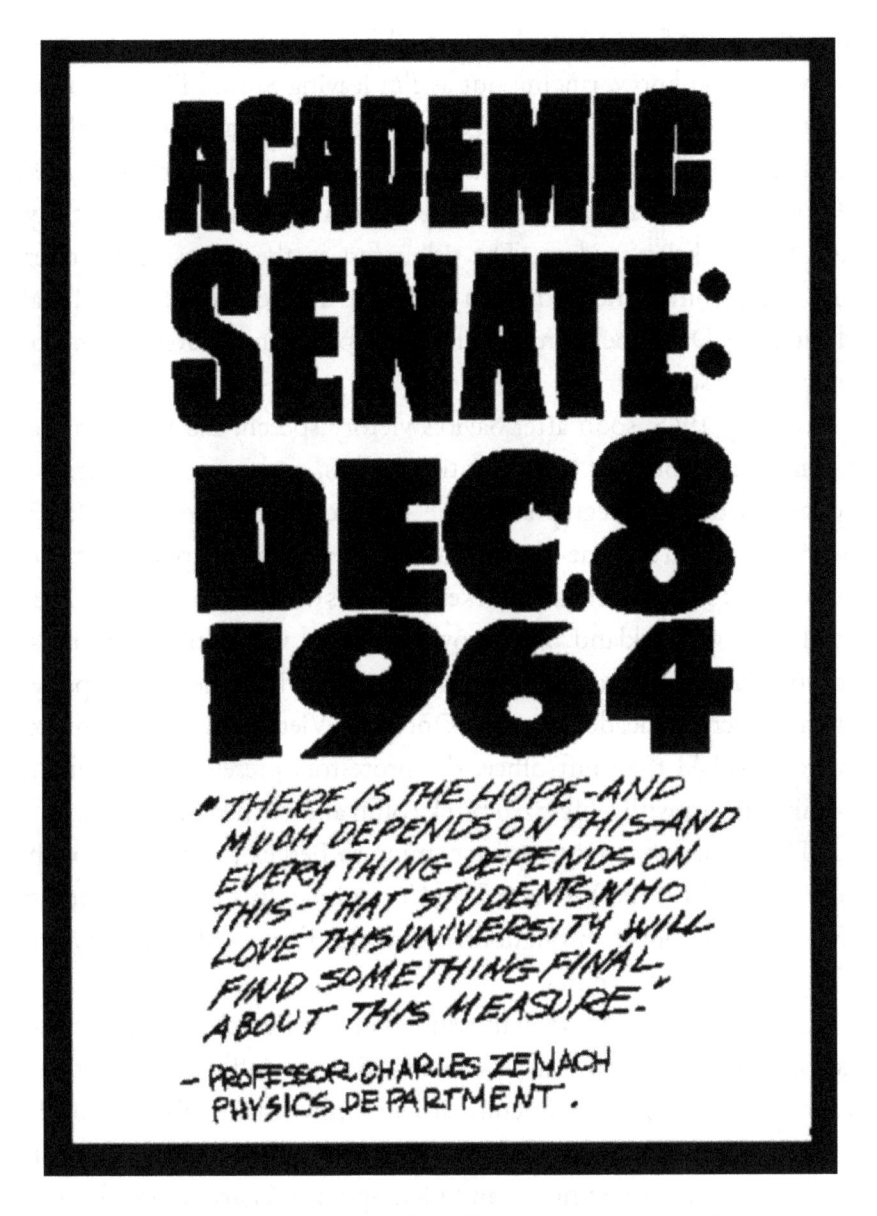

> **ACADEMIC SENATE: DEC. 8 1964**
>
> *"There is the hope – and much depends on this – and everything depends on this – that students who love this university will find something final about this measure."*
>
> *– Professor Charles Zemach, Physics Department.*

The faculty vote on Dec 8, 1964 affirmed students' freedom of speech on campus and marked the successful conclusion of the Free Speech Movement.
Courtesy of Wikimedia Commons.

At a FSM celebration speech on Sproul Plaza at the beginning of the spring term, Mario Savio urged students to consider a new cause: the Vietnam War. Jentri Anders, interviewed for the 1990 documentary

Berkeley in the Sixties, was there too. "I have this very clear memory of his voice, you know, ringing out as I'm leaving Sproul Plaza, and he's saying, 'Now don't everybody go walking away because we've still got a war to stop,'" Anders said at the time. Anders is the author of *Drag Me Out Like a Lady: An Activist's Journey,* a book that covers her days as a UC Berkeley student. The title refers to the harassment Anders and other women endured when they were dragged out of Sproul Hall during the December 3 mass arrest, the penultimate event that won over faculty support.

In early 1965, soon after Savio's victory speech, the Vietnam Day Committee took over the noontime rallies, and urged their crowds to march down Telegraph Avenue for a day of protest on May 5, 1965. Telegraph Avenue—named for the telegraph wire poles that once stretched from Oakland and Berkeley—leads directly from Sproul Plaza to downtown Oakland. Downtown Oakland was both the East Bay location of the Vietnam War draft office, and where the train departed with conscripts headed to war. Once the Vietnam Day Committee march reached the draft office, the protestors presented the military administrators with a life-sized black coffin and burned draft cards.

Thousands of activists, some coming to Berkeley to protest for the first time, joined the Vietnam Day Committee. In solidarity, Vietnam War protests spread throughout the world, first to Mexico City and Tokyo, then to other cities.

The Free Speech Movement remains one of Berkeley's proudest legacies. The Free Speech Café, located inside the Moffitt Undergraduate Library, displays photos, documents, and other memorabilia from the Free Speech Movement. With just a student ID, protest leaders can reserve Sproul Plaza at noon, and pick up a university-supplied sound system with microphones and speakers to address the crowd. Most speakers stand at the top of the Mario Savio Steps, where a plaque honoring Savio is embedded in the cement.

People's Park

*"Don't it always seem to go
That you don't know what you've got
Till it's gone
They paved paradise
And put up a parking lot"*

— Joni Mitchell, "Big Yellow Taxi"

"A People's History of Telegraph Avenue" Mural

After nearly 55 years of citizen occupation, People's Park no longer exists. It's now the site of new student housing. An open space designed by MacArthur Genius Grant winner Walter J. Hood will commemorate the historic site. Next to the new 12-story dormitory, "A People's History of Telegraph Avenue" mural remains at the corner of Telegraph and Haste Avenues, narrating the history of People's Park from the perspective of activists who fought for so many years to preserve it.

Artists Osha Neumann and O'Brien Thiele, later joined by Janet Kranzberg, Daniel Galvez, and crew of other local painters, created the People's Park mural on the north side of Amoeba Records for Berkeley's celebration of the U.S. bicentennial in 1976.

The mural sits just a stone's throw away from the famous signs that until January 3, 2024 welcomed visitors to People's Park with the slogans "Power to the People!" and "EVERYBODY GETS A BLISTER!"

The mural is designed as a book, with its pages open to Berkeley's civil rights activism. The pages show idyllic Berkeley as a paradise for Ohlone families, then the almost-complete harvest of the area's old growth redwood forests, and opens to the October 1, 1964 scene of Mario Savio, without his shoes, speaking from atop the police car in Sproul Plaza.

University President Clark Kerr—a political moderate whose career got caught between Governor Ronald Reagan's zeal for law and order and student activists' hatred of the university machine—is depicted in Nazi brown, clinging to one of the pillars of Sproul Hall.

Osha Newman touches up "The History of People's Park" Mural regularly. Here he greets Airbnb walking tour guests hosted by Pam Gleason during her Best of Berkeley Walking Tour.
Courtesy of Pam Gleason.

In 2020, Neumann explained in an email how he sketched out the mural's design: "I decided to start with the Free Speech Movement. I'd show a sit-in with Mario Savio, standing on a police car, and then the other movements of the time: the antiwar movement, a person burning his draft cards, the Third World Strike for ethnic studies, and then of course the Black liberation movements and the Black Panthers. And I wanted to show what we were fighting against, what we called, 'The System,' churning out blockheads and cannon fodder, but which seemed to be tottering on the brink of destruction; But the revolution wasn't just political. It was also cultural. I decided to show a Telegraph Avenue street scene, with hippies and Hare Krishnas, and a guy tripping, and I'd include folks who are still around such as Julia Winograd, Berkeley's wonderful street poet. And then, of course, I had to include People's Park, the building of it, and then the attack on it, Bloody Thursday, and the death of James Rector at the hands of the Alameda County Sheriffs. Finally I would come to the not-so-hopeful present—kids sitting on the sidewalk, a woman and her child just walking along, trying to survive, and a panhandler, but then end on a hopeful note breaking through behind them, a tree of life and a rainbow vision of the liberated reality we've been struggling for."

At the end of the mural, an idyllic future shows partially clothed revelers in bright colors, with their hands held high in celebration. A broken television screen lends the impression there's been a victory over media and technology—a vision of the future that, for now, is far from true.

People's Park

Nick Alexander is one of People's Park's last folk heroes. There won't be others. UC Berkeley finally won its campaign to bulldoze People's Park to build student dormitories, after its nearly 55 years of existence. The university promises that the dormitories will house around 1,000 students before the 2025-2026 academic year. On the night of January 3, 2024, the last residents of People's Park faced eviction. The next day, bulldozers and 16-wheeler trucks clogged Haste Street and Dwight Way, the streets that bound the park. Work crews stacked 160 shipping containers, each weighing 5,000 pounds, to create a 17 foot high impenetrable barrier so that construction work could begin.

Nick Alexander, People's Park activist and purveyor of the People's Park "Meat Kitchen," at a rally in November, 2021.
Courtesy of Berkeley Journalism alums Jennifer Wiley and Laura Garber.

Nick Alexander is a thirty-something alum of UC Berkeley and one of only a handful of protesters who maintained a permanent residence at People's Park for more than a couple of years. He ran the Park's

"Meat Kitchen"—a popular alternative to the healthy vegan meals set out on People's Park stage by volunteers from Food Not Bombs.

Alexander's "Food's ready!" announcements drew enthusiastic lines of people to his makeshift kitchen, which Alexander built from wooden pallets and make-it-work ingenuity. Food Not Bombs, an all-volunteer collective dedicated to combating poverty and homelessness, reliably provided meals using surplus food that would otherwise be wasted, but People's Park regulars greeted the vegan fare with resignation. Telegraph Avenue's nearby smorgasbord of fast food treats—pizza, pho, ice cream, boba tea, burgers, poké, cupcakes, kimchi, burritos, ramen, and artisanal salads—were what people wanted, and Alexander's hot dogs, hamburgers, and barbecued chicken drumsticks were an acceptable alternative.

Besides the lack of enthusiasm for the vegan-only Food Not Bombs fare, the donated food had another downside that irked Alexander: colonies of giant rats that took over People's Park, swarming the People's Park stage each night to gorge on the uneaten food. Alexander won the battle with one rat colony that had burrowed under his makeshift kitchen. After that, he kept a constant lookout, ready to bash returning strays with his shovel.

The rats are just one facet of the long and chaotic decay of People's Park. In 2023, UC Berkeley's People's Park Housing website summarized crimes committed within the three year period from 2020 through 2022 this way: "In the past 3 years, there have been 18 rapes, 19 robberies, 110 aggravated assaults, and 48 drug and 6 weapons arrests. In 2021, a UC Berkeley undergraduate was stabbed after walking past the park at night—the suspect has been charged with attempted murder. In 2017, a woman was arrested for attempted murder after feeding methamphetamine to a two-year-old."

For the final years of People's Park decay, Alexander faults the gray-haired hippies, "the elders," whom he's lost patience with many times. Alexander has bipolar disorder, grew up in foster homes after his mother died of cancer, and is triggered when things aren't moving in a positive direction. His equilibrium slipped whenever the elders' meetings devolved into griping sessions, and when the far-fetched proposals they pitched went nowhere.

As a symbolic talking stick was passed from one speaker to another during a Sunday afternoon meeting in People's Park in 2023, Alexander questioned the authority of a woman with short-cropped gray hair, who had explained to everyone how to share the talking stick. Alexander was bugged that the women could speak freely while everyone else was expected to keep quiet until she acknowledged them. He interjected. She shushed him. He yelled, she yelled back. The yelling escalated as others in the sharing circle looked down at their shoes. Finally Alexander walked away.

Before he voluntarily left People's Park with a security escort the night of January 3, 2024, Alexander spent days and nights working in the Meat Kitchen. He'd been robbed multiple times, also witnessing many late night brawls and the near-daily overdoses and territorial squabbles. He was there when they found a man dead in his tent. He figured it would all end when he was dragged away to jail as bulldozers finally leveled People's Park, as they had tried to do before. Even when he felt super-charged with purpose, he was braced for People's Park to have a nightmare ending. Some days he claimed he was ready to die for the Park, while on other days he longed for a quieter life where he could relax in a hot bath.

People's Park lasted for more than half a century, due in no small part to the die-hard support of activists like Alexander. UC Berkeley's first campus expansion scheme began in 1951, when plans for new student housing complexes were initiated. Since then, 15-year development plans have been issued, starting with the 1956 Long Range Development Plan, revised in 1962. The latest, the 2021 Long Range Development Plan, promises "up to 11,730 net new beds of housing."

Before People's Park, the university's use of eminent domain to seize property was not newsworthy. Like redlining in non-white neighborhoods, it was widely accepted as the price of modernization. People who spoke out against having their homes and neighborhoods seized for development were marginalized and ignored. Politicians barely acknowledged their plight. If the university had immediately developed the land it seized from eminent domain, People's Park would have never existed.

Through the 1950s, UC Berkeley's plans for expansion became more ambitious. University leaders, led by Chancellor Clark Kerr, tied California's economic future to the growth of higher education opportunities for high school graduates. These plans depended on exponential enrollment growth. The G.I. Bill's success in educating military veterans proved that students from all backgrounds could benefit from a university education. Campus expansion plans were spurred on by the idea that social mobility gained through higher education would fuel the California economy and build a strong workforce for generations to come.

To prepare for a surge of new enrollment, the 1956 Long Range Development Plan sketched out the plan to buy property south of campus, a neighborhood with a mix of small businesses and family-owned residences. In 1967, UC Berkeley used eminent domain to purchase south side land for student dormitories. The 2.8 acre block of land east of Telegraph Avenue, between Haste Street and Dwight Way—the future site of People's Park—was seized for $1.3 million. In 1968, UC Berkeley bulldozed the four one-block residential parcels the Regents had purchased to erect eight-story dormitory buildings. The first sets of dormitories, Units 1, 2, and 3, each on a separate block, were an immediate failure. Students complained of strict curfews and institutionalized meals. Unit 4, slated to be built on Block 1875-2, languished as an empty lot.

UC Berkeley's expansion plan to accommodate the first wave of baby boomer students in the 1960s misjudged the immediate need for dormitory housing. Housing vacancies in Berkeley had shot up during the postwar boom—families were moving in droves to the suburbs to live in brand new homes with two-car garages and modern plumbing. This left Berkeley's run-down multi-story Victorian-style homes available for affordable communal living. Students and young people lived together in large groups and enjoyed the groovy hippie lifestyle.

In 1967, Ronald Reagan ordered his motorcade to go to Berkeley for his first made-for-TV moment as California Governor. In University Hall on Oxford Avenue, with TV news cameras rolling, Reagan fired UC President Clark Kerr, the architect of the "multiversity" plan to offer a free college education to all Californians. Reagan was spoiling for a fight that would make national news, aiming to show voters his law-and-order chops as a candidate who would make good on his campaign stump speech promise "to clean up that mess in Berkeley."

By targeting Berkeley, Reagan knew he had a political foil that would showcase his fiscal conservatism. Reagan called Berkeley a "refuge for communism and immorality" and claimed the elitist faculty and their out-of-control students were wasting taxpayers funds and embarrassing upstanding citizens with their hippie antics. "How far do we go in tolerating these people and this trash under the excuse of academic freedom and freedom of expression?" Reagan mused in a 1966 speech titled "The Morality Gap at Berkeley."

Behind the scenes, J. Edgar Hoover ran one of the FBI's biggest spying operations in downtown Berkeley, in what is now the SkyDeck building. Nearly every activist group in Berkeley, from the Asian American Political Association to the Black Panthers, had infiltrators among their ranks. Berkeley's activists were at the top of Hoover's hit list, just behind his primary target, Dr. Martin Luther King, Jr.

Block 1875-2, slated to become Unit 4, UC Berkeley's fourth block in its cluster of south side dormitories, was bulldozed in 1968 despite the high level of vacancies in the newly finished dormitories of Units 1, 2, and 3. In its February 16, 1969 issue, *The Daily Californian* described the location of this block as "a concentration of hippies, radicals, rising crime, and a drug culture." Residents and neighbors surmised the university wanted to clear the area of undesirable left-leaning tenants with their counterculture tendencies.

After the block was bulldozed, it became an empty pit. Giant muddy moats formed in the imprint where house foundations had been, while broken down cars and heaps of garbage accumulated. Neighbors grew angry at the university's carelessness.

By this time political tensions in Berkeley were at a crisis level. Inspired and guided by the Black Panthers, in January, 1969, the Mexican American Student Confederation, the Asian American Political Alliance, and the Native American Student Alliance joined Black Student Union to create the Third World Liberation Front strike. To break up the swelling crowds of protestors, Berkeley police adopted the Oakland police's brute force tactics, preemptively swinging batons and shooting tear gas canisters.

That spring, the idea of transforming the bulldozed lot into a park for the Telegraph Avenue neighborhood captured violence-weary Berkeley residents' imaginations. The *Berkeley Barb*, a popular leftist pamphlet proclaimed,. "Hear Ye, Hear Ye, A park will be built ... Bring shovels, hoses, chains, grass, paints, flowers, trees, bulldozers, top soil, colorful smiles, laughter and lots of sweat ... Nobody supervises and the trip belongs to whoever dreams. Signed, Robin Hood's Park Commissioner." A park with lush gardens and a children's playground would be the ultimate gesture of community togetherness, an antidote to Telegraph Avenue's brutal confrontations by the police, and the opposite of the university's bureaucratic monolith, the "odious" machine that Mario Savio had railed against.

On April 20, 1969, 100 or so people showed up to create a park. Sod, shovels, and campfire pots of food were donated. At the nearby Red Square Dress Shop and at the Caffé Mediterranean—affectionately called "The Med"—volunteers kicked around ideas to create a poetry reading stage, a fish pond, a swing set play area for children, and a community vegetable garden. Over the next few weeks, the number of volunteers swelled to over 1,000. People's Park became a "peace and love" paradise, with rock band jam sessions, nudity, communal pot smoking, and a sense that differences could be worked out with a collective spirit of cooperation. Giant steaming caldrons containing soup or stew fed everyone who was hungry. One group of entrepreneurial young men made soup in a trash can.

"Everyone gets a blister!" and "Power to the People!" became People's Park mottos.
Courtesy of Wikimedia Commons.

Through the first couple of weeks after the creation of People's Park, Berkeley Chancellor Roger W. Heyns—a psychology researcher—managed a careful balance between the students' newly won free speech rights, the leftist activist culture of Telegraph Avenue, and Governor Ronald Reagan's political zeal to squelch student disobedience. He met with a coalition of People's Park activists and agreed to preserve a portion of the People's Park alongside the soon-to-be-built athletic field and parking lot. Heyns promised the organizers he'd let them know when work would begin.

Ten days into the creation of People's Park, Heyns announced that the university's development plans for Block 1875-2 would resume. He requested that People's Park leaders present the landscape designs that could be incorporated into the university's plans for the athletic field. Getting the People's Park leaders to meet proved difficult. People's Park activists were purposely non-hierarchical. "It was difficult to identify somebody with some kind of representational authority," said Heyns, who was quoted in the Daily Cal newspaper.

In the end, none of the negotiations mattered. Governor Ronald Reagan refused to condone any negotiations, and many of the People's Park leaders were equally stubborn, firmly refusing to relinquish any portion of the park for the university's development projects.

On Thursday, May 15, 1969, a violent standoff unfolded. "Bloody Thursday" is the name of the out-of-control melee that started before 5:00 a.m., when 250 officers from the Berkeley Police and the Highway Patrol cordoned off the south side neighborhood around People's Park, while workers erected an eight-foot high chain link fence around the perimeter. Once the fence stood, bulldozers plowed through the gardens, brick pathways, and playground area, returning the then-newly completed People's Park back to rubble. An electric bulldozer alarm system the activists had setup on a tall pole failed to sound. The person-to-person phone call tree set up to alert protestors of the bulldozers didn't do much better.

Berkeley activists had five years of protest practice, starting with the Free Speech Movement in 1964 and continuing throughout the Vietnam War protests. Everyone knew the drill: gather at noon in Sproul Plaza, listen to rally speeches, and then march down Telegraph Avenue towards Oakland. This time their planned march was shortened to just a few blocks, from Sproul Plaza to People's Park.

When the crowd, numbering around 3,000, began to march down Telegraph Avenue chanting "We want the park!," they were stopped by a barrage of tear gas canisters. Some officers carried shotguns loaded with birdshot, buckshot, and rock salt—considered nonlethal ammunition—presumably so officers could justify firing directly into the unarmed crowds, which they did.

Shots fired chaotically in every direction. They targeted protesters throwing rocks and bottles, but also bystanders who stood nearby. Protestors flipped over a City of Berkeley car and it erupted in flames. During the standoff, one police officer was stabbed. Dozens of protestors were taken to the hospital with gunshot wounds, including a student with a shattered leg, three students with punctured lungs, and one protester blinded by shots to his face. Law enforcement shot James

Rector, 25, in the chest while he watched the melee from a rooftop overlooking People's Park. Rector died a few days after.

Police shot James Rector in the chest as he watched the battle for People's Park on May 15, 1969 from the roof of Granma Books on Telegraph Avenue. He died of his wounds four days later.
Courtesy of Nacio Jan Brown.

By the afternoon, hundreds more law enforcement officers took over the streets of Berkeley. That evening, Governor Reagan called a "state of extreme emergency," mandating a two-week residential lockdown of the whole city, calling in tanks, tear gas loaded helicopters, and 2,700 National Guard troops. Tanks rumbled down University Avenue, assembling at the Berkeley Marina and on Durant Avenue, in front of the Berkeley Art Museum building, a concrete brutalist-style modern design by Mario Ciampi, then under construction. (This building is now the Bakar BioEnginuity Hub and Neurotech Collider Lab.)

During a Sproul Plaza vigil honoring Rector, helicopters swooped down to cover mourners and the entire UC Berkeley campus with a thick cloud of tear gas. The gas burned the eyes and lungs of children at the nearby elementary schools.

Governor Ronald Reagan called in the National Guard to quell the 1969 People's Park demonstrations. Tanks lined up at the Berkeley Marina and on Durant Avenue, ready for deployment against People's Park demonstrators.
Courtesy of Wikimedia Commons.

By the end of May, Berkeley residents solidly backed preserving People's Park. The Berkeley City Council voted 5-4 to lease People's Park from the university. The UC Berkeley's Faculty Senate voted to remove the chain-link fence from the park's perimeter, calling for a police conduct an internal investigation to determine why there was gun violence. In June, the University of California Regents voted to move forward with the construction of a soccer field with an adjacent parking lot at the site. Invigorated by their success and the Maoist-inspired slogan to "let a thousand parks bloom," more community garden sites appeared in Berkeley. For a few years after "Bloody Thursday," People's Park lawns and playground were kept immaculately, in honor of the struggle.

By the late 1970s, People's Park had become a haven for pervasive drug use. The People's Park Stage became Berkeley's epicenter of counterculture gatherings, a place where Joseph Campbell's "follow your bliss" and Timothy Leary's "turn on, tune in, drop out" meshed with

Summer of Love-style nudity and eyes-closed dancing to psychedelic rock music.

By the 1980s, crime spiked in People's Park. The down and out gathered there for refuge. It was one of the few places in Berkeley where people could sleep without being hassled by law enforcement.

In 1991, the construction of sand-filled volleyball courts touched off "Defend the Park" protests that resulted in 95 arrests. Eventually basketball courts replaced the sand courts. A dwindling number of students volunteered to tend to the People's Park gardens. Most students avoided the Park altogether. *Berkeleyside* reported that crime statistics kept by UCPD showed 10,102 criminal incidents at People's Park in between 2012 and 2017.

In its final decades, People's Park still showed remnants of Berkeley's marijuana-haze, tie-dyed past, especially in the spring and summer, when the lawn in front of the stage was still green and lush. People's Park Anniversary on April 20 coincides with the annual 420 celebration, when cannabis aficionados all over the world light up joints at 4:20 p.m. on 4/20 (April 20), assuring a reliably large crowd gathering. After the April 20 anniversary festivities, local groups hosted summer lineups of pop-up style festivals, featuring anti-establishment bands, poets, and performance artists. Old-timers took to the stage to reminisce and advocate for the Park's preservation, usually including a rant against UC Berkeley. A group called Save The Park showed films on summer nights to raise funds and attract new volunteers.

Poet Julia Vinograd, known to all as "Bubblelady," was a frequent performer on the People's Park Stage. Vinograd graduated from UC Berkeley in 1943, then joined the Iowa Writers' Workshop at the University of Iowa, where she received her Master's degree. She came back to Berkeley in 1967, at the start of the Summer of Love, when San Francisco and Berkeley were the destination for hippies from all over the world. Vinograd rented a room at the Berkeley Inn, just across the street from People's Park.

The cover of Street Spices, a poetry anthology by Julia Vinograd published by Thorp Springs in 1973.
Courtesy of Wikimedia Commons.

The evening before the May 15 "Bloody Thursday" standoff between police and protestors in 1969, Vinograd bought two large bags of soap bubble bottles—the kind sold in dime stores in garish colored plastic (usually pink) that included a plastic bubble wand (usually yellow) in each bottle.

Vinograd took the soap bubble bottles to People's Park, handing out a couple of bottles to the police on night duty, encouraging them to join her in blowing bubbles. They did. Vinograd blew bubbles all through the night and into the morning of Bloody Thursday, hoping the bubbles would diffuse the tension.

From that day forward, blowing bubbles became her calling card. At her beloved Caffé Med, where coffee-fueled activists plotted their next moves, Vinograd wrote five decades of poetry that captured the essence of Berkeley counterculture.

Vinograd's poetry readings and clouds of bubbles became a fixture at People's Park, where she performed regularly—and blew bubbles—until her death in 2018, at age 75. In her poem "People's Park" Vinograd wrote, "If they bulldoze People's Park / the blades of grass will fly like knives."

Despite the efforts of a few diehard activist groups, California's housing crisis eclipsed any lingering sentimentality to keep People's Park.

When Carol Christ became Berkeley's first woman Chancellor in 2017, one of her top objectives was to develop nine new student housing complexes with 7,500 new beds. Without enough available student housing, UC Berkeley struggled to keep up its ranking as the world's number one public university.

Activist groups, including Make UC A Good Neighbor, The People's Park Historic District Advocacy Group, and Berkeley Citizens for a Better Plan, filed lawsuits to stop the proposed student housing development at People's Park, but hardly any students joined their ranks.

The poster for the People's Park 53rd penultimate anniversary celebration on April 24, 2022.
Courtesy of Save People's Park.

According to UC Berkeley's People's Park Housing site, a historical tribute is planned for the outdoor space alongside the new student dormitories. Ideas for the tribute include "a memorial walkway that mimics the path of protestors walked in May 1969, murals or commemorative designs on the exterior of the buildings, displays of historic photos, and themed student housing floors around the topics of social justice, sustainability, and caring for the natural and human habitat." UC Berkeley Professor Walter Hood, a decorated urban designer and MacArthur Genius Grant winner for his landscape architecture that fosters community revitalization, is designing the outdoor space that commemorates People's Park for students and visitors in a way that simulates aspects of the original park. However, this newly designed outdoor space may not be open to the public.

The 2024 design for the Berkeley city block formally known as People's Park includes an outdoor space designed by Walter Hood.
Courtesy of UC Berkeley's People's Park Housing public information site.

The Black Panther Party and the Third World Front

"WE WANT FREEDOM. WE WANT POWER TO DETERMINE THE DESTINY OF OUR BLACK AND OPPRESSED COMMUNITIES."
—*First Point of the Black Panthers' Ten-Point Program*

Telegraph Avenue

Telegraph Avenue is Berkeley's most famous thoroughfare. On October 15-16, 1965, more than 10,000 Vietnam Day Committee Peace March participants marched down Telegraph Avenue from Sproul Plaza to the Oakland Army Terminal, the country's send-off point for men and supplies headed to Vietnam. Ever since, this route—from UC Berkeley to downtown Oakland— has served as arguably the world's most active protest march route. It's also where Berkeley's grittiness and funkiness is on full display, in what poet Julia Vinograd called "Desolation Row."

The intersection of Telegraph Avenue and Bancroft Avenue on the south side of campus is the busiest entrance to UC Berkeley.
Courtesy of Pam Gleason.

In 1858, the East Bay Area's first telegraph line was constructed between downtown Oakland and Martinez. The dirt road connecting the telegraph poles was named "Telegraph Road." Starting in 1873, a horse-drawn trolley carried students from their Oakland residences to the Berkeley campus along Telegraph Road. The Peralta family rancheria was located on the banks of Temescal Creek, the probable location of Sunday rodeos when nearby Telegraph Road was a path for vaqueros on horseback.

In 1903, after Telegraph Road became Telegraph Avenue, an amusement park called Idora Park opened on Telegraph between 56th and 58th Streets. Idora Park featured a Ferris wheel and dozens of other 5-cent rides. Visitors gawked at a pen holding grizzly bears and enjoyed Rocky Road ice cream, a locally invented flavor that quickly became a favorite.

Before Sproul Plaza's 1962 construction, Telegraph Avenue led up to Sather Gate. Residences and shops lined Telegraph Avenue all of the way up to the Sather Gate entrance, where the bridge crosses Strawberry Creek. One of the homes razed for Sproul Plaza's construction is where Ishi, the last known member of the Yahi tribe, spent the summer of 1915 with anthropologist Professor Thomas Talbot Waterman and his family.

Sproul Plaza architect Lawrence Halprin wanted to create a welcoming space dedicated to social interaction beckoning to passersby on Telegraph Avenue. In 1966, the university hired Halprin's mentor Thomas Church, to create a new university entrance at the end of College Avenue, in part to lessen the political activity that connected Sproul Hall and Telegraph Avenue. Nevertheless the Telegraph Avenue entrance to campus continues to be the hot spot for political activity. If you look up from this access point, you will see several security cameras pointed at you.

Telegraph Avenue is known for its characters. "Happy, Happy, Happy!" was J.J. Chin's near daily chant from the Telegraph entrance of Sproul Plaza. If provoked, the bespectacled and diminutive Chin growled, "CIA! CIA! CIA!" Other memorable regulars include Rick

Starr, a lounge singer whose Big Band hits were dedicated to attractive co-eds, and Hate Man, a street-styled philosopher-king who'd left his *New York Times* reporter job to live in People's Park. Hate Man, whose real name was Mark Hawthorne, started conversations with "I hate you!" This was his way of avoiding meaningless social niceties, so that "real" talk was unavoidable.

Mural of Hate Man painted in People's Park.
Courtesy of artists Bruce Duncan, Ace Backword, and other volunteer artists.

Hate Man also started a "hate drum circle" on Sproul Plaza so folks could join in and release their negative feelings. From Telegraph Avenue, passersby good hear (and join!) the drum circle, which continued on for a few decades as a weekend fixture at Lower Sproul Plaza. *San Francisco*

Chronicle reporter Rona Marech noted that the drummers brought a wide range of percussion instruments, including, "bongos, congas, dumbaks, timbales, djembes, bass drums, cowbells, agogo bells, cuicas, shakers and tambourines." The cacophony of banging and undulating dance styles emboldened novices—so long as you had something to bang or shake you fit right in.

Just off Telegraph Avenue, Bob Avakian's Revolution Books still advocates for "a radically different world." Avakian, chairperson of the Revolutionary Communist Party USA, is in his 80s, probably plotting his own five-year plan for a successor to run the Revolution Books bookstore and advocate for a new society based on "new communism." His posters proclaiming "WHY I'M *NOT* RUNNING FOR PRESIDENT" appeared all over Berkeley in the run up to the 2024 election.

One of Telegraph's most rascally characters, Ken Sarachan, is responsible for the Disney-esque monstrosity on the corner of Haste and Telegraph. Officially called the Enclave Dormitories, it's a student residence that some have affectionately nicknamed the "Flintstone Building." Local rumors say Sarachan wanted an outlandish design to piss off City of Berkeley officials.

Sarachan began his Telegraph Avenue business ventures out of a van, buying and selling books in front of Moe's Books, gleefully (rumors say) siphoning off of Moe Moskovitz's success. Sarachan used the proceeds to start Rasputin's Music, then expanded with Blondie's Pizza. He now also owns Bear Basics, Anastasia's Vintage Clothing, as well as the Mad Monk Center for Anachronistic Media, the latter of which is where Cody's Books was located before it closed in 2008.

Rasputin's Music display window shows historic photos of Barrington Hall, the infamous student cooperative known for acid-laced wine dinners and all-nude meetings. Another panel of photos and memorabilia shows off Berkeley's thriving punk scene, where thrashing, moshing, and stage dives into the audience could be enjoyed at places like the Gilman Street Project, an all-ages punk rock venue that advertises, "no violence or alcohol—have a nice day."

Perhaps the most poignant historic photos displayed in Rasputin's Music's window are of the Black Panthers, whose presence on Telegraph is also memorialized by the nearby images of Bobby Seale and Huey Newton on the "A People's History of Telegraph Avenue" mural. The Black Panthers hung out at Caffé Med and the Forum on Telegraph Avenue, where Bobby Seale and Huey Newton worked on their founding doctrines, "What We Want Now!", "What We Believe", and "The Black Panther Party for Self-Defense Ten-Point Platform and Program." These famous coffee shops, where countless revolutions and civil rights protests have been plotted, are now gone.

Telegraph Avenue still bustles with activity, but the heyday of its revolutionary fervor is fading into the past. A group called Telegraph for People wants to invigorate the area's community-minded spirit by making the northernmost portion of Telegraph Avenue a car-free plaza, an idea first proposed by Moe Moskowitz, owner of Moe's Books. A tweet from Telegraph for People announced its vision for a "future that isn't just sustainable, but contagiously fun!"

The Black Panther Party and the Third World Liberation Front

Oakland's Merritt College, which began in the 1920s as an elite school for the children of Berkeley faculty, attracted scholars and administrators who did not conform to UC Berkeley's more conservative standards. In 1962, Berkeley Ph.D. graduate Rodney Carlisle taught an "experimental" Black history sociology class at Merritt College, the kind of experimental class that wouldn't have a chance of being added to the course catalog at a UC campus before the civil rights era. "Black Studies came out of protest. It came out of the desire for students to take a hold of the academy and to force the academy to replace the emphasis from a eurocentric perspective to an African perspective," Siri Brown, Vice Chancellor and African American Studies Professor at Merritt College, said in a 2022 address commemorating Juneteenth.

Two of Carlisle's students were Huey Newton and Bobby Seale. In class, Newton challenged Carlisle on his university-authorized assumptions about the role of the United States in the slave trade, like the claim that slavery started as piracy. Newton saw these Berkeley-taught arguments as a way of skirting the economic deliberateness and state-sponsored role in perpetuating the slave trade. Seale, who liked to keep his local stand-up comedy gigs fresh with observations about the Black experience, knew Newton's rhetoric would grab any audience's attention. Both were fans of E. Franklin Frazier's *Black Bourgeoisie*, which advocated self-governance, healthcare for all, and militant unionization. Newton and Seale identified with Malcolm X's fiery rhetoric and passionate rejection of systemic anti-Black racism. His refusal to use the white last name he'd inherited was a powerful testament. "For me, my 'X' replaced the white slavemaster name of 'Little' which some blue-eyed devil named Little had imposed upon my paternal forebears."

Newton and Seale were disillusioned with the Berkeley hierarchy-styled Afro-American Association. Newton complained that the Afro-American Association's complacency acted as "a means to deceive Black people." The two decided to form their own group, the Soul Students Advisory Council, the precursor to the Black Panthers Party for Self-Defense.

Original Members of the Black Panther Party of Self-Defense. From top right: Elbert Howard, Huey P. Newton, Sherman Forte, Bobby Seale, Reggie Forte and Bobby Hutton.
Courtesy of the African American Library and Museum of Oakland (AALMO).

In 1966, the Soul Students Advisory Council held rallies that attracted audiences in the hundreds. Then, when Newton and Seale were arrested on Telegraph Avenue for blocking the sidewalk, the two decided it was time to carry guns. *In Seize The Time: The Story of The Black Panther Party and Huey P. Newton*, Seale explains what sparked the decision: While on their way to The Forum, a café with sidewalk seating across the street from Moe's Books, Seale began rapping a couple of his favorite street poems. As he walked down Telegraph Avenue, he launched into "Burn, Baby, Burn" written by Marvin X after the Los Angeles Watts Rebellion. A friend nicknamed Weasel joined them. He pulled out one of The Forum's sidewalk chairs and said. "Bobby, stand on this ... run it down again!" Seale complied, restarting his bars with "Uncle Sammy Call Me Fulla Lucifer" an anti-Vietnam poem, and belting it out louder as a white police officer approached—

> *Uncle Sammy don't shuck and jive me,*
> *I'm hip the popcorn jazz changes you blow,*
> *You know damn well what I mean,*
> *You school my naive heart to sing*
> *red-white-and-blue-stars-and-stripes songs*
> *and to pledge eternal allegiance to all things blue,*
> *true, blue-eyed blond, blond-haired, white chalk*
> *white skin with U.S.A. tattooed all over,*
> *When my soul trusted Uncle Sammy,*
> *Loved Uncle Sammy,*
> *I died in dreams for you Uncle Sammy...*

The officer lunged at Seale, and said, "You're under arrest!" Seale retorted, "Under arrest for what?" As he got down from the chair he was standing on, the policeman grabbed Seale's hands to handcuff him, and Newton shoved him off. A couple of other policemen jumped on Seale, laying him flat on the sidewalk, then several others joined Newton to fight the police off. Seale, Newton and the others escaped down the block, but the police caught up and arrested them. Newton spent several days in jail.

At the next meeting of the Soul Students Advisory Council, Seale and Newton stood resolute. They'd buy guns to defend themselves. If the others didn't agree, they'd form their own new group and insist on their Second Amendment rights to bear arms. Inspired by Malcom X, assassinated the year before, they adopted the motto "We want freedom by any means necessary."

Seize The Time: The Story of The Black Panther Party and Huey P. Newton by Bobby Seale, published by Black Classic Press.
Courtesy of Wikimedia Commons.

In *Seize The Time,* Seale also explains how they chose their name: "The nature of a panther is that he never attacks," Seale wrote. "But if anyone attacks him or backs him into a corner, the panther comes up to wipe that aggressor or that attacker out, absolutely, resolutely, wholly, thoroughly, and completely." Their name would be The Black Panthers Party of Self-Defense, and they'd have a ten-point plan, loosely modeled on Mao Tse Tung's revolutionary platform for China's Communist Party.

1

BLACK PANTHER PARTY FOR SELF-DEFENSE (BPPSD)

A source advised that the Black Panther Party For Self-Defense (BPPSD) was formed by HUEY PERCY NEWTON, Minister of Defense, and BOBBY GEORGE SEALE, Chairman, in Oakland, California, in December, 1966, as a militant black nationalist political organization to combat "police brutality," to unite militant black youth, to determine the destiny of black communities, and to educate black people in African history. The political philosophy of the organization was taken from the writings of MAO TSE-TUNG of Communist China and black militant writers.

The organizing principles for Black Panther Party for Self-Defense are outlined in its opening paragraph.
Courtesy of the African American Library and Museum of Oakland (AALMO).

Mao's teachings proved instrumental to the founding of the Black Panther Party in another way, too. Newton, Seale, and other early members were focused on obtaining guns. A few had been donated, including by Berkeley student and Japanese-Americans internment camp survivor, Richard Aoki, who served on the Berkeley Young Socialist Alliance's executive committee. Aoki was later outed as FBI informant. He'd amassed hundreds of spy dossiers on Berkeley's leftist organizations, including the Black Panthers in its earliest days.

Their quest to obtain more guns and their curiosity about Mao's *Little Red Book* presented a fundraising opportunity. Seale described their plan in "Red Books for Guns" in *Seize The Time*: "You know what? I know how to make some money to buy some guns ... We can sell those Red Books. I know that many brothers on the block would not buy a Red Book, but I do know that many of those leftist radicals at Berkeley will buy the Red Book."

Newton was so sure of his plan that he and Seale drove to San Francisco and bought 60 copies of the *Little Red Book* in Chinatown to sell on Sproul Plaza. They sold all of them within an hour for a dollar each, more than doubling their investment. Then they went right back to the same bookseller with the money they'd earned, asking for a discount to buy all of the *Little Red Books* left in stock for 30 cents a piece.

The next day, they perfected their sales pitch as they stood at Sather Gate, the busiest spot on the Berkeley campus. (Ironically, Richard Aoki warned them not to go near Sather Gate because FBI agents were waiting to bust them there.) Newton implored students within earshot, "Power comes out of the barrel of a gun. Quotations from Chairman Mao Tse Tung. Get your Red Book!"

Seale's pitch connected the Black Panther's Second Amendment pursuit with the Free Speech Movement's First Amendment struggle: "All you free speechers up here who lost Mario Savio must read the Red Book and do it like the Red Guards did it."

Bobby "Lil Bobby" Hutton, who at age 16 joined Newton and Seale as the first official member and treasurer of The Black Panthers Party, didn't yet have the gift of persuasion that came so easily for Newton and Seale. He simply shouted, "Red Book, Red Book!" In about two hours, they made $170, which they used to buy two shotguns.

With the Ten-Point Plan, the Black Panthers membership grew. Within two years of their 1966 founding, they had more than 5,000 members and 38 chapters across the United States. The Black Panther uniform—natural hair, black leather jacket, black beret, and a proud militant posture—attained global adoption.

Volunteers created community "survival programs" intended to serve the Black community in ways that local governments had failed them. They organized centers for the elderly, transportation services, clothing distribution centers, health care clinics that tested for sickle-cell disease, and created a Black Studies curriculum for children. One of their most successful programs, the Free Breakfast for Children program, at first rivaled then augmented the success of a nationwide School Breakfast Program, was permanently funded by Congress in 1975.

The success of the Black Panthers Free Breakfast for Children program influenced Congress to fund the expansion of the nationwide School Breakfast Program. Men served the breakfasts in a show of support for women's equality.
Courtesy of the African American Library and Museum of Oakland (AAMLO).

In April 1977, the Black Panthers delivered hot meals to the federal building in San Francisco, where disabled activists staged a sit-in that lasted 26 days in their fight for the passage of Section 504 of the 1971 Rehabilitation Act. Section 504 denies federal funding for organizations that do not provide access for individuals with disabilities, putting might behind eliminating barriers that disabled people face in their everyday lives.

"Crip Camp: A Disability Revolution," the 2020 documentary film, shows the Black Panthers efforts to fight oppression alongside the disabled activists. Many of the activists were from Berkeley's Center for

Independent Living, located near the UC Berkeley campus on Telegraph Avenue. Leaders including Ed Roberts, Hale Zukas, and Jan McEwan Brown—whose student group at UC Berkeley was called the "Rolling Quads"—welcomed the support from the Black Panthers.

The Black Panther Party newspaper on May 7, 1977 highlighted the struggle to enact Section 504, a provision mandating that organizations that benefit from federal funding must provide access for individuals with disabilities.
Courtesy of the African American Library and Museum of Oakland (AALMO).

The Black Panther Party of Self-Defense sparked UC Berkeley student demands for the serious treatment of Black history. Undergraduate students lobbied for an experimental course called Dehumanization and Regeneration of the American Social Order. In the fall of 1968, for the inaugural term of Social Analysis 139X, the students chose Eldridge Cleaver, then the Black Panther's Minister of Information, to give a series of ten lectures on "The Roots of Racism." According to *Black Against Empire: The History and Politics of the Black Panther Party* by Joshua Bloom and Waldo E. Martin, Jr., in less than 24 hours Governor Ronald Reagan demanded that Cleaver be uninvited.

Eldridge Cleaver of the Black Panther Party (center) on the UC Berkeley campus in October 1968. Cleaver had 900 students on the waitlist for his course "The Roots of Racism."
Courtesy of the Afrian American Library and Museum of Oakland (AALMO).

UC Berkeley students remained undaunted. When the UC Regents decided that Cleaver could only give one lecture, the Afro-American Student Union organized a sit-in at the offices of the Chancellor and the College of Letters and Sciences. Students also gathered around a huge bonfire in Sproul Plaza in protest. In opposition to Governor Reagan and the UC Regents, UC Berkeley's faculty Academic Senate voted 668 to 114 to allow Cleaver to teach the full term of ten classes. Course registration for Social Analysis 139X surpassed the hundred-seat limit, with 900 students on the waitlist.

Buffered by their success in securing Cleaver's "The Roots of Racism" lectures, the Afro-American Student Union (AASU) approached the Asian American Political Alliance (AAPA) and the Mexican-American Student Confederation (MASC) to form the Third World Liberation Front (TWLF).

Five UC Berkeley students, led by UC Berkeley's first recognized Native American student LaNada War Jack, formed the Native American Students United (NASU) and joined the coalition. Together, the four student organizations plotted a series of strikes starting in January 1969. For ten weeks, the Third World Liberation Front student leaders led UC Berkeley students in a series of strikes.

The Third World Liberation Front first demand was for the university to create four new departments, each with professors, courses, and curricula specific to each group's unique culture and history:

1. That funds be allocated for the implementation of the Third World College.
2. Department of Asian Studies controlled by Asian people.
3. Department of Black Studies as proposed by the AASU.
4. Department of Chicano Studies.
5. Department of Native American Studies.

The Third World Liberation Front held a series of marches on the UC Berkeley campus in the fall term of 1969.
Courtesy of the Bancroft Library.

Harvey Dong, a popular Asian Studies lecturer and PhD graduate of Ethnic Studies at UC Berkeley, remembers the friendships he formed with other TWLF strikers when he was an undergraduate. Dong's grandfather immigrated from China at the height of anti-Asian racism sanctioned by the 1882 Exclusion Act. His father was a decorated World War II veteran. Dong remembers hanging out with Black Panthers and Afro-American Student Union at TWLF gatherings and listening to music by John Coltrane, Miles Davis, and Thelonious Monk.

Protest songs and chants bonded the TWLF coalition together. When the Black students shouted, "I'm Black and I'm proud! Say it loud!" the Asian students chimed in with "I'm Asian and I'm proud! Say it loud!" Once every demographic was covered, Dong remembers it made everyone laugh when someone shouted, "I'm bougie and I'm proud! Say it loud!"

Ten weeks of strikes worked. The students of UC Berkeley's Third World Liberation Front won their number one demand when the Academic Senate voted in favor of establishing the Ethnic Studies Department with degree programs in African American Studies, Asian Studies, Chicano Studies, and Native American Studies.

In the book *Power of the People Won't Stop: Legacy of the TWLF at UC Berkeley,* Abraham Ramirez—an award-winning researcher and instructor of Chicana/o Latina/o Thought and the Philosophy of Race in UC Berkeley's Ethnic Studies Department—lists the events that followed the Third World Liberation Front victory.

Depressingly, many of the entries note cuts in funding, citing for example UC Berkeley's 2011 Operational Excellence plan, which implemented significant cuts in staffing, halted faculty hiring, and centralized administrative services such as human resources and financial record keeping. Under Operational Excellence, the Ethnic Studies Department lost five staff members, crippling its programming.

Despite setbacks, campus leaders forge ahead. In 1989, the Senate Faculty instituted the American Culture course requirement, designed "to introduce students to the diverse cultures of the United States through a comparative framework" according to UC Berkeley's American Culture website.

At least 40 departments now offer courses adhering to the American Culture requirement, ensuring that each UC Berkeley undergraduate student—a number expected to surge to past 35,000 students—has ample opportunity to meet this requirement by taking one of the 400 or so American Culture courses offered.

The front page of the Daily Californian leads with the article "American Cultures Passes" on April 26, 1989.
Courtesy of the Daily Californian.

UC Berkeley has made strides in tenuring Black faculty members. In 2023, *The Daily Californian*'s reported that the number of Black ladder faculty had more than doubled in 40 years. "From the 1980s to the (2000s), there were usually only a couple Black ladder faculty hired in a given year," Fabrizio Mejia, UC Berkeley Associate Vice Chancellor, told the newspaper. "In the last few years, that pattern has shifted to around 5-7 Black ladder faculty hired in a given year which has been the major driver in the increase from earlier decades."

Administrators struggle to address low enrollment numbers of Black students at UC Berkeley. Affirmative Action modestly increased the number of Black students in the 1970s, and this increase held steady until 1996, when Californians voted to approve the passage of Proposition 209. Proposition 209 prohibited California state institutions from considering race, sex, or ethnicity in public employment, public contracting, and public education.

African American Studies Association march on campus at UC Berkeley on March November 6, 1987.
Courtesy of the African American Library and Museum of Oakland (AAMLO).

The City of Berkeley is also coming to terms with anti-Black racism. While Berkeley's Black history has its share of triumphs, the setbacks are glaring. Berkeley's jagged southern border with Oakland was decided in 1854 based on which blocks were most desirable to include. Black, Japanese, and other non-white families lived on less desirable land that was marshy or prone to flooding, like Berkeley's Lorin District, centered on the corner of Alcatraz and Adeline Avenues.

A Thomas Brothers map of Berkeley from 1937 shows the redlined areas that were determined to be a risk for home loans. These areas, in South Berkeley and West Berkeley, had suppressed property values. This practice of redlining—the discriminatory practice of denying home loans in "risky" neighborhoods, which were most often predominantly Black—caused Berkeley's Black population to plummet in the 1940s and 1950s. Though the Fair Housing Act of 1968 made the practice of redlining illegal, very few Black families remained in Berkeley.

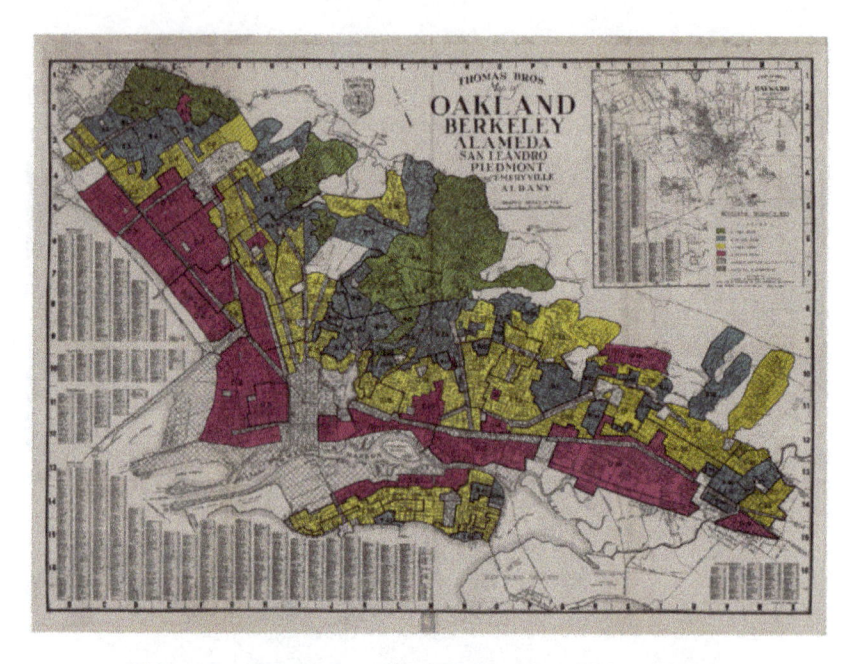

Homeowners Loan Corporation (HOLC) produced this "redlining map" in 1937. Red areas on the map indicated D-grade high risk neighborhoods for loans. Black families living in these areas were not able to secure bank loans to own their homes. Berkeley's Black families, along with Black families in cities across the U.S., were locked out of the wealth accumulation afforded to middle class white families because of this redlining system.
Courtesy of Wikimedia Commons.

In addition, residents in Berkeley's non-white neighborhoods were expected to have less political power to fight evictions for homes that could be bulldozed for new highway construction. For this reason, routes for the expansion of the East Bay's freeway system and for the Bay Area Rapid Transit (BART) System were designed to cut right through South Berkeley. In 1956, UC Berkeley evicted Black families from their homes in the West Berkeley neighborhood called Codornices Village to make room for a new subdivision called University Village. UC Berkeley demolished nearly 2,000 Codornices Village homes, 90 percent of which were occupied by Black families.

In 1968, Mable "Mama" Howard filed a lawsuit to stop BART from dividing her community, the Lorin District of South Berkeley, where many Black, Japanese, and other families of color lived. She succeeded:

BART moved underground up to the Oakland border. Every Juneteenth, Berkeley celebrates its Black heritage in the Lorin District, where the BART tracks would have divided the community if it hadn't been for Mable Howard.

Mabel "Mama" Howard stopped the above-ground construction of BART tracks in the Lorin District of South Berkeley.
Courtesy of the African American Library and Museum of Oakland (AALMO).

During the 1970s, the progressive coalition Berkeley Citizens Action (BCA) led by former Berkeley City Council member Ronald V. Dellums, rallied UC Berkeley students to the ballot box on a slate of progressive issues. BCA's primary issue was police reform, to stop Berkeley Police brutality regularly inflicted upon protestors and political activists. Other progressive issues, like rent control and marijuana deregulation, also served as BCA political agenda mainstays.

Dellums, who earned a Master of Social Work from UC Berkeley in 1962, had been instrumental in making Berkeley one of the first places where African American history was taught in public schools. In 1970, he became Northern California's first Black Congressman.

City of Berkeley voter registration flyer distributed on UC Berkeley campus for the April 19, 1977 election. Registering students to vote turned Berkeley politics from conservative to liberal in this election. *Courtesy of the David Mundstock Collection.*

On April 7, 1971, Berkeley voters elected three new progressive City Council members—called the April Coalition—and approved a new civilian-run police conduct review commission, one of the first of its kind in the U.S. The efforts of Dellums, the BCA, and other left-leaning political operatives in rallying students to vote changed Berkeley city politics from a conservative Not-In-My-Backyard style governance to one of the most politically progressive cities in the United States.

Recently UC Berkeley's Black student population has increased, in large part because of the leadership of Olufemi Ogundele, appointed associate vice chancellor of admissions and enrollment at UC Berkeley in 2021. Ogundele looked at the restrictions of Proposition 209 as an opportunity to formulate a new, more refined admissions process. UC Berkeley stopped requiring high school achievement tests, like the SAT, for undergraduate admissions. Instead, the admissions team relies on grades and evidence of excellence in extracurricular activities.

"I do not think there is any race-neutral alternative to creating diversity on a college campus," Ogundele told a local news outlet. "However, I do think we can do better than what we've done." Ogundele's efforts showed immediate results. Berkeley's new student enrollment since 2021 is the most diverse in school history.

The legacies of people and achievements in UC Berkeley's Black history continues to be discovered and published, part of the Black Panther's broader legacy on campus. Black Lives at Cal (BLAC), an initiative that began in 2021, supports the research of Black people at UC Berkeley and current "living history" in order to "to celebrate, defend, and advance" the Black experience on campus. According to its website, "BLAC advances these goals by (1) exhibiting in digital form the images, documents, and interviews in the archival record; (2) fostering and presenting new research by students and scholars; and (3) serving as a resource on the Black experience in the twenty-first century. To accomplish this, Black graduate students mentor Black undergraduate students through the Undergraduate Research Apprentice Program."

The Black Panther Party of Self-Defense left another Berkeley legacy that thousands still enjoy: the music of Tupac Shakur. Tupac's song "California Love" blasts over the speakers at Memorial Stadium when the Cal football team explodes onto the field at the beginning of each home game. Shakur's mom, Afeni Shakur, was a section leader for the Black Panther Party and brought Tupac to Party meetings.

Black Lives Matter activist wearing a t-shirt of Tupac, who often met friends on Telegraph Avenue in Berkeley.
Courtesy of Wikimedia Commons.

When Tupac started writing poetry and rapping, he often walked along Telegraph Avenue with his friends, seeking out the same Berkeley record stores and social spots as Bobby Seale and Huey Newton, and walking on the same sidewalk where the Black Panther founders rumbled with the Berkeley Police.

In a 1994 *Entertainment Weekly* interview, Tupac explained that his tattoo—THUG LIFE, inked in large letters across his abdomen—wasn't about criminal life, but about the pride and resiliency that he learned as a Black Panthers kid: "My mother was a woman, a Black woman, a single mother raising two kids on her own. She was dark-skinned, had short hair, got no love from nobody except for a group called the Black Panthers... I don't consider myself to be a straight militant. I'm a thug, and my definition of thug comes from half of the street element and half of the Panther element, half of the independence movement. Saying we want self-determination. We want to do it by self-defense and by any means necessary. That came from my family and that's what thug life is. It's a mixture."

Tupac's "California Love" is about hard-earned freedom, "Only in Cali where we riot, not rally, to live and die." In "California Love" Tupac calls out Oakland in his lyrics, but he doesn't call out B-Town, Berkeley's rap name.

Despite the hard-earned victories of civil rights activists, the City of Berkeley's diversity is largely due to its student population. Berkeley's housing is not affordable for working class families. Its aging demographics have preserved its identity as an intellectual and elitist enclave, kryptonite for modern politicians. In 1962, President John F. Kennedy was the last person to choose Berkeley for an important address. Now, no ambitious politician wants a photo op with Berkeley backdrop.

Kamala Harris proclaimed she was "so proud to be a daughter of Oakland, California!" upon declaring her candidacy for President of the United States in 2019 before a crowd of 20,000. Although Harris grew up in Berkeley, Oakland was perhaps a more campaign-friendly locale because it celebrates its Black roots, and its blue-collar resiliency. It's accessible to people of all walks of life in a way Berkeley isn't.

Despite Berkeley's lack of off-campus diversity, the city's civil rights roots gives it deep ties to Black culture and history in the Bay Area. Kamala Harris remembers struggling to stay close to her mother on

Telegraph Avenue during civil rights marches. Shyamala Gopalan Harris received her PhD from Berkeley in 1964. Her thesis, "The Isolation and Purification of a Trypsin Inhibitor from Whole-Wheat Flour," led to a career in breast cancer research on progesterone receptors for the Lawrence Berkeley National Laboratory. Gopalan was a founding member of Berkeley's Afro-American Association. At a campus racial justice meeting in 1962, she met Donald J. Harris, a Berkeley graduate student in economics from Jamaica who later joined the faculty at Stanford.

Kamala Harris (center) with her mother Shyamala Gopalan Harris, her grandparents, and younger sister Maya in front of their Berkeley home at 1227 Bancroft Way in 1972.
Courtesy of Kamala Harris campaign media.

In an exchange with Joe Biden on the Democratic debate stage in 2019, then California Senator Kamala Harris caught the nation's attention when she described herself as "a little girl in California who was part of the second class to integrate her public schools, and she was bused to school every day. And that little girl was me... I was part of the second class to integrate Berkeley, California public schools almost two decades after Brown v. Board of Education." Harris was referencing her childhood in Berkeley in the 1970s.

Harris's mother arrived in Berkeley for her PhD in nutrition and endocrinology just as Martin Luther King, Jr., Malcolm X, and the Black Panthers were raising issues of racial equity. Kamala Harris said she "grew up with a strollers-eye view of the civil rights movement" while being pushed in her stroller down Telegraph Avenue during protest marches.

Harris credits this era of fierce and courageous Black women in Berkeley as a major influence on her life and aspirations. In 2020, she proudly told members of the Omega Psi Phi, one of the oldest Black fraternities who had gathered at Harrah's Resort Atlantic City, "My sister, Maya, and I, we joke that we grew up surrounded by a bunch of adults who spent full time marching and shouting for this thing called 'justice.'"

Fires and Faults

"You could feel the heat coming up through your boots, you could hear a sound like a train coming, and the ground started rumbling... you saw the debris under the trees, especially the pine trees and the eucalyptus... the ground was so hot the leaves would catch on fire... then it would just explode."

— Dee Rosario, one of 1,500 firefighters at the 1991 Oakland Berkeley Firestorm, remembering the helplessness he felt watching trees and houses explode as the firestorm destroyed 3,500 homes and killed 25

Tilden Park

The best place in Berkeley to be enveloped by the scent of a Eucalyptus forest is in Tilden Park. But maybe not for long. Berkeley firefighters at nearby Station 7 on Shasta Road would probably sleep much more soundly at night if all of Tilden Park's Eucalyptus trees were removed. A wildfire that spreads from Wildcat Canyon in Tilden Park to the Berkeley Hills could be unstoppable. To mitigate this danger, workers cut thousands of giant Eucalyptus in recent years, with thousands more scheduled to get the axe. In a 2021 interview with *The Daily Californian* about wildfires, UC Berkeley wildfire scholar Matteo Garbelotto warned of the extreme fire danger the Eucalyptus trees pose. Eucalyptus oil causes an "explosive combustion" when ignited, Garbelotto explained.

Tilden Park covers 2,709 acres and its main entrance is located just east of Grizzly Peak Boulevard at the crest of the Berkeley Hills. The park features a botanical garden, an eighteen-hole golf course, a merry-go-round, a mini-sized passenger steam train, a native plant nursery, around forty miles of hiking trails, and campgrounds. In the summer, Lake Anza is a popular swimming and hangout spot for Berkeley High School students.

Guests dance the night away in Tilden Park's Brazilian Room, a posh venue for wedding parties. The Brazilian government donated the elegant hardwood paneling from its Brazilian Pavilion exhibit at the 1939 San Francisco World's Fair. Funding from the New Deal's Works Progress Administration (WPA) paid for Brazilian Room's construction, including its rich paneling.

Tilden Park's Environmental Education Center, located at the site where the WPA Civilian Conservation Corps camped while constructing the park's bathrooms, trials, stone bridges and picnic areas, offers family-oriented programs. "Creatures of the Night," is a naturalist-guided screening of night vision trail camera footage that documents Tilden Park's wide variety of nocturnal animals including skunks, raccoons, coyotes, foxes, and possums. In "Bugs for Lunch," a naturalist teaches about cuisines made from edible bugs and the program ends with a special treat: homemade ice cream topped with bugs. Kids also can eat mushroom-flavored ice cream at the annual Tilden Fungus Fair.

The Tilden Fungus Fair, held every January at the Environmental Education Center, exhibits over 300 types of mushrooms and offers mushroom-flavored ice cream making workshops and expert presentations on topics like the science of fungal bioluminescence.
Courtesy of Pam Gleason.

    Next to the Environmental Education Center is the Little Farm, open year-round. The farm buildings were built by local boy scout troops at 62 percent scale, making everything kid-sized. Little Farm has cows, chickens, goats, rabbits, sheep, and two 500-pound spotted pigs named Pinky and Perky. Guests are limited to feeding Little Farm's animals low calorie produce, like celery and lettuce, to prevent health issues caused by an overly rich diet.

    Neighborhoods next to Tilden Park enjoy a daily parade of wildlife. Berkeley Hills residents regularly host deer, raccoons, possums, coyotes, foxes, and skunks. Occasionally, Tilden Park visitors also report seeing mountain lions, rattle snakes, bobcats, or weasels. In 2010, a two-year-old male mountain lion made its way down the hill to Berkeley's famed gourmet food neighborhood, home to Chez Panisse, the restaurant Alice Waters made famous for sourcing local farms for high quality produce, and a forerunner of the farm-to-table movement. A wildlife officer shot the mountain lion in a parking lot at the corner of Cedar Street and Shattuck Avenue, instantly killing the 100-pound cat, causing a public outcry and demands for an investigation. For months, mourners left flowers, wreaths, and cards honoring the dead wildcat.

The park is also home to much smaller but no less beloved creatures. Each November, Tilden Park's South Park Drive is closed to vehicles for the annual newt crossing. At the start of the fall rainy season, California Newts (*Taricha torosa*), the orange and rust-colored native salamanders, cross South Park Drive in droves to seek water-filled culverts along the road where they can mate.

Fires and Faults

Bay Area residents who've lived here for several decades are familiar with the anxiety-provoking refrain "The Big One is coming!" Earthquakes are part of life in California. It's normal to experience one or two small jolts a year, but the threat for one much bigger is ever present. The Association of Bay Area Governments predicts 55,000 destroyed homes totaling $11.2 billion in damage from a 7.0 earthquake on the Hayward Fault. The Hayward Fault runs directly under Berkeley.

Berkeley High School's chimney's collapsed during the 1906 San Andreas Earthquake. Berkeley's population skyrocketed after much of San Francisco was destroyed by fire after the earthquake.
Courtesy of the Bancroft Library.

"San Francisco is gone!" wrote Jack London for *Collier's Weekly* in his report of the 1906 earthquake, on record as California's deadliest natural disaster. It killed as many as 3,000 and destroyed 80 percent of the city. San Francisco burned for four days. Busted pipes were largely responsible for most of the damage. Ruptured gas lines added fuel, and broken water lines frustrated the exhausted firefighters.

UC Berkeley Professor Andrew Lawson, famous for identifying and naming the San Andreas Fault as the source of the 1906 earthquake in his report, "The California Earthquake of April 18, 1906: Report of the State Earthquake Investigation Commission," understood that another powerful tremor could strike at any time. In 1908, the same year as his career-defining report, Lawson asked up-and-coming architect Bernard Maybeck to construct a house of solid concrete, strong enough to withstand the next great earthquake.

Andrew Lawson (front row, far right) with mining students in front of the Lawson Adit next to the Hearst Mining Building in 1917.
Courtesy of the Bancroft Library.

What Professor Lawson didn't know was that the land he chose for his Maybeck house is situated right on top of one of the most dangerous faults in the world. A short distance from the Lawson House is the Lawson Adit, a mining pit used for educational purposes and shuttered for good once its position of extreme danger arose. Professor Lawson's walk from his house to the pit—the two Berkeley sites still carrying his name—follows the exact path of the Hayward Fault. Lawson had discovered the San Andreas Fault, but he had no idea that the most lethal fault resided directly under his feet.

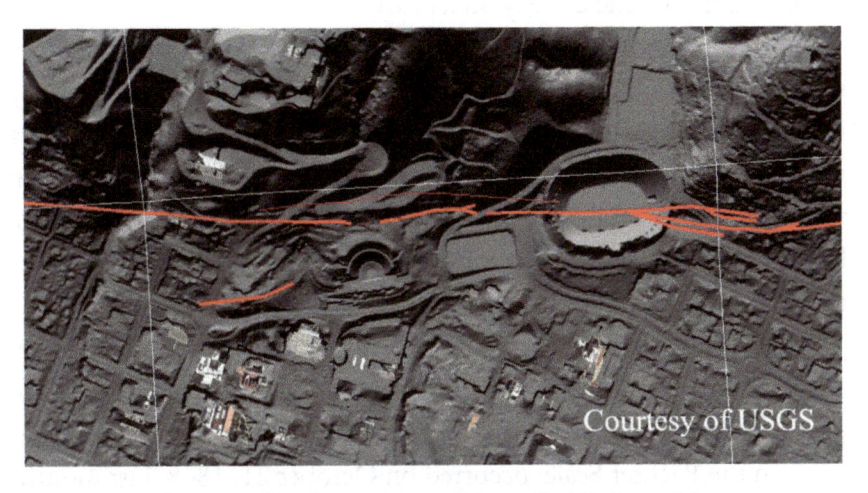

The Hayward Fault runs from north to south at the base of the Berkeley Hills and through the center of Memorial Stadium.
Courtesy of the USGS.

Under Berkeley, the continental North American Plate and the Pacific Plate—two massive continental plates several million more square feet across than any of the other plates—grind past each other at a rate of about three to four inches per year. The Bay Area is composed of gigantic shards of land squeezed haphazardly between these two mothers-of-all-plates. As the Pacific Plate moves south, it bulldozes parts of the California coastline with it. Some joke that the land under San Francisco will eventually move far enough south that it will align with Los Angeles, perhaps finally ending the intrastate SoCal versus NorCal rivalry emblazoned on shirts, baseball hats, and surf gear.

A few giant California faults hold the lion's share of tectonic strain. The San Andreas Fault, which runs along the coastline, caused the 1906 earthquake and fire that leveled San Francisco. The Loma Prieta Fault, which runs through the South Bay Area, caused the 1989 Loma Prieta earthquake. Neither are considered as deadly as the Hayward Fault, which runs south to north along the base of the Berkeley Hills. This is the fault that scientists predict could generate one of Mother Nature's most dangerous moments in world history. For a century and a half the Hayward Fault has been dormant, allowing a population approaching three million to settle densely on its edges.

The United States Geological Survey calls the Hayward Fault "the single most urbanized earthquake fault in the United States." Berkeley is divided between two of the most dangerous places to experience a major earthquake: West Berkeley structures may fail from liquefaction, where landfilled areas will wobble like jelly. East Berkeley structures, built directory over the Hayward Fault, could violently shake off of their foundations. Water and gas pipes will fail everywhere.

Geologist James Lienkaemper famously estimated in 2010 that a recurrence of a Hayward Fault earthquake would happen every 161 years, plus or minus 65 years. The last big earthquake on the Hayward Fault, a 6.7 on the Richter Scale, occurred on October 21, 1868, just months after the University of California's charter. There were only a few simple structures in Berkeley in 1868. According to local lore, Jose Domingo Peralta's small adobe home collapsed. If Lienkaemper's estimates stand correct, this means the "Big One" could hit any day now.

Berkeley is now home to some of the tallest and heftiest buildings outside Los Angeles and San Francisco. Its biggest structure is the university's Memorial Stadium, which sits directly on top of the Hayward Fault and holds 63,000 fans. Memorial Stadium's renovation in 2012 included some earthquake-proofing design elements, including steel beam bracing, surface rupture blocks to prevent the stadiums from sinking into the fault, and expansion joints—essentially shock absorbers for massive structures. The new "coffee bean" structure was built with seams to absorb shaking under the seats at the northern and southern far ends of the stadium.

Ominously, there is a squiggly line of discolored turf discernible on the surface of the field, perhaps indicating a crack along the fault line has already developed. The famous crevasse in section KK, called the KK crack, will continue to slowly separate since it is being pulled in opposite directions by the North American and Pacific Plates. For most games, section KK seats are reserved for fans from the opposing team.

Memorial Stadium's "Section KK Crack."
Architects designed this feature to help the stadium withstand a large earthquake.
Courtesy of Wikimedia Commons.

Already, previews have arisen for what a "Big One" could look like. At 5:04 p.m. on October 17, 1989, the Loma Prieta earthquake struck, California's first multi-county, high-population-density earthquake since the 1906 San Francisco earthquake. Along San Pablo Avenue, once Berkeley's sole wagon road, car alarms sounded as the asphalt swayed and buckled. In nearby Oakland, a mile-long section of the double-decker freeway collapsed, trapping hundreds and killing 42 people. A section of the old eight-mile-long Bay Bridge fell, plunging a 23 year old driver to her death. Around ten seconds of violent shaking left 63 people dead and caused $6 billion in damages.

Although it affected the lives of millions, the Loma Prieta earthquake had a mercilessly low death toll for a magnitude 6.9 earthquake —just 11 months prior, a magnitude 6.9 magnitude earthquake in Armenia killed 25,000 people. Loma Prieta's worst scene unfolded under the collapsed Cypress Freeway. Emergency workers crawled through the guard rails into the dark abyss of the sandwiched upper and lower decks, listening for sounds of life amidst rubble and twisted rebar.

Emergency workers rescued people trapped under the collapsed Cypress Freeway after the October 17, 1989 Loma Prieta earthquake.
. *Courtesy of Wikimedia Commons.*

Every October, around the anniversary of the Loma Prieta earthquake, the City of Berkeley hosts an emergency preparedness fair. The Quake Shake Trailer is a big hit for anyone wanting to practice the "Drop, Cover, and Hold On!" safety drill. Inside, the cabin looks like a life-sized doll house, with stuffed animals on the bookshelves and faux living room furniture. A powerful jolt of hydraulics—the same used for lowrider cars—bounces everyone around at the same velocity as a 7.0 quake, while stuffed animals fall from the shelves above.

To educate people, the Berkeley Fire Department showed a video clip of the Great Hanshin Earthquake during its safety training for Berkeley citizens. The Great Hanshin Earthquake is another 6.9 that hit on January 17, 1995 in Kobe, Japan. The video shows people hurled to the ground, buildings and freeways collapsing, trains jackknifing off tracks, and uncontrollable fires raging across the city. With a landscape is a lot like Berkeley's, Kobe is a small, bustling city on the shoreline capped with picturesque hills perched on millions of years of tectonic plate movement still rumbling underneath. After just 20 seconds of shaking, the fault line under Kobe jumped five feet, irreparably damaging more than a 100,000 buildings and causing $132 billion in damage. Some 6,433 people died.

Berkeley firefighters stopped showing this video in 2018, when the Camp Fire in a small town called Paradise made it clear that even the biggest possible earthquake would be far less fatal than an out-of-control fire. Berkeley's topography is similar to Paradise's, but Berkeley is much, much more populated.

The Camp Fire on November 8, 2018. The town of Paradise, 90 miles north of Sacramento, was completely destroyed in the firestorm.
Courtesy of NASA.

Early in the morning of November 8, 2018, Diablo winds howled through the Berkeley Hills. A Red Flag Warning issued by the National Weather Service had gone into effect the night before for all East Bay locations above 1,000 feet in elevation. As the sun rose, an eerie orange glow enveloped the landscape, and the acrid smell of burning wood caused eyes to water.

The Berkeley Fire Department responded to a grassfire near Highway 13 on the western side of the Caldecott Tunnel, along the Berkeley Oakland border. This area, along with Wildcat Canyon on Berkeley's eastern border, is where the most dangerous wildfires start. A few hours later, with the grassfire out, Berkeley firefighters turned their attention to the Sierra Foothills, just northeast of Sacramento. There, hundreds of firefighters assembled from throughout California to fight the deadliest fire in state history in a place no one had heard of before: Paradise.

The Camp Fire, named for the Camp Creek Road in a valley adjacent to Paradise, had become so big that it could be seen from outer space. The smoke that polluted Berkeley's normally crisp, clear-air and sunshine wasn't from the nearby grassfire the Berkeley fire department put out that morning, but had traveled some 160 miles from the northeast across California from Paradise. Thick smoke stagnated over the San Francisco Bay Area for days.

By Thursday, November 15, 2018, the Air Quality Index measured above 200, causing the UC Berkeley campus, all K-12 schools, and all government offices to close. Berkeley residents were told to seal their houses from outside air and stay inside. Essential workers were advised to wear high-quality N95 respirator masks, which filter out 95 percent of particles as small as 0.3 microns, smaller than the size of a human cell. These microparticles wreak havoc in the lungs and with the immune system, and the known list of health risks they cause is long. Ace Hardware near Berkeley's City Hall sold out of respirator masks within hours.

Perhaps the most wide-spread disruption was for the tens of thousands of loyal Cal fans. The Big Game, Cal's traditional rivalry with Stanford, was canceled and postponed for the first time since President John F. Kennedy's 1963 assassination. Berkeley's Big Game Bonfire Rally, a tradition since 1892, was canceled altogether. Many Cal alums will miss the calls of "Freshmen, more wood!" and the four- story-high flames that cast an orange glow throughout the majestic Greek Theater.

The stack of 126 wooden pallets traditionally used in the fire generated enough heat to cause the faces of students in the front rows to glisten with sweat. To keep the fire going strong, Rally Club members threw more and more wooden pallets into the roiling flames. Audience members offered items of red clothing to add to the blaze. Anyone who's seen videos of a raging firestorm can understand why these traditions will never take place again.

As details of the Camp Fire were revealed—the wrenching, apocalyptic photos showing $16.5 billion dollars in damage, and the heartbreaking stories of the 85 people who died trying to escape or trapped in their homes—it became clear that Berkeley could be the site of an even worse scenario.

The warm, dry winds howling through the Berkeley Hills from Mount Diablo are more and more frequent each autumn. As Berkeley historian Charles Wollenberg points out, the Berkeley Hills residential area has become "the Berkeley Forest" from a century's-worth of nonindigenous trees, grasses, and shrubs that have grown with abandon. Each house in the Berkeley Hills adds to the danger. "There is actually more flammable material in a house per square yard than in a forest," said UCLA's Michael Ghil, a professor of climate dynamics and geosciences, summing up his research in a 2007 article published in the *Proceedings of the National Academy of Sciences*.

Two previous fires in Berkeley's history demonstrate the danger that lurks in these hills. In 1923, a fire started in Wildcat Canyon near the crest of the Berkeley Hills and quickly spread downward through the newly populated Cragmont, Northside, and La Loma neighborhoods. The winds whipped the flames from structure to structure.

Students mobilized on Hearst Avenue, on the north side of campus, and were able to save a few residences, but the fire didn't stop until the dry southwesterly Diablo Wind was subdued by the cool, moisture-filled breeze that comes off the Pacific Ocean through the Golden Gate on most Berkeley afternoons.

The September 17, 1923 fire in North Berkeley destroyed 640 buildings. Most were houses. No deaths were reported.
Courtesy of the Bancroft Library.

On October 19, 1991, twenty-five firefighters responded to a grass-fire just north of Caldecott Tunnel on the border of Berkeley and Oakland. They put the fire out, but the next day, October 20, the fire reignited. 65-mile-an-hour winds whipped the blaze, spreading it in all directions.

Oakland Fire Captain Donald R. Parker, in charge of the firefighters who gathered at Berkeley's historic Claremont Hotel, in the immediate path of the raging fire, explained: "The fire quickly established four fronts, west downhill toward state Highway 24 and the Rockridge District, north toward the Claremont Hotel, south toward Broadway Terrace and east toward Contra Costa County."

Within 30 minutes, the Tunnel Fire, as it's popularly known, had jumped across both Highway 13, a four-lane freeway, and all eight lanes of Highway 24, an eight-lane freeway and reached up into the upper-middle-class neighborhood of Broadway Terrace. There it jumped from one house to the next at an average speed of eleven seconds. Twenty-five people died, including two firemen who were trying to evacuate residents.

The Tunnel Fire was equivalent to a 107-alarm fire. The firestorm crossed into Berkeley and stopped just behind the Claremont Hotel, when the wind finally eased. The Claremont Hotel was built on the site where a similar fire burned residences to the ground in 1901.

The present danger for a firestorm could be far worse. Berkeley's leafy neighborhoods, featuring all-wood Craftsman-style houses, some kept charmingly private by overgrown trees and foliage, offer an unprecedented level of fuel mass. The number of elderly and disabled residents who live on the narrow, winding streets of the Berkeley Hills are particularly vulnerable since it will be difficult for them to evacuate quickly.

The 1991 Oakland Hills firestorm could not be stopped from its spread to the Berkeley Hills above the Claremont Hotel.
Courtesy of Wikimedia Commons.

The climate crisis means that Red Flag Warnings are the new normal whenever the hot and dry Diablo winds start whistling over Grizzly Peak. Since the Camp Fire, every Red Flag Warning comes with apprehension. If any of the narrow, windy roads that crisscross throughout the Berkeley Hills gets blocked, the chances of survival for those trapped while trying to escape are dim. This is why the Camp Fire in Paradise was so deadly—people died in their cars, under their cars, in their driveways, unable to get out quickly because the roads were clogged.

A 2019 USA Today-California Network analysis of California communities found that Berkeley's 94708 zip code area was in the top one percent of danger for fatalities in the event of an out of control wildfire. This conclusion was based on the population density and the number of roads that could serve as escape routes.

About 11,000 people reside in the Berkeley Hills, a three-square-mile area in the 94708 zip code. That's around 3,666 residents per square mile; compared with Paradise's pre-Camp Fire population density of 1,431 residents per square mile. California's dry winds, which have become more frequent with ever-warming temperatures, create fires that burn through acreage faster than ever. At its top velocity, the Camp Fire grew about 10,000 acres in 90 minutes, the equivalent of burning more than a football field each second, and the equivalent of devouring a city block in a few seconds.

The City of Berkeley emergency evacuation maps show there are six main escape route roads for the 11,000 residents living in its hills. It doesn't take complicated math to realize that the Berkeley Hill escape routes could immediately clog with traffic if a quick evacuation is necessary. A few hundred residents participated in Berkeley's first-ever evacuation drills in August, 2019.

The main lesson learned from the evacuation drills was: Get out of town (or at least get out of the Berkeley Hills) whenever the National Weather Service issues a Red Flag Warning. UC Berkeley is considering flexible days off during the fall semester to allow students, staff and faculty to stay home during Red Flag Warnings, akin to the stay-at-home snow days in other parts of the country that get heavy snow fall.

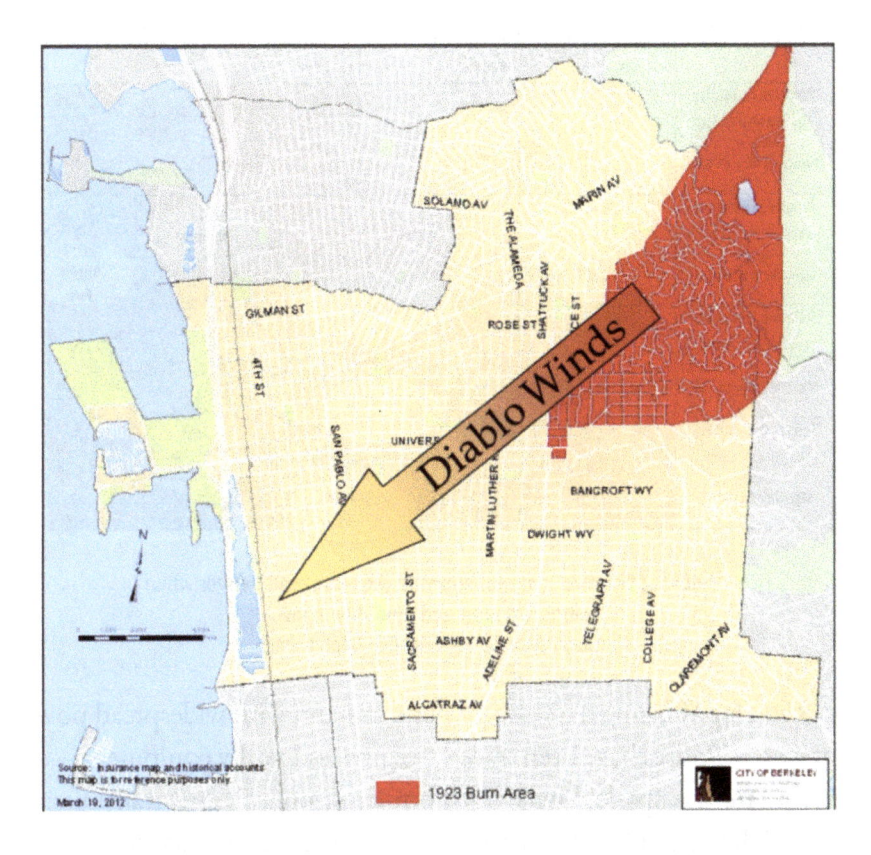

Map from Berkeley Fire Mitigation Plan showing the area burned in the 1923 fire, which was fanned by Diablo winds.
Courtesy of the City of Berkeley.

The National Weather Service uses a formula to determine the Red Flag threat level based on humidity, temperature, and expected wind gust speed. Once a Red Flag Warning is issued, normally twenty-four to forty-eight hours before Red Flag weather begins, this information is distributed widely by automated texts, phone calls, and by local officials and news networks. East and North Bay Area residents now brace for several Red Flag Warnings per year. The fire season in California used to be in the fall, when foliage is at its driest point, and wind patterns shift to create the Diablo winds from the east. Fall is still the most dangerous time, but surging temperatures have expanded the fire season.

	Sustained Wind 6-11 mph	Sustained Wind 12-20 mph	Sustained Wind 21-29 mph	Sustained Wind 30+ mph
Relative Humidity Daytime Min: 29-42% and/or Nighttime Max: 60-80%				
Relative Humidity Daytime Min: 19-28% and/or Nighttime Max: 46-60%			2017 Thomas Fire	2017 Tubbs Fire
Relative Humidity Daytime Min: 9-18% and/or Nighttime Max: 31-45%	Red Flag Weather (25 days in 2020)	2018 Camp (Paradise) Fire 2017 Atlas Peak Fire	Extreme Fire Weather (2 days in 2020)	
Relative Humidity Daytime Min: <9% and/or Nighttime Max: <31%		1991 Hills Fire		

Red Flag Warning diagram showing the increased danger when winds are high and humidity is low.
Courtesy of the Berkeley Fire Department.

Red Flag Warning days also go hand in hand with widespread power outages. Wildfires have been traced to aging and faulty equipment—the Camp Fire was sparked by a worn-out hook on a PG&E transmission line. High winds blow tree branches into the transformers, causing the circuits to spark and overheat. PG&E declared bankruptcy in 2019 when it faced $30 billion in liability for its faulty equipment, and made a deal to pay out $13 billion to wildfire victims to emerge from bankruptcy. PG&E is now turning off the power grid in areas with Red Flag Warnings, calling them "public safety power shutoffs."

There are no easy solutions to protect Berkeley from the dangers of earthquakes and wildfires. In an opinion article published in the *Berkeleyside* on July 25, 2023, UC Berkeley graduate researcher Harrison Raine wrote, "As someone who spent seven years fighting America's western wildfires, I worry. I know a catastrophic wildfire can happen here... In Berkeley, residents are organizing and carrying out on-the-ground cleanups to reduce the risk for everyone. The Berkeley FireSafe Council monitors and implements projects focused on removing hazardous vegetation, such as Eucalyptus debris. They have cleared almost 75 tons of hazardous fuel from our neighborhoods."

Susan Wengraf, the City of Berkeley councilperson representing the Berkeley Hills from 2008 to 2024, proposed that PG&E underground the electrical grid, starting with the higher elevations of the Berkeley Hills where the hot Diablo winds are most likely to turn a spark into a full blown fire. Wengraf spearheaded efforts to get drivers to avoid parking on the narrow roads that zigzag through the Berkeley Hills. She knows of instances where poorly parked cars have blocked emergency vehicles from getting to their destination—with dire results. "Red paint is cheap," she likes to say, but she also knows not everyone agrees. One of her constituents said she would lie down in the street to prevent a city vehicle from coming through to paint the curbs on her block.

The City of Berkeley's efforts are ramping up, hopefully on time to prevent a nightmare scenario. In 2023, the City Council approved a Community Wildfire Protection Program, the City's most aggressive fire prevention plan to date. Fifteen new speaking emergency sirens are part of the plan, they're programmed to broadcast real-time evacuation instructions throughout the city. The focus of the plan is to get 8,500 Berkeley Hills property owners to "harden" their properties by clearing all vegetation within five feet of their homes. It also urges neighbors to work together to clear dangerous vegetation within a hundred feet of their homes.

It's hard to imagine that enough residents of the Berkeley Hills will comply, given how attached they are to their lush gardens and tree covered privacy. As one resident said, "You'd have to have chainsaws running 24/7 to clear out a significant amount of fuel around here."

Another Berkeley Hills resident, knowing his chances of outrunning a firestorm aren't good, spent a couple thousand dollars on a sleeping bag-like fire shelter that he can crawl into as the fire roars around him.

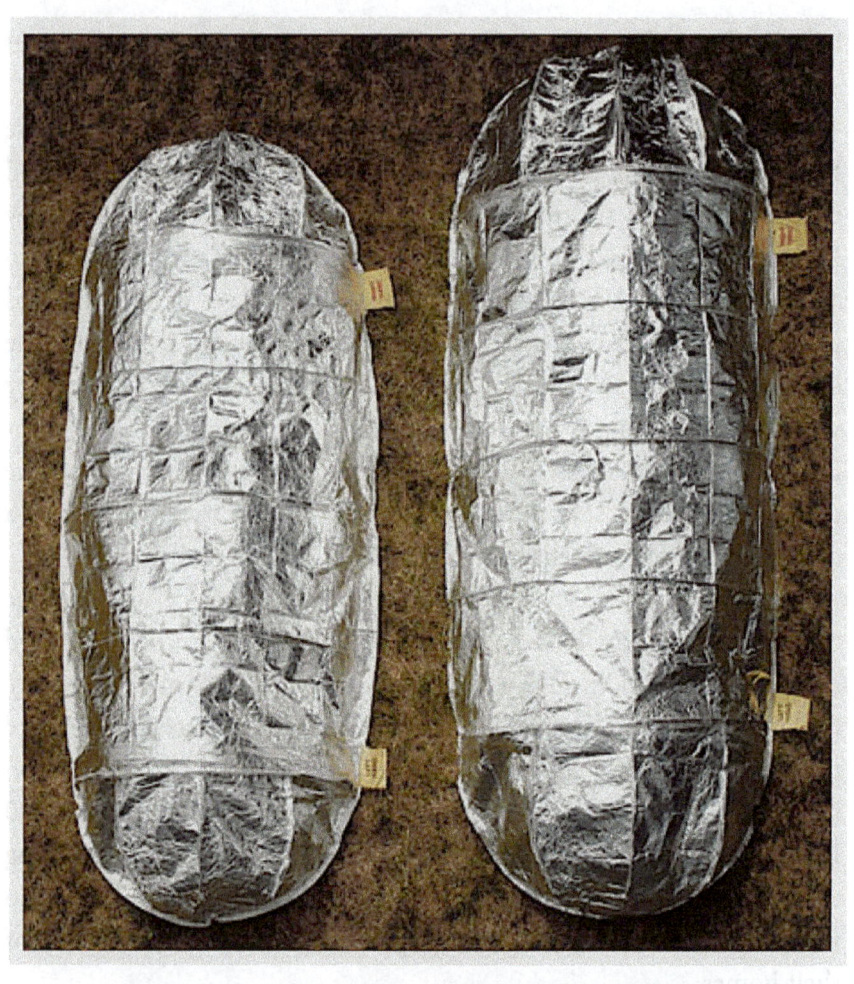

Regular and large-size emergency shelters for wildland firefighters.
Courtesy of NIFC.Gov.

Bleeding Blue and Gold

*"I'm about to pick up the world and shake it
Throw it to the ground and laugh as I break it
Let the whole world know that I'm gonna make it
And if you don't give it to me then I'm gonna take it
BEAST MODE, I'M IN BEAST MODE"*

— "A Boogie Wit Da Hoodie - Beast Mode" by Ludacris. Marshawn Lynch stars in the video.

Memorial Stadium

Red is not allowed in Memorial Stadium—unless you are a Stanford fan bunched in with other Stanford fans for the "Big Game." Cal fans will mercilessly heckle anyone caught wearing red to a football game: "TAKE OFF THAT RED SHIRT! TAKE OFF THAT RED SHIRT!" Once the person wearing the red shirt peels it off, or heads towards the exit, cheers erupt. Occasionally a Cal student will wear red on purpose: Once the chants reach a crescendo, they'll rip off the offending red shirt and show off their blue and gold painted torso underneath. Sometimes the surrounding crowd will lift a non-compliant offender high overhead, passing them hand by hand over the crowd and out of the stadium. This Memorial Stadium "crowd surfing" technique is the same as what you'd see at local punk clubs, like Berkeley's 924 Gilman, where the band Green Day got its start.

Built in 1923, California Memorial Stadium is the epicenter of Cal traditions. Memorial Stadium's name honors American veterans of World War I. It reached its maximum capacity of 83,000 in 1947, a jubilant post-war time when maximum safety capacity was not set, and Americans weren't raised on corn sweetener products and could fit into smaller sized seats.

Even after its several hundred million-dollar upgrade in 2012 and higher quality seating for its new capacity of 63,186, Memorial Stadium is rarely over half full these days. There is hope that Cal's entry into the colossal 17-team Atlantic Coast Conference will increase audience numbers.

In the days leading up to Cal's first home game in the ACC, Berkeley's online fans—collectively calling themselves the "Calgorithim"—trolled Miami Hurricane fans, memeing taunts for a "Woke vs. Coke." showdown.

O-T-T T-O G-O

Callie, an anonymous Cal student using the handle @wokemobfootball, created and posted the music video "OTT TO GO" to troll fans of opposing teams in the ACC on Sept 28, 2024. Courtesy of @wokemobfootball.

The hype worked. On October 5, 2024, ESPN's "CollegeGameDay" set up their outdoor studio on the Berkeley campus, perched over a sea of fans celebrating on Memorial Glade, for the first time. Marshawn Lynch joined the fun, reprising his golf cart joy ride, tickling old Bear fans with good memories of his Beast Mode days at Cal. Bear fans are used to heartbreak, but losing in the final minutes to Miami with a score of 39-38 stung worse than usual. No matter, Cal fans will always win hearts with the playfulness of their traditions, both old and new.

The student section, at the 50 yard line on the east side of the stadium, needs to be near capacity to effectively use card stunts to entertain the alumni, who sit on the opposite side of the stadium. Card stunts were started by Cal students in 1910 and then spread to dozens of other athletic stadiums. Hundreds of fans flashing colored cards to create giant pixelated designs—including the original depictions of the Stanford Axe and a blue C—are precursors to the elaborate crowd shows for the Olympics opening and closing ceremonies. In recent years, drones replace card stunts for night halftime shows, making elaborate 3-D images in the airspace over Panoramic Hill.

Early in the morning on a game day, the UC Cannoneers move Cal's cannon from an undisclosed location up to Charter Hill. The Cannoneers rush to light the fuse of the cannon after every time Cal scores, in addition to signaling the start and end of the game, and halftime. The cannon's BOOM ricochets across Berkeley.

A rally committee member runs down the hill to clean and reload the Cal Canon so it can be fired again when the football game scores. *Courtesy of Pam Gleason.*

The section of Charter Hill above Memorial Stadium is commonly known as Tightwad Hill, for the refuseniks who stake out a hillside view above the stadium to avoid buying tickets or adhering to stadium rules. Below Tightwad Hill, Berkeley's firefighters start their day early. They know that the folks on Tightwad Hill will be enjoying cigars, cigarettes, and joints. Any carelessness could light the whole hill on fire. Green Day's song "Tight Wad Hill" describes the joint-smoking camaraderie.

Fans who watch Cal football games from Tightwad Hill enjoy beverages, food, cigars, cigarettes, and joints. Berkeley firefighters stand by in case someone accidentally starts a fire.
Courtesy of Pam Gleason.

Before the start of a football game, the Cal Band begins its Victory March through campus and into Memorial Stadium. To conclude the pregame show, the Cal Band plays "Fight for California" as they spell out "Cal" in scripted form, with the giant tuba horns providing the final punctuation flourish. Smoke bombs and pyrotechnics explode on the field as Cal football players charge into the stadium. Tupac's "California Love" blasts throughout the stadium from a rock concert quality speaker system. The DJ works in tandem with the Cal Band to keep the energy high throughout the game.

Crowd antics begin with the National Anthem: Cal fans belt out "UC" in place of "you see" for the first line of the song. In the third stanza, it's "the rockets BLUE glare," and in the last stanza, fans shout out "GOLD" (modifying "spangled") and substitute "brave" to end of the song with "and the home of the BEARS!" Bear fans sing out this last line of the National Anthem as loudly as they can: "O say does that star-spanGOLD banner yet wave, o'er the land of the free, and the home of the BEARS!"

The student section, led by the Rally Committee, the Mic Men, and Oski the Bear, rile up the crowd with a series of well known chants, beginning with the student section shouting, "Hey Alumni! Go!" The alumni section responds by shouting "Bears!" The call and response sequence of "Go!" and "Bears!" echoes loudly throughout the stadium for a few rounds, then the whole stadium erupts into cheers. BOOM! The cannon signals everyone's attention to the field, where the special teams players run their first kickoff play.

During the game, the entertainment and antics continue. The Cal Band keeps its song list fresh with K-Pop, the theme song from Game of Thrones, and rotates in rebellious favorites from Green Day ("Basket Case" and "Welcome to Paradise") and Nirvana ("Smells Like Teen Spirit"). During tense moments—for third downs and goal line stands—Oski the Bear, Cal's nerdy-looking mascot, appears overhead on the jumbotron with laser beams coming from his eyes. At the end of the game, the Cal Band serenades the departing crowd with the song "Lights Out." Later, when all is quiet again in Strawberry Canyon, stadium workers spot coyotes wandering down the hill and into the stadium, looking for scraps and tearing up seat covers.

New traditions are on the rise. The Bearettes, an all-Black majorette dance troupe started in 2015 by LoRay Davis, blend popular styles including hip hop, dance lines, and majorette dancing. The Bearettes talked about barriers they've faced at UC Berkeley in a documentary called *Berkeley Dance Project 2021: Turntables*. Director Latanya Tigner told *Berkeleyside* that "the inequalities and mistreatment experienced by the Bearettes at an institution whose outward facing message on diversity doesn't reflect the reality of the students." Tigner is hopeful that UC Berkeley will move decisively "to examine their systems and genuinely realign them with anti-racist and equitable practices."

Trombone players click their heels together during the Cal Band Victory March through campus.
Courtesy of the Cal Band.

Bleeding Blue and Gold

Ike's Love and Sandwiches next to the downtown Berkeley BART station has a giant sandwich called "Beast Mode" after running back Marshawn Lynch, who holds the Cal football record for gaining over 100 rushing yards in 17 games. Lynch earned the nickname Beast Mode at Cal for relentlessly out-juking defenders and plowing into men twice his size to advance the ball. Lynch's grandfather claimed he ate full jars of peanut butter as a toddler. In 2011, at the peak of his NFL career, Lynch caused the "Beast Quake", a 2.0 earthquake from the eruption of fans in Lumen Stadium when Lynch broke nine tackles on a 67-yard touchdown run to secure a playoff win for the Seattle Seahawks over the New Orleans Saints. (Swifties caused a 2.3 earthquake in Lumen Stadium during a Taylor Swift concert in 2023.)

Marshawn Lynch's goofy, irreverent charm is well-suited for commercials and reality TV appearances. Lynch's "Beast Mode" brand is everywhere, selling clothing, blenders, video games, and BMX bikes. Lynch is an easily recognizable star in Super Bowl commercials, reality TV shows, and movie cameos. On *Running Wild With Bear Grylls*, Lynch hunted wild boar on a mountain top in Corsica and used the bloodied knife to cut off one of his dreadlocks to start the roasting fire. On *Stars On Mars*, Lynch showed off his joy riding skills on the celebrity crew's space rover missions. Lynch's disarming playfulness wins hearts. He easily eclipsed star NFL quarterback Aaron Rodgers as Cal's most popular football player even before Rodgers lied about his COVID-19 vaccine status, and he is more famous than Janet Yellen, a UC Berkeley professor whose leadership at the Federal Reserve and as Treasury Secretary has the power to stabilize world markets.

Marshawn Lynch is Cal's most beloved football player. Hundreds of fans wear his number 10 jersey to Cal football games.
Courtesy of Wikimedia Commons.

    Cal football has been at the center of students' social life since football was introduced as a modified version of rugby in the late 1800s. A statue called "The Football Players" sculpted by Douglas Tilden for the 1893 Paris Exposition was San Francisco Mayor James Phelan's prize for Cal's wins over Stanford in 1898 and 1899. It's been embraced by the LGBTQ community as a symbol of gay pride because of the tender and caring bond the statue shows between the two athletes.

Postcard of "The Football Players" by Douglas Tilden. This statue was the original trophy to Cal after winning against Stanford twice. Since then, the axe is the trophy for the winner of the Big Game.
Courtesy of Wikimedia Commons.

Berkeley's most famous gay hero is Mark Bingham, who was overheard saying "Let's roll!" when he and three other men stormed the cockpit of Flight 93 on September 11, 2001. Bingham was a star rugby player in high school, at Cal, and then later as a leader of the gay-inclusive San Francisco Fog. Melissa Etheridge wrote the song "Tuesday Morning" in tribute to his bravery as a gay man and as an American hero who chose to die so that the 9/11 terrorists piloting Flight 93 would not make it to their target.

> 10:03 on a Tuesday morning
> in the fall of an American dream
> a man is doing what he knows is right
> on flight 93

Loved his mom and he loved his dad
loved his home and he loved his man
but on that bloody Tuesday morning
he died and American

Now you cannot change this
You can't erase this
You can't pretend this is not the truth

Even though he could not marry
Or teach your children in our schools
Because who he wants to love
Is breaking your God's rules

He stood up on a Tuesday Morning
In the terror he was brave
And he made his choice and without a doubt
A hundred lives he must have saved

And the things you might take for granted
Your inalienable rights
Some might choose to deny him
Even though he gave his life

Can you live with yourself in the land of the free
And make him less of a hero than the other three
Well it might begin to change ya
In a field in Pennsylvania

Stand up America
Hear the bell now as it tolls
Wake up America
It's Tuesday Morning
Let's roll

"Roll on you Bears!" is one of Cal's old-timey cheers, and maybe Bingham's last words "Let's roll!" braced him and the others as they shoved their way through the cockpit door. "Rose Bowl Before I die!" is another one of Cal's old-timey cheers, shouted out by alums who are hopeful Cal will someday make it to the national playoffs.

The Rose Bowl chant hasn't been used much since the eras of Marshawn Lynch and Aaron Rodgers played at Memorial Stadium. Even when NFL quarterback Jared Goff played for Cal from 2013 to 2015, there was not much hope for Cal fans that their team would ever make the championship game. The last time Cal played in the Rose Bowl was 1958, when Joe Kapp, who spoke proudly of his Mexican-American heritage, was quarterback. Kapp died in 2023, and an autopsy by the University of California San Francisco showed he suffered from the most advanced form of Chronic Traumatic Encephalopathy (CTE).

The image of Jahvid Best lying unconscious in the end zone is burned into the minds of Cal fans who were at Memorial Stadium on November 7, 2009. CTE was all over the news. A few days before, Dr. Robert C. Cantu had testified in Congress about the "growing and convincing evidence that repetitive concussive and subconcussive blows to the head in NFL players lead to a progressive neurodegenerative brain disease called chronic traumatic encephalopathy or CTE … which causes serious progressive impairments in cognition, emotion, and behavioral control, and eventual full-blown dementia."

In 2010, Best was a first round NFL draft pick for the Detroit Lions. In 2011, Best suffered two more concussions. This brought him to a total of five concussions, two at Cal and three with the Detroit Lions, and ended his career as a football player. Representing St. Lucia, Best ran the men's 100 meter at the 2016 Olympics against Usain Bolt. His time was 10.39 seconds, barely a second slower than Usain's world record. Best returned to Berkeley to coach high school football and make music. He reached out to offer his support to Miami Dolphins quarterback Tua Tagovailoa after Tagovailoa suffered another very scary concussion early in the 2024 NFL season.

Since 2008, when UC Berkeley's Brain Imaging Center began using a state-of-the-art Siemens Trio Tims 3T scanner to study brain functions and abnormalities, UC Berkeley has been a leader in brain scanning technology. Students analyzed brain images with dark spots—indicating major impairments that could never be healed. Now, UC Berkeley's Brain Imaging Center uses newer scanner technology, produced by Tesla Siemens TIM/Trio scanners that shows brain damage even more vividly. In 2017, using similar technology, Boston University researchers revealed in the Journal of the American Medical Association that of the brains they tested, 99 percent of the NFL players' brains, and 91 percent of college football players' brains showed signs of CTE.

Meanwhile, some of Berkeley's faculty continue to struggle with the financial cost of running a Division 1 football program. They wonder about the debt-heavy fiscal responsibility left after refurbishment of Memorial Stadium, which typically hosts only six home football games a year.

A 2011 *New York Times* article by Ryan Phillips, who was a graduate student at Berkeley Journalism at the time, revealed faculty dissent for the financial model used to cover the cost of Memorial Stadium's upgrade. Professor Brian Barsky, an expert in computer modeling, questioned whether an adequate endowment could be raised to avoid the budget-strangling interest payments. For years, the faculty had struggled to accept the skyrocketing salaries of the head coaches, who earn as much as five to ten times the average salaries of professors. The stadium upgrades forced the university's budget plans to include structured multi-million-dollar debt payments stretching a hundred years into the future, until 2113. In "Cal's Football-Stadium Gamble," an investigative report by the *Wall Street Journal*, confirmed that the debt obligation would ultimately cost over a billion dollars, with $18 million dollar payments stretching over a hundred years. Under the leadership of Chancellor Carol Christ, this debt was restructured by offsetting $200 million in earthquake retrofitting costs.

The proposed stadium renovation rankled others too, and sparked what would be known as the "Berkeley Oak Grove Controversy." The renovation plans included clearing about an acre of land for a Student Athlete High Performance Center, a necessity to attract and retain top athletes for the university. In a lawsuit to stop the construction, expert arborists testified that most of the grove—including sixty-five oak trees and eight redwood trees—was planted in the years after the Memorial Stadium was built in 1923, but a handful of oaks predated the construction. Experts also testified that the grove was the site of Indigenous graves.

As part of the protest, tree sitters set up a platform at the top of one of Memorial Stadium's threatened redwood trees near the stadium and lived there for nearly two years. The "Berkeley Oak Grove Controversy" started at the end of the 2006 football season and ended before the 2008 football season, overlapping the time that Jahvid Best was recruited to play as a running back for Cal.

In 2006, Berkeley mayoral candidate Zachary RunningWolf made protecting the grove of 90 or so trees on the west side of Memorial Stadium the focus of his activist campaign. RunningWolf told the *Economist* magazine that building on the site would be "a hate crime; we call it Guantánamo Berkeley."

During the almost two-year takeover of the grove, there was plenty of drama. A couple of the tree sitters rotated their protest to an oak tree on a main campus thoroughfare, between Wheeler Hall and Sather Gate, where they could shout their appeals to the hundreds of students walking to and from class. They sawed off a few branches at the top of their redwood tree home to fortify their treetop platform, which they claimed didn't hurt the tree. A few months into the protest, photographer Jack Gescheidt, whose TreeSpirit Project focuses on naked people hugging trees, photographed one hundred nudists at the grove in a photo titled "Last Stand." A year later, he came back and took another photo of the nude demonstrators called "Law of Attraction." Until 24/7 security guards were stationed at the site, the protesters could come down from the trees to eat, sleep, defecate, and argue with anyone who doubted their cause.

Protesters lived in the redwood trees next to Memorial Stadium to protect them from removal.
Courtesy of Wikimedia Commons.

Fearing scuffles between the tree sitters and football fans, UCPD (the university's police department) erected a chain-link fence around the trees before the 2007 football season opener against Tennessee. Throughout the rest of the 2007, season fans and passersby could watch the cat-and-mouse chase between the security guards and the protesters, who climbed up and down the trees. Friends of the protestors threw food and water bottles to the tree sitters from the top rim of the stadium, and the activists threw refuse over the chain link fence, sometimes near the guards. "One of the tree-sitters threw his poo-bag at the police!" HBO Director David Simon, on campus to talk with documentary film students, called his wife to report.

Finally, on September 9, 2008, after 649 days, contractors erected a 90-foot scaffolding to bring down four tree-sitters who remained at the top of a redwood tree. Police officers arrested four tree sitters, plus five others who tried to defend them, and the redwood tree that they inhabited was cut down. After lawyers settled all of the lawsuits, the controversy ended. There are a few redwoods and oak trees left near the northwest stadium entrance, at the site of protest.

Cal—the nickname Berkeley uses for all non-academic purposes—fielded its first football team in 1882, just after rules introducing a line of scrimmage and the ball snap to the quarterback were agreed upon. In 1899, Cal proved it was the best football team in the West when it played Glenn "Pop" Warner's Carlisle Indian School in the media-hyped "East-West Championship" in San Francisco on Christmas Day. Though Cal lost the game 2-0 on a fluke safety play, the Cal players proved they could keep up with Pop Warner's team of all-Indigenous players, whose speed, finesse, and cleverly executed offense made them the undisputed national champions. The close score gave Cal football a media reputation of being scrappy and clever, and confirmed that football fans were hungry to see champion teams travel across the country to play each other in the postseason.

"Get the RED out!" is the slogan for Berkeley's Red Cross blood drive during Big Game Week, usually in mid-November, a week or two before the Thanksgiving holiday. During Big Game Week, which culminates on a Saturday when Cal plays Stanford in their annual "Big Game" rivalry derby, UC Berkeley students are discouraged from wearing the color red, Stanford's color.

Throughout Big Game week, blue and gold signs, balloons, and streamers decorate campus buildings. The Rally Club informs students of each day's spirited festivities. The Campanile Bell Tower and Sather Gate are flooded by blue and gold lights at night.

The 1965 Stanford versus Cal Football Program cover depicts frenemy couples enjoying a Big Game tailgate party in front of Memorial Stadium. The background shows an over-dramatized rendition of the dome on top of the International House.
Courtesy of the Bancroft Library.

The winner of the Cal versus Stanford Big Game takes home the trophy: an axehead mounted onto a trophy plaque. According to the (agreed upon) rivalry lore, the exchange of the axehead started out as a prank in 1899, when a Stanford student used it to hack up blue and gold ribbons during a baseball game between the two colleges. After the game, Cal students stole the axe. Sometime during their escape romp around San Francisco, the handle was sawed off. One student snuck the axehead onto an Oakland-bound ferry boat to bring it to the East Bay.

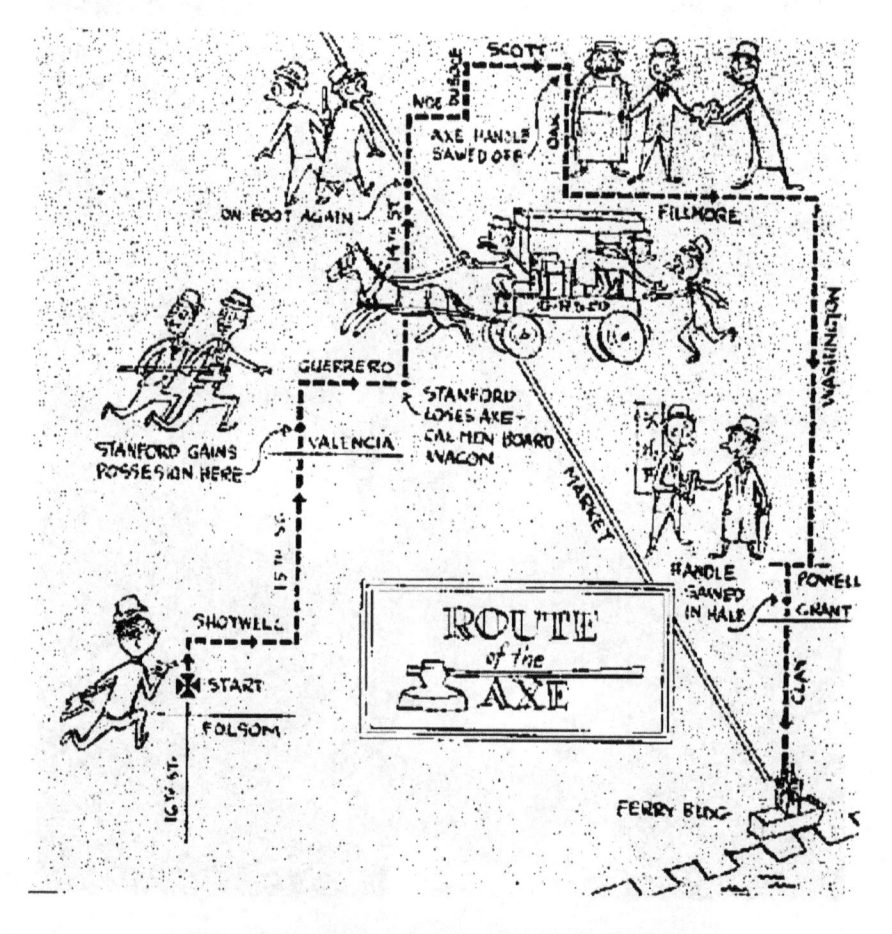

A sketch of the April 15, 1899 route of the stolen Stanford Axe through the streets of San Francisco shows the Lower Haight Ashbury area where the axe handle was sawed off during the caper.
Courtesy of Wikimedia Commons.

Once safely in Berkeley, the Stanford Axe was locked away in a fraternity bank vault for the next three decades, and only brought out for Big Game baseball and football rallies.

In 1930, Stanford students disguised as Cal students stole the axehead back at the spring baseball rally, and secured it in a Palo Alto bank vault. In 1933, the two sides agreed to use the axehead as a Big Game trophy, though each side continued to concoct elaborate schemes to steal it from the other. It's been stolen back and forth seven times, in addition to being passed (or kept) by the victor of each Big Game.

The Stanford Axe in 1899.
Courtesy of Wikimedia Commons.

"The Play" is Cal's most famous moment in football. With four seconds left on the clock, rival Stanford started celebrating its win of the 1982 Big Game. While the Stanford band and cheerleaders stormed the field to celebrate, the Cal team returned the final kickoff with a series of five rugby-style back passes. Cal player Kevin Moen, who played rugby with his teammates to stay in shape during the off-season, started out the series of passes and ran to the end zone to catch the final pass in the series. As Moen plowed over the goal line for the surprise win, he knocked over a Stanford trombone player. The videotape of those last four seconds is one of the most watched moments in sports.

With Cal competing against sixteen other teams in the giant Atlantic Coast Conference, they'll need another superstar like Lynch to make a mark on the national stage. Meanwhile, Cal fans have traditions and stories—old and new—that endear them as fans for life.

The Atlantic Coast Conference scheduling model for 2024-2030. The model stipulates that Cal plays Stanford and SMU each year, but fans will miss the annual trips to play the old Pac-12 rivals, like USC and UCLA at the Los Angeles Coliseum. It's unclear how the increased cross-country travel will inflate the Cal Athletics budget and affect student athlete's class attendance.
Courtesy of the ACC.

How Berkeley Can You Be?

*"You are quite something else!
As God looks down on you today he's saying,
'Hey! Hey! Have you seen my children in Berkeley? Hey!
Don't you think that they are something else?'"*

— Bishop Desmond Tutu on May 14, 1985, speaking to a crowd of 9,000 at Berkeley's Greek Theater during the zenith of Berkeley's anti-apartheid racial justice movement

Berkeley Bowl

Shouting matches sometimes break out in the crowded aisles of the Berkeley Bowl, a grocery store that carries somewhere around 200 different types of vegetables and 150 types of fruits. It was the first grocery store featured in the reality competition show "Top Chef." Berkeley Bowl's shopping cart traffic jams can bring out the worst in people, but for those in a suitably zen state of mind, it's a treasure trove of delights.

The Berkeley Bowl produce section has 200 different types of vegetables and 150 types of fruits.
Courtesy of Pam Gleason.

Berkeley author and professor Michael Pollan called the Berkeley Bowl "heaven for omnivores" in an article in the *New York Times* that rapturously described the store's vast selection, including its 20 varieties of heirloom tomatoes. California's commodified wellness culture is on full display at the Berkeley Bowl. There's an entire refrigerator display of probiotic supplements, a kombucha bar, and a vegan cheese section; yoga and meditation magazines are for sale next to fluffy eco-friendly slippers; one aisle displays hundreds of kinds of tea leaf concoctions touting every healing property imaginable.

"If we can find it, we'll buy it," is the store's long-standing motto. In 1977, husband and wife team Glenn and Diane Yasuda converted the bowling alley next to their South Berkeley home into a produce store. First, though, they sought out mentor Tom Fujimoto's blessing.

Tom Takumi Fujimoto is the founder of North Berkeley's Monterey Market, Berkeley's less famous foodie-lovers grocery paradise. In 1961, when Tom and his wife Mary Noburi Fuimoto opened Monterey Foods (its original name), they sourced fruits and vegetables from a network of small farms. The Fujimotos were farmers until their land was confiscated. The family, including their children Kenneth, Robert, and Gloria, were incarcerated at the Gila River War Relocation Center in Arizona, and later at the Topaz War Relocation Center by President Franklin D. Roosevelt's Order 9066 after the Japanese attack on Pearl Harbor.

Glenn and Diane Yasuda's families were also forced off of their California farms and incarcerated in camps. Glenn Yasuda learned about produce from his father and grandfather, immigrants of Japan who bought and sold produce in Los Angeles's fresh food markets. During World War II, the entire Yasuda family was sent to an internment camp in Cody, Wyoming, with its formidable, bitter cold winters and scorching summers.

With the Fujimoto family's guidance, Glenn Yasuda built a loyal clientele for the Berkeley Bowl by driving across the Bay Bridge to South San Francisco every morning at 2 a.m. to buy the best-tasting produce from small farm wholesalers, then driving back to the produce wholesalers at Oakland's Jack London Square to taste and buy more, all before the sunrise. Yasuda continued this into his 80s, though by the time he died in early 2020—a month before the COVID-19 pandemic's shelter-in-place order forced Berkeley businesses and schools to close temporarily—he'd cut back from seven to three days a week.

Both Berkeley Bowl and Monterey Market are thriving under the leadership of the younger generations. Bill Fujimoto, born after his family were allowed to move back to California, is at the helm of Monterey Market, and has maintained its neighborly folksiness. Gen, Glenn and Diane Yasuda's son, leads the team at the Berkeley Bowl, with its hip and edgy vibe.

Today, the Berkeley Bowl is more crowded than ever. The parking lot can descend into pure mayhem as cars angle every direction, jonesing for a free parking spot. Gen Yasuda leads the team of some 250 employees at its location across from the original bowling alley, as well as a second Berkeley Bowl, opened in 2009, in West Berkeley near the Ashby freeway entrance. Local chefs are invited to arrive before the store opens to do their shopping. When the doors open, long-timers dash to the discounted produce section to fill their shopping carts with slightly blemished fruits and veggies.

Arguably, any day at Berkeley Bowl beats Telegraph Avenue for the sheer number of characters jumbled together. Those who miss the How Berkeley Can You Be Parade can get a taste of the city's anything-goes sensory experience by shopping at its favorite grocery store.

How Berkeley Can You Be?

Local lore blames nudists for the demise of the How Berkeley Can You Be Parade, held every summer from 1996 to 2009. Allegedly, critics complained that a group of aging nudists, the X-plicit Players, was not family-appropriate parade entertainment. The X-plicit Players marched in semi-choreographed abandon, and parade goers cheered their body-positive enthusiasm.

Sporting tufts of body hair in varying shades of gray, the Players walked the parade route arm-in-arm in a chorus-line formation, while chanting anti-war slogans like, "Breasts not Bombs" and "Get Your Bush Out to Get Bush Out." Occasionally the whole line would rotate 180 degrees to give sidewalk onlookers full views of front and back sides.

Nudity is a cherished freedom in Berkeley. One notable resident, the militant nudist Andrew Martinez, a.k.a. "Naked Guy," was lauded as a Berkeley icon. Thousands joined Martinez in unity at the UC Nude-In demonstration on Sproul Plaza in 1993. His Adonis-like physique won him appearances in both *Playgirl* and *Playboy* and he was invited to CNN's *Hardcopy*—with his crotch blurred out—to discuss his only-in-Berkeley lifestyle.

The How Berkeley Can You Be Parade featured locals outdoing each other with harmless outrageousness. Women from a local health collective squatted down every block or so to act out the full drama giving birth; Synchronized cyclists circled and posed, lifting their arms skyward and extending their legs sideways in clumsy-kaleidoscope unison; Fashion police hassled people along the crowded sidewalks with citations for poor clothing choices. Berkeley-esque attire—tie-dyed t-shirts, Birkenstocks, peasant skirts, long beaded necklaces, copious amounts of hair unbound by convention—earned praise. Anyone with a conservative look or boringly ordinary attire was issued a warning ticket.

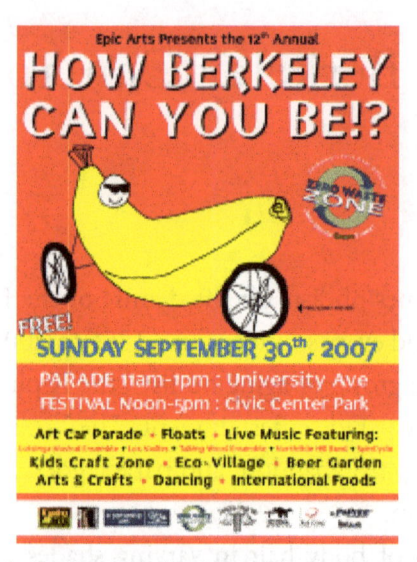

Marchers in the How Berkeley Can You Be Parade competed for attention with anti-establishment silliness.
Courtesy of Wikimedia Commons.

People Eatin' Them Animals, a large squad of meat lovers, spoofed the national animal activist group People for the Ethical Treatment of Animals (PETA) to show their carnivore pride. The pro-meat evangelists wore fur coats, waved skewers with uncooked chicken feet, and passed out Marlboro cigarettes to bemused onlookers.

One fur-clad parader held a red flare in one hand and a forked morsel of pork in the other so that he could barbecue as he marched. A faux-butcher with a bushy handlebar mustache and a blood-spattered "Goodbye Kitty" t-shirt revved his meat chainsaw on the back of the group's flatbed truck. Barbecuers stationed at the truck's tailgate lobbed grilled hotdogs into the crowd.

Behind the truck, a counterprotest group calling itself the Veget Aryans held placards saying "Brownshirts & Birkenstocks Forever" and "I DON'T ENVY YOUR COLON!" They chanted "Beans Not Bunnies!" and "Meat People Suck!" as hotdogs rained down on them from The People Eatin' Them Animals barbecuers. Following the Veget Aryans were three forlorn-looking monks, wearing head-to-toe burlap robes tied with thick rope belts cinched around their sizable girths. Their sign identified them as the "Deep Fat Fryers."

Pink Man, a self-styled superhero on a unicycle, served as the unofficial grand marshal for the How Berkeley Can You Be Parade.
Courtesy of Wikimedia Commons.

Despite the nudist-blaming, public safety concerns were the true factors that shut down the How Berkeley Can You Be Parade in 2009. To keep parade-goers reasonably safe—for example, from unpredictable hazards caused by flame-throwing art cars and motorized couches—the City of Berkeley and other sponsors would have to foot the bill for dozens of additional police officers and firefighters.

Berkeley firefighters, who serve both campus and city residents as first responders, were already understaffed on the other 364 days of the year. The demographic explosion of two high-need segments of Berkeley's population—medically-fragile senior citizens and the unhoused sleeping on Berkeley's streets—was costing hundreds of thousands of dollars in wages for overtime pay. Full deployment of the Berkeley Fire Department for an afternoon of cliché-busting antics wasn't a defensible municipal expense. Besides, most Berkeley firefighters cannot afford to live in Berkeley, adding salt to the wound of having to be on standby to respond to prop-inflicted accidents along the parade route.

To many, the end of the How Berkeley Can You Be Parade signaled the end of a free-wheeling era in Berkeley—no more naked people, no more art cars, no more Pink Man doing tricks on his unicycle in his hot pink unitard and streaming hot pink cape emblazoned with a big letter "P".

"Everyone knows I've had some harsh words for this slow food, locavore, patchouli superfund granola dumpsite," said satirist Stephen Colbert about "Hippie Haven UC Berkeley" on *The Colbert Report* in 2011, a few years before he became host of *The Late Show with Stephen Colbert* on CBS. Colbert was ribbing Berkeleyans for their commitment to protest after students took over the top floor of Wheeler Hall in a precursor to the Occupy Movement protests against corporate greed.

It's true. Berkeleyans take their progressive bonafides seriously. Berkeley's the first city to replace Columbus Day with Indigenous People's Day; the first city to declare itself a nuclear free zone; the first to legalize marijuana; the first to call pet owners "guardians" and dedicate a park for dogs to run free; the first to introduce curbside recycling; the first to ban styrofoam; and the first to tax sugary drinks.

In the 1960s and 1970s, Berkeley's Baby Boomers set the pace for counterculture fads. Young adults moved to Berkeley for its everyday-is-a-Summer-of-Love lifestyle. Berkeley was San Francisco's sunnier counterpart for those who wanted to hang out while letting it all hang out. New arrivals were thirsty for creative life choices that expressed their inner desires, and communal sharing made employment optional, and exploring sexuality a given.

In the 1980s and 1990s, Berkeley's cooperatives—communal living houses—represented the ultimate counterculture lifestyle choice. Local classified ads for communal living broadcasted personal proclivities: 420-friendly, vegan curious, TV tolerance, music tastes, attitudes towards consumerism, bathing frequency, noise level needs, sexual identity, chore work ethic, openness to pets, kids, clutter, and kitchen chaos.

Those who could live with just about anyone—or who could pretend to live with just about anyone—could earn a place in a cooperative household with rock bottom rents, close-quarter sleeping arrangements, and all-evening house meetings with vegan casseroles, intentions to cultivate collective harmony, and the ever-present risk of devolving to invective airings of irks and ire.

For decades, Berkeley's gold standard of cooperative harmony has been the Cheese Board Collective, a worker-owned enterprise beloved by gourmands. The Cheese Board—with devotees who line up around the block for pizza, then eat it picnic-style in the middle of the street on the grass-covered median—is a marvel of modern-day communism. The employee-owner meetings are legendary: Decision-making processes are said to be honed to an art form.

Berkeley's communal spirit attracted religious practitioners from all over the world. The Berkeley Psychic Institute, with a clairvoyant alumni in the thousands, originated in Berkeley, touting its sheer variety of colorful auras. In the 1980s, Berkeley's Graduate Theological Union expanded its original Protestant-based mission to include all religions. Holy Hill, the nickname for Berkeley's north side campus area—where monks are neighbors with Tellefsen House Cal Band members—became the communal center for Jewish, Islamic, Buddhist, Orthodox, Hindu, Jain, and Swedenborgian practitioners. Psychics and Wiccan witches were welcomed to join Holy Hill's Interfaith Choir, where songs like "Imagine" by The Beatles proved particularly adaptable to the span of spiritual beliefs.

Queerness flourished. It was a *What Color is Your Parachute* approach to everyday living, with vivid palette choices and showy tie-dyed plumage. Tattoos, piercings, and immodest jewelry expressed a spectrum of experimentation.

This multi-color kaleidoscope of Berkeley living is what I expected people would want to hear about when I first started leading walking tours of Berkeley. I thought folks would ask about why Berkeley is considered a "Hippie Haven," as Stephen Colbert put it. I researched the Free Speech Movement and I was ready to talk about Berkeley's quirky characters and the "truthiness" of the "People's Republic of Berkeley" commie-pinko clichés. But no one's asked me about Berkeley hippies. Not once. Instead, within the first few minutes of a tour, someone inevitably asks, "Why does Berkeley have so many homeless people?"

As a college student, I'd thought Berkeley's homeless were folks who'd overdosed on acid too many times and hadn't found their way back to reality. However, when I heard a homeless advocate speak at a Berkeley City Council meeting in 2018, I felt that I finally understood why homelessness is such a pervasive and intractable problem. The advocate cited research from Stanford that showed severe mental illness was often a result of homelessness, not necessarily a cause of it. The more sleepless nights a person endures on the street, the more likely their mental health will deteriorate, especially if they are already in a vulnerable mental health state. Anyone will lose their mind if they are deprived of sleep long enough. Professor Matthew Walker's groundbreaking sleep research at UC Berkeley's Center for Human Sleep Science, described in his book *Why We Sleep: Unlocking the Power of Sleep and Dreams,* shows how crucial sleep is to mental health.

Sleep-deprived individuals experience extreme fear and paranoia, which compounds the difficulty of administering treatment. Many turn to alcohol and drug use for temporary relief, but dependency on substances for a quick fix easily slips into addiction and overdoses. The obvious solution is to not allow people to become "unhoused" in the first place.

Berkeley is fondly called "The People's Republic of Berkeley" for its leftist politics, yet in the past couple of decades the cost of housing has made it an emblem of wealth disparity. Living in Berkeley may be a utopia for the wealthy, but it's a financial struggle for everyone else. Professor Brad DeLong, one of the world's most influential economists and author of *Slouching Towards Utopia: An Economic History of the Twentieth Century,* confirms this dilemma: "Half a mile from where I live in prosperous and smug liberal Berkeley, California, there are people living in cardboard boxes."

When 200,000 San Franciscans became homeless after the 1906 earthquake, civic-minded Berkeleyans proudly erected tent cities to house anyone in need. UC Berkeley administrators and students set up state of the art sanitation and social services. Many of the homeless stayed and became Berkeley residents, increasing Berkeley's population from 13,000 in 1900 to 40,000 in 1910.

UC Berkeley students and administrators set up a tent city on California Field to care for the people made homeless by the 1906 earthquake, which destroyed 80% of San Francisco.
Courtesy of Wikimedia Commons.

Today's housing crisis in Berkeley started in the 1990s, when local news outlets reported that students who could not find housing were sleeping in the Downtown Berkeley BART Station. In 2010, Berkeley voters overwhelmingly approved Measure R—by a vote of 44,177 to 8,014—to permit new high rises up to 180-feet tall in the downtown area. Until Measure R, Berkeley had only two high rise buildings, the SkyDeck Chase building at 186 feet and the Wells Fargo Bank at 176 feet, each 13 stories high and across the street from each other at the Berkeley downtown intersection of Center Street and Shattuck Avenue.

Since the enactment of Measure R, giant cranes have taken center stage in Berkeley's skyline, with the high rise-filled downtown almost unrecognizable to anyone who has been away for more than a few years. The 307-foot-tall Campanile Bell Tower built in 1914 reigned as Berkeley's tallest structure for over 110 years, but the passage of Measure R paved the way for even taller buildings. By the end of 2025, a 28-story apartment building at the corner of University Avenue and Shattuck Avenue will rise to 317-feet and add 599 apartments to Berkeley housing supply. A 26-story 285-foot apartment building was approved for the corner of Center and Oxford Streets, adding another 456 units. Yet despite adding thousands of new housing units, Berkeley's rents continue to rival the world's most expensive cities.

"We really have two Berkeleys," Jesse Arreguín, Berkeley's first Latino mayor, said on the eve of his successful 2016 bid for Mayor, according to *Berkeleyside*, an independent news site. "I want a more equitable future for Berkeley with housing for many income levels. We need a Berkeley where everyone has a fair shot, where the prosperity is shared with everyone." For eight years as Mayor, Arreguín dedicated his agenda to increasing Berkeley's affordable housing. Now he's venturing to do more for the entire East Bay Area as a state senator.

In the past couple of decades, the number of people living in tents and RVs has skyrocketed throughout California. California's homes cost on average more than double of the cost of homes in other states. "I just think it's fundamentally wrong that we are literally pricing out future generations from being able to own a home," Arreguín told the *Business Insider* in 2021.

A son and grandson of California Central Valley migrant farm workers, Arreguín remembers the "Si, Se Puede!" protest chant he first hear when marching with Dolores Huerte when he was ten years old. In 2016, Arreguín won with 51% of the votes.

Photos from Jesse Arreguín's State Senate District 7 election website includes (from left to right) Arreguín with civil rights hero Dolores Huerta, Arreguín interviewed in San Francisco while participating in the action to rename Army Street to Cesar Chavez Street, and Arreguín in the Berkeley Mayor's Office.
Courtesy of Jesse Arreguín's campaign.

In his first weeks of office, Arreguín doubled the number of emergency beds available to Berkeley's homeless population and launched Vision 2050, a plan to bring an economically and ecologically sustainable infrastructure plan to make Berkeley vibrant for decades to come. In 2020, Arreguín won with 63% of the votes. Arreguín promises to use his platform in the California State Senate to create affordable housing. Berkeley's new mayor, Sophie Hahn, vows to continue Arreguín's local initiatives.

Despite a contentious and ongoing multi-million dollar lawsuit between the City of Berkeley and UC Berkeley, when with Carol T. Christ became UC Berkeley's first female Chancellor in 2017, Arreguín—a UC Berkeley alumnus—partnered with Christ to resolve Berkeley's housing crisis.

As Chancellor, Christ steeled herself to solve UC Berkeley's budget and housing problems, the two issues that threatened to topple UC Berkeley's preeminence. She pledged to go forward with dormitory housing at the site of People's Park and balance UC Berkeley's budget, the latter a byzantine tangle that had a decades-long pattern of rewarding high profile faculty members and their departments—with advantages such as well-funded marketing and fundraising teams and state-of-the-art facilities—at the expense of investment in undergraduate student needs.

Berkeley's flagship status and $3 billion budget also leaves it with one intractable budgetary feature: the increasing cost of maintaining aging and earthquake-vulnerable buildings built before 1980. Many of Berkeley's campus buildings are in need of major repairs. Politically mandated budget cuts that began in the 1970s have lowered the portion of state funding for UC Berkeley's budget. Funding from California taxpayers has declined to a new low, somewhere between 12 and 14% of UC Berkeley's budget, an amount that irrationally varies from year to year, depending on the outcome of the annual California state budget negotiations and the boom and bust cycle of political promises. In effect, in financial terms UC Berkeley is more of a private university than a public university because of the lack of state support.

To resolve inequities, Christ launched Berkeley's "Light the Way" campaign in 2014, the most ambitious fundraising campaign in Berkeley's history. By the end of 2022, Christ announced the campaign had reached its $6 billion fundraising goal more than a year early. In her annual December address to the Berkeley community, Christ's explanation for the unprecedented success was that "the pandemic seemed to increase people's philanthropy." In 2024, after the campaign ended, Gretchen Kell of *UC Berkeley News* reported that the total was "$7.37 billion raised—the largest total in history for any public university and for any university without a medical school."

While Christ worked on taming UC Berkeley's budget, the wheels of development kept turning: UC Regents gave her a green light for building housing, backed up by adequate legal support to repossess People's Park and permission to raze outdated buildings and replace them with new structures that cost hundreds of millions of dollars.

The UC Regents also approved the 2022 Campus Master Plan for the Berkeley campus, a 15-year plan for capital investments. The plan in calls for nearly 60 new buildings and emphasizes natural open outdoor spaces throughout campus. One of the new buildings, the 14-story Helen Diller Anchor House, opened in 2024 with 772 deluxe student apartments, accommodates transfer students at an affordable price. Rent collected at the Anchor House is reinvested as financial aid for students who need it.

Already there are only a few universities with a larger student population than UC Berkeley. With the California Legislature's 2021 decision to lift limits to the number of students who can enroll at Berkeley, no one would be surprised if Berkeley enrollment surpasses the goal of 51,201 set for the 2029-2030 academic year a few years early.

Chancellor Carol T. Christ, wearing her signature blue blazer, hosted an ice cream social for the UC Berkeley campus community on July 16, 2021 to celebrate the reopening of campus after a university-wide pandemic vaccination campaign made in-person work on campus safe again. The campaign surpassed the 90% target vaccination rate.
Courtesy of Pam Gleason

With her goals for Berkeley on track, in 2021 Christ splurged a little on her own interests by teaching a Freshman seminar called "Monsters and Robots: Boundaries of the Human." The course description reads:

> Mary Shelley's novel *Frankenstein* has so much cultural resonance that Frankenstein itself has become a word. Reflecting a slippage

between the scientist and the being he creates, Frankenstein has come to mean a monstrous creation that destroys its maker. No less an economist than Milton Friedman writes, "How can we keep the government we create from becoming a Frankenstein that will destroy the very freedom we establish it to protect?" With Hurricane Sandy, we even had Frankenstorm. We have Frankenfood. As cultural historian and collector of Frankensteiniana, Susan Tyler Hitchcock observes, Frankenstein is both a joke and a symbol for a profound ethical dilemma. Frankenstein is instantly recognizable as a cultural icon and has an enormous richness of referential context. In this seminar we will study Mary Shelley's novel, and several contemporary novels and films that re-imagine its central idea in the context of robotics, artificial intelligence, and genetic engineering.

Perhaps Mary Shelley's most famous quote from *Frankenstein* is: "Nothing is so painful to the human mind as a great and sudden change." Chancellor Christ's successor, Richard K. Lyons, holds a different view. Lyons has built his academic career as a champion of change. A Haas School of Business professor and former dean (from 2008 to 2018), Lyons was appointed in 2020 as UC Berkeley's first Chief Innovation and Entrepreneurship Officer.

At Haas, Lyons developed four Defining Leadership Principles that encourage "students to develop the mindset and behaviors of innovative leaders." In a nutshell, these four principles encourage entrepreneurialism and collaboration while promoting ethical and responsible contributions that support the collective good. The "Berkeley Changemaker" curriculum that Lyons piloted challenges students to find their passion and to use it to make the world a better place.

Despite the praise heaped on Lyons by many for his likability, his charisma, and his proven record of administrative leadership, the UC Regents announcement appointing Lyons as Chancellor was met with a stern letter of warning from the Berkeley Faculty Association. An excerpt typifies the faculty letter's blunt language:

"Faculty have never been more demoralized. For the past 25 years, your predecessors have tried to make up for dwindling state support by soliciting philanthropic gifts, pursuing commercial income, raising tuition fees, and cutting costs. It is a strategy that has demonstrably failed. Private funds cannot begin to replace the scale of lost public investment. You will inherit a campus that is close to breaking point."

Controversies over money, principles, and priorities are inextricably intertwined between UC Berkeley and the City of Berkeley. "Berkeley vs. Berkeley is a Fight Over the California Dream" is the title of a 2022 *New York Times* article that revealed the tensions between The City of Berkeley, residents, UC Berkeley, students, housing, and moneyed interests. Chancellor Christ and Mayor Arreguín negotiated an $82.6 million deal to compensate the city for the cost of policing, firefighting, and other services through 2038. The deal included Arreguín's blessings for UC Berkeley to move ahead with plans to build student housing in place of People's Park.

To outsiders, Berkeley politics can seem like a blur of righteous bickering. By the time I'd met Starr Watkins, I'd tried to answer questions about Berkeley's unhoused population dozens of times on my walking tours. I'd switched to saying "unhoused" instead of homeless because it recognizes that people living on the streets had a home before and endeavored to have one again. Inevitably, a person surrounded by personal items would be sitting or laying on the sidewalk near the starting point of my tour, prompting questions about why California cities such as San Diego, Los Angeles, San Francisco, San Jose, Oakland, and Berkeley have such a large unhoused populations. There's no easy answer. Even the idea that down and out folks are attracted to the mild California weather has been debunked since studies show people living on the streets often live within a few miles of where they were once housed.

The good intentions to address the housing crisis—signified by all of the new downtown apartment buildings—seem to be nullified by stubbornly high rents. Berkeley's biggest landlords, Square One

Management and Sterling Berkeley Collection, control rent for 16 apartment buildings in the Berkeley downtown area.

Square One Management properties, with ten downtown properties, inherited much of its original portfolio from the 1,000-unit Berkeley property empire owned by convicted sex trafficker Lakireddy Bali Reddy and his family. In 1999, Berkeley High student journalists Megan Greenwell and Iliana Montauk uncovered Reddy's sex trafficking business when a 13-year old girl held captive by Reddy was found dead in the stairwell of one of his properties. Reddy, who died in 2021, oversaw the construction of a mansion for himself in the Berkeley Hills during his seven year prison sentence. After prison, he lived the rest of his life as a registered sex offender as his Berkeley properties skyrocketed in value.

Starr Watkins was 17 years old and living with her mother and younger sister in an REI pop-up tent when I first met her in 2019. Her mother had secured a campsite at the Here There homeless encampment at the Berkeley border next to the BART train tracks. Here There was a model encampment that started in 2017, with portable toilets and residents who agreed to keep their sobriety and adhere to the camp's quiet hours, among other mutual living agreements. A couple of large community tents sat at its center, one for a makeshift kitchen and the other for community meetings.

The group First They Came for the Homeless began the Here There encampment modeled on the protest camp they started in front of the downtown Berkeley Main Post Office in 2015, after the Berkeley City Council passed a new set of restrictions, including limiting belongings to a two-by-two-foot area. Jesse Arreguín, who had announced his bid for mayor a few weeks prior, was one of the three council members who voted against the punitive restrictions.

The name Here There is from the art installment of giant block letters that say HERE (on the Berkeley side of the border) and THERE (on the Oakland side of the border). It's where the BART tracks emerge after the Berkeley Ashby Station on the way to the Oakland MacArthur Station.

Here There sculpture at the Berkeley Oakland border.
Courtesy of Wikimedia Commons.

Here There founders Mike Zint, who died of pulmonary disease a month before the pandemic started in 2020, and Sarah Menefee, a poet and board member of the People's Tribune, based the organizing principles of the encampment on what they learned from the OccupySF Movement.

Volunteers kept the Here There encampment well supplied with electricity, food, hand washing stations and portable toilets. The cooking tent was outfitted with a stove, refrigerator, and pantry. Patches of flowers and vegetables were grown near the solar panels that were set up along Adeline Street. It was arguably the best supported encampment in the Bay Area, though it didn't start that way. In 2017, First They Came for the Homeless organized a "Party for a Potty" to raise funds for their first portable toilet.

Three of the Here There founders died before the end of the pandemic. After Mike Zint, founders Mike Lee and Clark Sullivan died.

Gertrude Stein had famously said of Oakland, "There's no there there." Stein was bemoaning the loss of a rich mix of ethnic cultures that Oakland was known for until the city's vibrancy declined after World

War II, when freeways were built that divided neighborhoods and its electric streetcar network was dismantled. Also a riff on Stein's quote, *There There* is an Oakland-based novel about Indigenous identity and urban culture by Tommy Orange, who was the keynote speaker for the incoming UC Berkeley students in 2018.

The first time I stopped by the Here There encampment I brought a to-go order of hot biscuits to share from Lois The Pie Queen. Activist artist Toan Nguyen invited me to join him, Watkins, and a few others in the Here There meeting tent. Nguyen, an activist artist for First They Came for the Homeless (TCftH), was one of the activists who set up the WHERE DO WE GO tents that hauntingly glowed next to the University Avenue exit of I-80 freeway in Berkeley and other high-visibility locations.

Tent art by artists Suzi Garner and Toan Nguyen in support of the residents of Berkeley's Seabreeze encampment near the University Avenue Exit in Berkeley.
Courtesy of Wikimedia Commons.

Nguyen gathered a few more HERE THERE residents to join us in the meeting tent to discuss two candidates who were vying for an open campsite, vacated by a hospitalized elderly man who was not expected to return. Nguyen asked Watkins to run the meeting, then explained to the candidates that Watkins would ask each of them to take turns stating their reasons for joining the Here There community while the other waited by the portable toilets at the edge of the encampment.

Starr Watkins, a former resident of the Here There encampment, says prayer kept her and her family going through the tough times.
Courtesy of Peter Bittner.

Watkins tucked her pink hair extension braids over one shoulder and called the meeting to order. She listened carefully as each man made his case.

The first candidate, a curly haired man with hiking boots, said he was a seasonal worker for the Humboldt County marijuana harvest, but with the new legalized regulations these jobs had disappeared. He'd been living in People's Park and selling joints to passersby. He planned to continue this line of work, but wanted a safer place to sleep. He was matter-of-fact, and his voice sounded weary and defeated.

The second candidate gave an energetic and self-assured pitch, mentioning he respected the rules of the Here There community and already knew some of the people living there, including the hospitalized man whose space was available. He lived at the Wood Street encampment, Oakland's biggest homeless encampment that covered several blocks and had as many as 200 residents.

Nguyen asked both men to step away while Watkins led a discussion of which man would be chosen. In a low, cautious voice, one resident said the second candidate had a reputation as a troublemaker at the

Wood Street encampment, and he did not believe that the candidate would abide by Here There's sobriety rule.

Everyone stayed quiet for a few moments. Nguyen suggested that the group vote to give the open spot to the first candidate, the street dealer. The assembled residents voted unanimously in favor of Nguyen's proposal. Nguyen called both men back to give them the news. The street dealer seemed mildly surprised, while the Woods Street resident's face flushed red with anger, but he walked away quietly, with one shoulder stooped low as though disjointed.

Watkins and her mother and younger sister are a Berkeley housing success story. They moved from the Here There encampment into the back of a dilapidated moving van, which they parked near Berkeley's Aquatic Park. In 2020, Alameda County leased a couple of University Avenue motels for unhoused people, with priority for those who caught COVID or had other medical conditions. The Watkins family were given two side-by-side motel rooms. After a few months, city workers helped them move into an apartment just down the street from their motel on University Avenue. Social workers signed the family up for a number of services.

Starr and her sister attended art classes at Youth Spirit Artworks, a Berkeley non-profit whose stated mission is "to create spaces of safety, dignity and belonging for healing, transition, growth and development of TQBIPOC [Trans/Queer, Black, Indigenous, People of Color] youth experiencing various vulnerabilities and challenges." Social workers signed up Watkins for a monthly Medicaid salary to compensate her for the care of her mother, whose health worsened. The Berkeley Fire Department responded to Watkins's emergency phone calls each time her mother needed immediate hospitalization. Throughout, Watkins's Facebook feed shows her devotion to gospel music. I recognize the names of Berkeley officials and employees who've posted encouraging messages on her newsfeed.

It's heartening to see positive policy results. Berkeley hosts one of the largest communities of social scientists the world has ever known. Every August, thousands of incoming students stake out their path as changemakers, each striving to improve the human condition while choosing among thousands of classes that prepare them to tackle society's most entrenched problems. One of UC Berkeley's core principle statements is: "We believe that active participation and leadership in addressing the most pressing issues facing our local and global communities are central to our educational mission."

Charged with fulfilling noble, earth-saving dreams, modern day Berkeleyans seem too busy and purposeful for the antics of the How Berkeley Can You Be Parade. Instead of vegans with placards, maybe it's vegans coaxing their meat-eating brethren to make better life choices, maybe over a full course brunch featuring tasty plant-based Eggs Benedict, sausage, and bacon created at UC Berkeley's Alternative Meat Lab.

Berkeley talent is less "let it all hang out" these days, and more "let's crunch the data to see if we can make something healthy and feasible." Many aspire to be the kinds of steadfast problem-solvers featured in *The Fifth Risk* by Berkeley author Michael Lewis, who interviewed unsung heroes keeping the public safe from catastrophe for his book. Being silly and frivolous isn't very Berkeley anymore. Nowadays, being very Berkeley means getting things done and making a positive impact.

Epilogue

Gaza protestors block Sather Gate on Cal Day, April 13, 2024.
Courtesy of Pam Gleason.

Berkeley's Gaza protests are professional and orderly compared with the violence unleashed by anti-immigrant speakers who visited campus between 2015 and 2019. Post-pandemic, Berkeley seems a gentler place. Folks are focused on getting ahead. Disruptors who traffic in outrage are largely ignored.

Along with Portland, Berkeley was a destination for political street fighting before 2020. Far right outsiders traveled to Berkeley to "own the libs" and far left anarchists reveled in opportunities for hand to hand combat. But for the Gaza conflict, both outgoing Chancellor Carol Christ, and newly minted Chancellor Rich Lyons appeared as featured guests on news shows to talk about UC Berkeley's commitment to supporting peaceful protests. In May, 2024 Christ successfully negotiated with a group called Free Palestine Encampment to take down tents set up on the grass outside Sproul Hall. The protestors agreed to a timeline to remove all items, and in return Christ agreed to "support a comprehensive and rigorous examination of our investments and our socially responsible investment strategy" according to the *Daily Cal*. Berkeley's making news for being measured and reasonable.

"No Coulter! No I - C - E! Berkeley is a SANCTUARY!" chanted protestors from By Any Means Necessary (BAMN) before Ann Coulter's Berkeley appearance on November 20, 2019. Ann Coulter was the last Free Speech Week speaker invited by Berkeley's Republican Club students. She was also the last speaker to be escorted onto the Berkeley campus by the Proud Boys before January 6, 2020. Coulter was plugging her book *Adios, America: The Left's Plan to Turn Our Country into a Third World Hellhole.* Riling up Berkeley's "snowflakes"—as her former significant other Bill Maher calls them—and targeting Berkeley's DREAMers was her plan.

Conservative author Ann Coulter spoke on November 21, 2019 to a crowd of about 400 in UC Berkeley's Wheeler Hall, as more than a thousand protested her appearance outside.
Courtesy of Amber Tang for the Daily Cal.

Coulter claimed that "Most public schools are, at best, nothing but expensive babysitting arrangements, helpfully keeping hoodlums off the street during daylight hours. At worst, they are criminal training labs, where teachers sexually abuse the children between drinking binges and acts of grand larceny." Consistently ranked as the top public university in the world, Berkeley provided the perfect backdrop for Coulter's provocative sound bites. Big protests bring out the news helicopters that vie for airspace above campus, swooping down for video closeups of students' anguished faces. For Coulter this meant money in the bank.

Before Coulter arrived at Wheeler Hall for her speech, a Twitter war was brewing between the By Any Means Necessary (BAMN) antifa group and the Proud Boys. One of the Proud Boys' initiation rights is to get into a violent fight in the cause to preserve their brand of chauvinism. From their founding in 2016, Proud Boys routinely traveled hundreds of miles to Berkeley for the chance to fight antifa protesters and anyone else who argued against their anti-feminist, anti-immigrant, anti-LGBTQ agenda. Both BAMN and the Proud Boys counted on videotaped arson, blood, and mayhem to trigger a new flood of donations and recruits.

Throughout the Coulter protest I followed the Twitter feed of Amber Tang, a pre-med turned political science undergrad, and a senior staff writer for the Daily Cal. The next day Tang tweeted, "I am so proud of the @dailycal staff for getting this article out last night. I bumped into colleagues from multimedia and photo in the field, and several fellow newsies stopped by just to make sure I was safe. Student journalism at its finest folks." Tang graduated in 2020. She was one of the many students reduced to lego-like blocks at UC Berkeley's Blockeley Minecraft Commencement, the students clever alternative to an in-person ceremony during the pandemic.

Berkeleyans endured violent standoffs between antifa and far-right agitators like the Proud Boys for several years before Ann Coulter's speech. In 2011, the Berkeley College Republicans staged an antagonistic "Increase Diversity Bake Sale." This publicity stunt made them darlings of a then-emerging alt-right, and secured on-going support for future provocations. The bake sale featured discounted prices for anyone not white and male. The biggest discounts were for Black and Native American students. Native American women could have pastries for free. The timing of the "Increase Diversity Bake Sale" coincided with Robert Mercer's $11 million Breitbart News investment and Steve Bannon's ascent to political prominence as a Republican operative.

Up until their bake sale stunt, the Republican Club at Berkeley had been known for their moderate and tolerant political rhetoric. By 2016, Milo Yiannopoulos, the caustic editor at *Breitbart News*, was their new hero.

Yiannopoulos rose to prominence in Republican politics for marshaling the venom of Gamergate supporters—accused of organizing threats of doxing, rape and death to women in the video game industry on 8chan and Reddit. The Republican Club students invited Yiannopoulos to speak at the beginning of the spring semester in 2017, just after the first wave of MAGA Republicans were sworn into office.

Two hours before Yiannopoulos's scheduled speech, police whisked him to safety. As night fell, more than a hundred protesters—many wearing the all-black clothing and masks of Black Bloc anarchists, and some identifying as members of the antifa group By Any Means Necessary (BAMN)—lit fires and rioted in Sproul Plaza. They smashed the glass of the Amazon Fulfillment Center, which had recently replaced the Associated Students of University of California (ASUC) Bookstore in the Martin Luther King Jr. Student Union Building.

No Berkeley students were implicated in the melee. ASUC student leaders had scheduled a dance to celebrate gender fluidity as a counter event to encourage students to boycott Yiannopoulos. The LGBTQ rainbow lights student leaders set up to illuminate the Roman columns of the Sproul Hall served as a backdrop to the anarchists' melee.

By the time Yiannopoulos was asked back to headline the Republican Club's Free Speech Week, scheduled for September 24-27, 2017, Berkeley's new Chancellor Carol Christ had already begun a fundraising campaign to raise nearly $1 million to pay for increased campus security to keep students safe when controversial speakers were scheduled to speak at UC Berkeley.

Antifa and far-right agitators battled in front of Sproul Hall on Feb 1, 2017. Meanwhile students celebrated LGBTQ pride with a dance.
Courtesy fo Wikimedia Commons.

 Christ began her term with a $70,000 settlement to the Republican Club and to the Young America Foundation, an organization that promotes conservative activism on college campuses funded by the Koch Brothers, Betsy DeVos and other so-called alt-right conservatives. They sued and won because Berkeley's events policy was "unconstitutionally vague" and used its "unwritten and unpublished High-Profile Speaker Policy to repeatedly suppress conservative speech on campus."

 Though Coulter, Steve Bannon, and other speakers backed out of the Republican Club's Free Speech Week, Yiannapolous appeared on schedule on Sunday, September 24, 2017, accompanied by a dozen or so supporters and almost as many reporters. During the rally, few could hear what Yiannopoulos said because the student organizers had neglected to arrange microphones and speakers.

 The broadcast footage shows Yiannopoulos posing with supporters for selfies while angling an American flag for optimal positioning. Around 100 or so viewers milled around after they'd made it through the heavily policed security lines. Yiannapolous left shortly after taking a few selfies. "It feels like probably the most expensive photo opp in the university's history," said Berkeley spokesman Dan Mogulof. Yiannopoulos left Sproul Plaza after about 15 minutes. The event cost $800,000 in security costs, used mostly for the police reinforcements needed to ensure campus safety.

The November 20, 2019 Coulter protest was the last controversial protest before the Berkeley campus closed for the pandemic in March 2020. With the campus empty, Black Lives Matter protests were held in Oakland. Berkeley was a ghost town. With all-online classes, students abandoned the dorms and pricey Berkeley apartments and moved back in with their parents or to other cities with more affordable rent prices.

Construction in downtown Berkeley continued after the Bay Area COVID-19 shelter-in-place began on March 17, 2024.
Courtesy of Peter Bittner.

After the murder of George Floyd, Cal basketball players Cailyn Crocker and Sierra Richey formed the Racial Justice Council to address issues of racism and discrimination. To speak out against the Black Lives Matter silence on campus, the the Racial Justice Council held campus conversations on Zoom, the only place students were allowed to meet during the pandemic. Thousands of Zoom conversations later, Berkeley's new student enrollment was the most diverse in Berkeley's history. For Black Futures Month in 2022, Black Lives Matter co-founder Alicia Garza served as the basketball team's honorary captain. If it weren't for these student-initiated efforts, the Black Lives Matter movement would have missed Berkeley completely.

If you had secure housing, Berkeley was a pretty good place to be during the pandemic. Besides a few superspreader student parties in the early days, the number of COVID-19 cases remained low.

The pandemic decimated the already struggling publishing industry. When I finished the first draft of this book, the market for local-appeal books had completely collapsed. Unsurprisingly, I lost my book contract. I stopped writing and applied for PPP funds to interview Berkeleyans on video.

Peter Bittner and Omar Rincon film Corrina Gould at the West Berkeley Shellmound site on the pavement of Spenger's parking lot.
Courtesy of Pam Gleason.

Peter Bittner, a talented videographer and drone footage specialist, and Omar Rincon, a world-wise Berkeley PoliSci major I'd met while working on Elizabeth Warren's presidential campaign, joined my venture. Together, we interviewed several of Berkeley's luminaries in an effort to turn my book material into an accessible documentary.

Chancellor Carol Christ in conversation with Jennifer Douda in the lobby of the Hearst Mining Building on May 15, 2020. A few months later Douda won the Nobel prize in Chemistry.
Courtesy of Omar Rincon.

We filmed Chancellor Carol Christ in conversation with CRISPR trailblazer Jennifer Doudna. Doudna was game enough to allow us to follow her with a drone to film her as she walked past the reserved parking signs marked "NL" for Nobel Laureates. (It was my hunch that she would win the Nobel Prize for her gene-editing research, and she did just a few months later!) We filmed Mayor Jesse Arreguín in his City Hall office talking about how his political career was shaped by Dolores Huerta, Cesar Chavez, and Bernie Sanders. We filmed Ohlone spokeswoman Corrina Gould at the site of the West Berkeley Shellmound at Spenger's parking lot, the very place she was fighting to save.

At dawn on the Sunday after we wrapped up filming, a phone call jolted me awake. Peter called with shocking news: All of his gear was stolen, including his cameras, laptop, drone, and hard drives. Our footage was gone—we'd delayed backing it up on the cloud. Peter explained that theft had just happened, and the Berkeley Police were on their way to his Airbnb rental. The despondency in Peter's voice was heartbreaking.

Though I was groggy with sleep, I had an idea of where the thieves would unload their stolen loot. I jumped out of bed and raced my car to Martin Luther King Jr. Park, next to City Hall, with a half-baked plan to catch the thieves red-handed.

I was right. As soon as I got within a block of Martin Luther King Jr. Park, I saw two men dragging suitcases behind them, headed directly to the park, where another man waited for them.

I rolled down my window and shouted to them my made-up-on-the-spot pretext for finding out if they had Peter's stuff: "My laptop just crashed on me. Someone told me this would be a good place to buy a really cheap used laptop. Do you know where I could buy one?" I was posing as a student who was desperate to finish a final assignment and was willing to pay cash for a stolen laptop.

The two men stopped to look at me, then they looked at each other. One shrugged and politely answered, "I don't know." I carefully searched his expression: He seemed to be telling the truth. The suitcases looked stolen, but if they didn't have a laptop, then I didn't think it was Peter's stuff. I drove away in disbelief, thinking about the hours of footage we'd lost.

A few days later, it occurred to me: Maybe all of the stolen stuff was in the suitcases the men were dragging behind them. I'd imagined the thieves would separate the most valuable items and discard the rest, as thieves do with wallets. I texted Peter, "Was your stuff in suitcases with wheels?" Peter texted back, "Yes. Navy blue. Rollar. Initials JDB or PBB on it."

Oh no. The men dragging the suitcases to Martin Luther King Jr. Park *were* the thieves with Peter's stuff and all of our footage. I played the scene over and over again in my head. Why didn't I realize those were Peter's suitcases? Why didn't I alert the police as I should have? I was obviously too sleep-deprived to think straight. Maybe I would have put myself in danger if I'd confronted the men.

I pined over the lost footage: Jennifer Doudna explaining to Chancellor Christ about the challenges in her career ascent as a woman scientist; Professor Lucia Jacobs, a neuroscience professor who founded Berkeley's Jacobs Lab of Cognitive Biology, surrounded by squirrels that she'd magically beckoned in the Eucalyptus Grove next to Strawberry Creek. Jacobs demonstrated her squirrel-whispering abilities and explained how she and her students designed groundbreaking experiments on Berkeley squirrels—how they remember where hundreds of nuts are buried and how their evaluation and accumulation of wealth is similar to humans—without causing any harm. (Unless you count painting brightly colored stripes on their tails to identify them as harm.)

The footage we all grieved for the most was the incredible music video Peter produced of Rich Lyons (now Berkeley's chancellor) singing his newly penned song "Long Semester"—a riff on the Counting Crows "Long December"—about the devastation of the pandemic. We filmed in the cavernous lobby of the Hearst Mining Building, with the sunlight filtering through its 50 foot majestic domes. The acoustics were superb. Lyons's voice and expert riffs on the guitar filled the space completely and exquisitely. Peter, Omar, and I were awestruck. It was truly one of the most incredible musical experiences I've ever had.

In August of 2020, Peter came back to Berkeley and he, Omar, and I started the shoot all over again. Though Lyons agreed to reprise his performance, we knew we could not recreate the magic from the lost video footage. I left the new footage unedited and restarted my book.

Pretty much every day I discover some intriguing anecdote about Berkeley and wonder how I could shoehorn it into one of these chapters. Berkeley is chock-full of people with fresh ideas and the audacity to create something new.

A month after her 2020 Blockeley Minecraft Commencement ceremony, Amber Tang wrote: "What I'll miss most about Berkeley is the people, the culture and the never-ending influx of information. The people in this city have a wealth of knowledge and are not afraid to share their opinions about the social and political climates. When you're in Berkeley, you can't help but learn new things from the people around you, even if you don't want to. It's easy to often take for granted the constant flow of knowledge that is unique to Berkeley, but it's this that I'll miss the most about this city." Berkeley's new generation of leaders and innovators make me excited and confident about what's next.

The Daily Cal reporting team in 2019. Amber Tang is in a jean jacket.
Courtesy of the Daily Cal.

Endnotes

Foreward

1. Adam Hochschild teaches narrative writing at the Berkeley Graduate School of Journalism. He's earned three decades worth of the world's most prestigious book awards. I'll never forget the day he let me tag along with him as he descended into Berkeley's Main Stacks library—with five underground floors and 52 miles (84 km) of bookshelves—to find the books he needed for his research. As a UC Berkeley student, I spent a lot of time on the so-called "Berkeley Beach" lawn (officially called Memorial Glade) *above* the 14 million or so books kept underground in the Main Stacks, but I sheepishly admitted to him that I hadn't spent time *in* the Main Stacks, as every Berkeley undergrad should.
2. Adam Hochschild's bestselling and most critically acclaimed book is *King Leopold's Ghost: A Story of Greed, Terror and Heroism in Colonial Africa* (1998) about the King Leopold of Belgium's murderous plunder of the Congo Free State from 1885-1908.

Introduction

1. In 2017, I joined the pilot Airbnb Experience program with my Best of Berkeley Walking Tour, available at airbnb.com/experiences/63973. At first I thought a quick read of Charles Wollenberg's *Berkeley: A City in History* along with my personal anecdotes would suffice, but my tour guests asked excellent questions that I couldn't answer. This started my 7-year odyssey of research about Berkeley, which turned into this book.

2. My arrival at Barrington Hall in 1985 coincided with Barrington's drug-fueled downward spiral into mayhem, forcing its closure in 1989. Up until the 1980s, Barrington Hall residents were known as proud standard bearers for civil rights and community stewardship. Residents of Barrington organized against Joseph McCarthy's House Un-American Activities Committee (HUAC) hearings staged in San Francisco City Hall in 1960. Their sit-in protests made national news when firefighters used high pressure hoses to force them down City Hall's pink marble steps. The 1990 film *Berkeley in the Sixties* opens with this dramatic footage of this protest.

3. Barrington Hall, originally located on Ridge Road, was founded in 1933 as the world's first student-run cooperative. The Berkeley Student Cooperative describes its founding values to "further the principles of tolerance and cooperation through mutual, self-help living at minimal cost" on its website, bsc.coop. These values can be traced to Rochdale, England, where the Rochdale Pioneers founded the world's first cooperative shops, based on a model of community-run ownership. The formation of Berkeley's co-ops was aided by Finnish immigrants, who in 1911 founded The Finnish Hall (Berkeley Lodge 21) at 1970 Chestnut Street near University Avenue. According to *West of Eden: Communes and Utopia in Northern California*, Berkeley had two Finnish nationality halls, both socialist. "The Communist or Red Finns, joined by WWI activists ("Wobblies") took over Finn Hall on Tenth St. after 1917. The anti-Bolshevik socialist met on University Avenue." Berkeley's moniker as "The People's Republic of Berkeley" aptly captures its proud history of communal living.

4. Idiosyncrasies of life at Barrington Hall are chronicled in *Animal House on Acid: The Barrington Hall Saga* by Beverly Potter, who lived in the house next door. Potter turned her detailed log of all of Barrington's illicit happenings into a memoir. Potter's memoir ends with the 1989 incident when evicted residents threw a

washing machine from Barrington's three story roof onto the roof of her house.

5. Kamala Harris avoided mentioning her childhood in Berkeley in her DNC nomination acceptance speech on August 22, 2024. Instead, she described growing up in the "flatlands" of the East Bay. Her omission was reported in *The New York Times* article titled, "As Kamala Harris Claims Oakland, Berkeley Forgives" with the tagline, "The vice president has virtually erased Berkeley, Calif., her hometown, from her campaign biography. The residents of 'the People's Republic' say they get it." Charles Wollenberg, author of *Berkeley: A City in History*, opines the reason for Harris's omission: "I'd be willing to bet a lot the reason they're not saying Berkeley is just because of the stereotype."

6. In *The Truths We Hold: An American Journey*, Harris writes about the Rainbow Sign, a Black cultural center open in Berkeley from 1971-1977, where "artistic expression, ambition and intelligence were cool." The Rainbow Sign hosted book readings with Maya Angelou and Alice Walker, held concerts for Nina Simone, and featured art by Betye Saar and others featured in the De Young Museum's 2019 exhibition Soul of a Nation: Art in the Age of Black Power 1963–1983. The Rainbow Sign was located near the corner of Derby and Grove Streets. Grove Street was renamed Martin Luther King Jr. Way on November 8, 1983.

The Sacred Land of Xučyun

1. Local farmers and vendors used horse drawn carts to remove the top portion of Shellmound to use and sell as nitrogen rich fertilizer. Some of the remaining top portion of the West Berkeley Shellmound is visible in the 1909 photo by archeologist Nels C Nelson, the UC Berkeley archeologist who named the site CA-Ala-307 and assisted in the removal of human remains for study. All of the above-ground portion of the West Berkeley Shellmound was removed in subsequent years.

2. The Berkeley Landmarks Preservation Commission declared the West Berkeley Shellmound a historical landmark in 2000.
3. In 2018, Developer Ruegg & Ellsworth sued the City of Berkeley for blocking their plans to build 260 apartments on the land. Their case is based on SB35, a 2017 law signed into law by Governor Jerry Brown to override zoning regulations and local barriers so affordable housing can be fast-tracked.
4. In 2020, the National Trust for Historic Preservation named the West Berkeley Shellmound as one of America's 11 Most Endangered Historic Places.
5. *Bad Indians: A Tribal Memoir* (2013) by Deborah A. Miranda is described by *Kirkus Reviews* as "A searing indictment of the ravage of the past and a hopeful look at the courage to confront and overcome." Miranda demonstrates how archival research can dispute harmful narratives and revitalize the Indigenous stories of California.
6. Deborah A. Miranda explains the recent changes in California's fourth grade curriculum in an interview on November 9, 2023 with David Heska Wanbli Weiden for Alta California's Book Club, in "Reinventing Indigenous California," available online at altaonline.com/california-book-club: "In 2017, the California legislature announced a new History-Social Science Framework, de-emphasizing the building of mission dioramas and suggesting curricula that teaches 'missions were sites of conflict, conquest, and forced labor. Students should consider cultural differences, such as gender roles and religious beliefs, in order to better understand the dynamics of Native and Spanish interaction.' This was a big step; however, legislation does not *mandate* such a change and, perhaps more important, doesn't provide funding for curriculum development, teacher training, collaboration with local California tribes, or even alternative textbooks."
7. In 2018 California expanded its K-12 Native California curriculum with the passage of AB 738, which encourages high schools to create an elective Native American studies class, and AB 2016,

which requires a high school ethnic studies course that may include Native American history and culture.
8. The original Contra Costa East Bay El Camino route was a Spanish bridle path from Mission San José to San Pablo Bay. This same route is now California State Route 123, also known as San Pablo Avenue.
9. *Grave Matters: Excavating California's Buried Past* (2011) by Tony Platt details the desecration of Indigenous graves by hobbyists and academics in pursuit of science, profit, and prestige. Platt further focuses on UC Berkeley's "large-scale hoarding of Indigenous remains" in *The Scandal of Cal* (2023). Both are published by Heyday Books, a publishing house founded in 1974 by Malcolm Margolin. In 1978, Margolin wrote the groundbreaking book *The Ohlone Way: Indian Life in the San Francisco–Monterey Bay Area* and more recently, in 2021, *Deep Hanging Out: Wandering and Wonderment in Native California*, a compilation of 50 years of academic research articles about Native Californians.
10. *There There* by Tommy Orange, a fictional book about twelve Native characters who travel to the Big Oakland Powwow, was selected as the top book on UC Berkeley's 2019 Summer Reading List for New Students.
11. Berkeley alumnus Dr. Lanada War Jack presented her book *Native Resistance* to an overflowing audience at a lecture on the UC Berkeley campus in 2017. Dr. War Jack was one of the first Indigenous student activists in Berkeley and fought to decolonize Alcatraz Island, which is sacred to the Ohlone people. The popularity of War Jack's lecture is an example of how UC Berkeley students have focused on local matters addressing justice for Indigenous people and culture. Courtesy of The Native American Health Alliance.
12. Trinity College Dublin removed George Berkeley's name from its campus in 2023 in light of new research showing Berkeley owned slaves and wrote in support of slavery and forcibly

kidnapping Indigenous people for reeducation in Christianity. Source: "Working Paper on Berkeley's Legacies at Trinity" by Dr. Mobeen Hussain, Dr. Ciaran O'Neill and Dr. Patrick Walsh, March 2023.

13. Each October, the Ohlone celebrate their ancestors' spiritual journeys with a tule boat race to Alcatraz Island. The boats are made from handwoven tule bulrush found in bunches on the Chochenyo Trail on the shores of Coyote Hills East Bay Regional Park District.

14. The *PBS* series "Tending the Wild" (2017) explores how Indigenous people have tended the land and developed a deep knowledge of plants and animals. In the PBS series segment "Untold History: The Survival of California Indians" (2016) *KCET*'s environment writer Chris Clark further examined the decimation of California's Indigenous population. Researchers estimate that roughly 100,000 to 300,000 Indigenous people lived in California before colonization. The 1870 federal census—taken 20 years after California became the 31st state—counted a mere 7,241 California Indians. This census was probably short by several thousand who managed to avoid the count, along with many hiding their identities by claiming to be Mexican-American, but the population loss was enormous and the textbook definition of genocidal. Sherburne Cook's *The Population of the California Indians, 1769-1970*, written in 1976, uses mission records to trace this demographic data.

15. "Nearly 11 million acres of Indigenous land. Approximately 250 tribal nations. Over 160 violence-backed treaties and land seizures. Fifty-two universities. Discover the bloody history behind land-grant universities." This tagline summarized the findings of reporters Robert Lee, Tristan Ahtone, Margaret Pearce, Kalen Goodluck, Geoff McGhee, Cody Leff, Katherine Lanpher and Taryn Salinas in a *High Country News* Investigation in 2022 titled "Land-Grab Universities: How the United States funded land-grant universities with expropriated Indigenous land." This

reporting, available at landgrabu.org, focused on the treaty-violating federal government transfer of Indigenous land to the state governments as a result of the enactment of the 1862 Morrill Land Grant Act that created land grant universities like UC Berkeley.

16. In addition to unnaming Kroeber Hall in 2021, the UC Berkeley Building Name Review Committee also recommended unnaming Boalt, LeConte, and Barrows halls in 2020. In 2023, Moses Hall was additionally unnamed. The Committee concluded that each of these buildings' namesakes wrote profoundly offensive and racist statements. Both LeConte (from 1875 to 1881) and Barrows (from 1919 to 1923) served as presidents of the University of California at Berkeley. LeConte Hall is now the Physics Building and Barrows Hall is the Social Sciences Building. Bernard Moses, whose scholarly works stated Indigenous population in Latin America was genetically inferior to the colonial Spanish population, was a professor of history and political science and founded UC Berkeley's Department of Political Science in 1903. Elizabeth Boalt donated $100,000 to construct the Boalt Memorial Hall of Law, a small building at the center of campus in honor of her husband, John Henry Boalt, who was not affiliated with UC Berkeley. Boalt was an influential attorney in nearby Oakland who championed the Chinese Exclusion Act of 1882. Boalt Memorial Hall of Law has been renamed Durant Hall, after UC Berkeley's first president Henry Durant. UC Berkeley's law school was renamed Berkeley Law.

17. The course syllabus for Nuzune Menka's Legal Studies 190: Racial and Colonial Foundations of UC Berkeley can be found on the Legal Studies Undergraduate Program website.

18. *ProPublica's* story "Senate Committee Probes Top Universities, Museums Over Failures to Repatriate Human Remains" by Mary Hudetz and Graham Lee Brewer is available on propublica.org.

19. American novelist and science fiction writer Ursula Kroeber Le Guin was born in Berkeley to parents Alfred L. Kroeber and

Theodora Kroeber. Theodora "Krakie" Kroeber wrote *Ishi in Two Worlds* using notes collected by her husband Alfred L. Kroeber and his colleagues, possibly because Alfred L. Kroeber was too depressed about Ishi's death to do it himself.

20. *Truthout* reporter Tyler Walicek interviewed Nuzune Menka in 2023 for the article titled, "UC Berkeley Holds Thousands of Native Remains Despite Repatriation Requests," available at: https://truthout.org/articles/uc-berkeley-holds-thousands-of-native-remains-despite-repatriation-requests.

21. Indian Rock and its sister Mortar Rock are important Ohlone landmarks in Berkeley. Located on Indian Rock Avenue, a block or so above the Marin Circle, the Ohlone carved bedrock mortars into the volcanic rocks to process acorns, fish, and other plants and meats. *Berkeleyside's* Ally Markovich reported that it's a place "of contemplation, ceremony, gossip and industry for the Ohlone...and a symbol of a destroyed cultural landscape." Markovich also interviewed Muwekma Tribe member Gloria Arellano-Gómez, who said the rock formations were called "gossip stones" because of Ohlone people gathered there to converse, perhaps while enjoying the sweeping view of the Bay. After becoming a public park in 1917, it was used for rock climbing. Indian Rock is where Dick Leonard, considered the father of modern rock, and environmentalist David Brower first learned their climbing techniques. In 2010, Hank Pellissier of *The New York Times* noted there are an estimated "1,000 problems" to challenge boulders who use the rocks to practice climbing techniques. Pellissier noted in that same article that many of the rock climbing route problems have "colorful names like White Men Can't Jump."

37°52'N

1. Mariners will recognize the imprecision of 37°52'N since a nautically correct reading should show degrees, and minutes, and

seconds. Now we all carry GPS on our phones, and latitude and longitude is pin-pointed digitally to the thousandth degree. The Golden Gate Bridge is assigned the latitude of 37.8199°, which is mid-span. UC Berkeley's Campanile is 37.8721°. Using minutes and seconds would make 37°52′N equivalent to 37 degrees and 52 minutes. Essentially the span of the Golden Gate is between 37.8106° and 37.8255°, just short of a nautical minute of difference.
2. A Franciscan Friar named Bernardino de Sahagún described the encounters between the Spanish and the Aztec Empire and the cultural and history of the Aztecs in *Florentine Codex,* circa 1580.
3. John Frémont was the first to describe the opening of the San Francisco Bay as the "Golden Gate". He chose the name in what might be considered California's first branding and marketing campaign — wooing Congress to approve California as the 31st state. Frémont proclaimed "to this Gate I gave the name of 'Chrysopylae' or 'Golden Gate' for the same reasons that the harbor of Byzantium was called Chrysoceras, or Golden Horn." His intent was to liken the Golden Gate to the Golden Horn in Turkey in order to convince Congress that bringing California into the Union would provide lucrative trade opportunities with China.
4. Berkeley's love affair with coffee began on April 1, 1966 when Alfred Peet opened his first coffee shop on the corner of Vine and Walnut Streets, a ten minute walk from campus. Alfred Peet was from the Netherlands and apprenticed at Twinings in London and as coffee and tea taster in Indonesia. When he moved to San Francisco he asked himself "I came to the richest country in the world, so why are they drinking the lousiest coffee?" He shared his coffee knowledge with a start-up called Starbucks in 1971.
5. Yorkshire commoner and clockmaker John Harrison won the Longitude Act prize money with his design of a chronometer that measures longitudinal time with dials and springs. Essentially the

chronometer is a timekeeper, with the same elements as a Rolex watch.

6. In 1747 Scottish physician James Lind conducted a series of diet trials on sailors with scurvy. He discovered that a diet with lemons or limes added to a sailor's daily grog was the cure. Subsequently, Sicily was planted with lemon groves and British sailors became known as "Limeys."

7. Junipero Serra, Juan Crespí, Pedro Fages, Gaspar de Portolá and others were the first Spaniards to explore the interior of California. They spoke Catalan. The Bourbon Reforms included the expulsion of Jesuits, who controlled wealth and profited from the slave trade in the Americas. Catalans, particularly those who subscribed to the teachings of Francis of Assisi (San Francisco's namesake) were trusted because of their vows of poverty.

8. An 1876 map by Charles Brooks shows Japanese shipwrecks just outside the San Francisco Bay, suggesting that the Pacific coastal route was known to Japan.

9. In 1774, after the 37°52′N coordinate discovery was the toast of the Spanish court, another royal decree arrived in California: Crespí's successful trailblazing earned him a spot on Juan Perez's 1774 expedition to map and claim the Pacific Northwest coast all the way to 60° North. Not bad for a little man from Mallorca!

10. The cattle voraciously sought out the nutrient-rich California bunch grasses. Over time the straw-like European grasses grew in their place. *Cattle Colonialism: An Environmental History of the Conquest of California and Hawai'i* by John Ryan Fischer University of North Carolina Press, 2015 explains the role of cattle in California's transition to a capitalist society. Giant caldrons to boil tallow and clean cattle carcasses were California's first means of mass production. From the 1820s through the 1840s, cattle hides, dubbed "California banknotes" because of their utility as a means of exchange, filled the ballasts of ships headed to New England. Leather strips from the hides were for use as factory machine belts until rubber-made belts proved more durable.

11. Luís Maria Peralta's daughters filed a California Supreme Court case against their brothers to receive a larger share of their father's estate. The *Sisters Title* case failed, and the Peralta family was compelled to sell large amounts of the estate to pay the legal fees of their American lawyers. Oakland's first mayor, Horace W. Carpentier, infamous for ballot box stuffing and land swindles, leased Peralta land in Berkeley and Oakland and then sold it off in parcels. Those who settled on Berkeley's first parcels of land became Berkeley's first elites: Their land shot up in value when lawmakers chartered the University of California.
12. After Frémont served a term as California's first United States senator in 1850, he turned his focus on bringing the railroad to California. Frémont formed a partnership with his wife Jessie's father, Thomas Hart Benton, to build the transcontinental railroad at 38.0° North. The Bentons were from St. Louis, Missouri, located at 38.0° North. Their idea was to use Frémont's political power to advocate that the train tracks follow 38.0° North from St. Louis all of the way to Sacramento, California. Thomas Hart Benton, the Regionalist painter, was named after his great-uncle, a major proponent of western expansion who earned the nickname "Old Bullion."

Victorian Blueprints

1. Jack London was a student at UC Berkeley for one semester. He was a reporter for the *San Francisco Examiner* and wrote "Simple, Impressive Rite at Cornerstone Emplacement of the Hearst Memorial Mining Building," published on November 19, 1902. The ceremony for placing the cornerstone for the Hearst Memorial Mining Building was hosted by benefactress Phoebe Apperson Hearst. Her son, media magnate William Randolph Hearst was also in attendance. The campus architect John Galen Howard was also honored.

2. George Berkeley's Bermuda scheme is spelled out in a Utopian Studies article by Costica Bradatan, a professor at Texas Tech University: BRADATAN, COSTICA. "Waiting for the Eschaton: Berkeley's 'Bermuda Scheme' between Earthly Paradise and Educational Utopia." The article is available through JSTOR at *Utopian Studies*, vol. 14, no. 1, 2003, pp. 36–50 at jstor.org/stable/20718545.

3. George Berkeley was one of the first proponents of separating young Indigenous people from their families for Christian re-education. He dreamed of founding the first university in the Americas, and may have chosen Bermuda because the labor of enslaved people could make his 'city on a hill' vision for a university possible.

4. Joe Humphreys of the Irish Times reports on Trinity College's decision to remove George Berkeley's name from campus in "What to do about George Berkeley, Trinity figurehead and slave owner? Unthinkable: Ireland's most celebrated philosopher was 'also extremely morally fallible'" published on June 18, 2020 on the website irishtimes.com.

5. Ed O'Loughlin of *The New York Times* wrote "A Philosopher and a Slaver, but No Longer a Name on a Library" published on May 8, 2023. O'Loughlin reports that at UC Berkeley "there has been no serious discussion at the university of changing its own name."

6. Historian Elizabeth Kiszonas wrote her dissertation in 2019 about how a single line of George Berkeley's poetry "Westward the course of empire takes its way" became a nationalist slogan of manifest destiny and the subject of Emanuel Leutze's mural *Westward the Course of Empire Takes Its Way* (1861) that hangs in the U.S. Capitol buildings west staircase.

7. Founders' Rock was intentionally chosen as the northeast cornerstone for the Berkeley campus because it signaled that the property was delineated and ready for the construction of buildings. Traditional practices for ceremoniously placing a cornerstone at

the northeastern corner of a building site before construction begins goes back to biblical times and before, when building owners made live sacrifices and buried the bodies under the cornerstone to assure a building would stand strong for many years. Beginning in Victorian times, VIPs and public officials have been invited to give auspicious speeches at a laying of the cornerstone ceremony to proclaim the longevity of the building and the success it will bring to the community, much like the ceremony to christen a boats before its first voyage with a bottle of champagne.

8. UCLA also has a Founders Rock. It's a 75-ton granite boulder that was hauled from the desert to the Westwood, Los Angeles site that was chosen by one of UCLA's founders, Edward Augustus Dickson. UCLA is on Indigenous land unceded by the Tongva people.

9. Cory Hall was named for Clarence L. Cory, who designed the first electrical wiring for campus buildings, and was appointed dean of the College of Mechanics in 1901. Cory Hall houses the Department of Electrical Engineering and Computer Science. Its fifth floor was added in 1950 with computer chip design on its façade. Students work on electronic microfabrication used in robotics, integrated circuits, lasers in labs dedicated to nanoelectronics, cryoelectronics, biomimetics, organic electronics, and optoelectronics. Principal Investigator Jeffrey Bokor of the Ultrafast Laser Lab is one of Cory Hall's prolific researchers. He co-authored " Picosecond spin-orbit torque–induced coherent magnetization switching in a ferromagnet" published in *Science Advances* on September 6, 2023.

10. Ted Kaczynski, known as the Unabomber, planted two bombs in Cory Hall. According to Katie Dowd at SFGATE, one of the bombs went off in July, 1982 in a break room, causing flying shrapnel wounds on a professor's face. The other went off in a computer lab in May, 1985, causing a graduate student to lose several fingers.

11. UC Berkeley celebrates Charter Day on March 23, but a bigger event, Cal Day, has taken its place as UC Berkeley's annual celebration and open house. University leaders invite the community to enjoy a packed day of lectures and family-friendly activities for Cal Day, but the focus has become recruiting newly admitted students who bring their families to decide if they would like to enroll at UC Berkeley.
12. According to *The Centennial Record of the University of California, 1868-1968,* compiled and edited by Verne A. Stadtman, the fledgling College of California had barely any students, and "bill collectors routinely waylaid Durant in the streets of Oakland." Verne A. Stadtman was part of a group of Cal alumni editors who founded *The Chronicle of Higher Education*.
13. Two other colleges, Santa Clara College (now Santa Clara University) and California Wesleyan College (now University of the Pacific) were founded in Santa Clara, California, in 1851. Santa Clara College started as a Jesuit seminary led by Italian Catholic priests, and California Wesleyan College started as a Methodist college, which based its instruction on a liberal arts curriculum. University of California (Berkeley), according to Stadtman's *The Centennial Record,* was chartered in 1868 as a public trust "independent of all political or sectarian influence and kept free therefrom in the appointment of its regents and in the administration of its affairs."
14. Joy Fisher's lively account of "The Handsome Town" in the USGenWeb Archives describes Henry Durant's "family high school for boys." Durant started with three pupils in his home on Broadway and Fifth Avenue in Oakland. "The course of instruction comprised, according to an announcement in The Pacific, "besides those [subjects] usually taught in high schools, the Latin, Greek, and, if desired, the French, German, and Spanish languages . . . The price for board, washing, domestic care, and School Instruction will be $12.50 per week, payable monthly, in advance: for Tuition alone $10.00 per month. Each boarder will

provide his own chamber furniture." Durant wrote to ministers and others interested in the school, asking them to send pupils, who he promised would be considered a part of his family and always be in his care. He hired a Mr. and Mrs. Quinn as housekeepers for $150 a month and began operations." According to Fisher's research, Durant could not pay the Quinns as promised, and Durant had to take the Quinns to court for trying to turn the lower part of the house into a barroom to bring in more revenue. http://files.usgwarchives.net/ca/alameda/history/1941/berkeley/18661878251gms.txt

15. The plaque still visible on Founders' Rock is from 1896, when the graduating senior class affixed a chiseled monument stone with the inscription "Founders Rock California College April 16, 1860" to commemorate the Founders' Rock story.

16. In 1960, California's political heavyweights, including Pat Brown, the governor of California, and Clark Kerr, the president of the University of California, stopped by Founders' Rock for a centennial celebration photo opp. However, rather than waxing poetic about the university's beginnings, Brown and Kerr's agenda was to implement the new "California Master Plan for Education." Founders' Rock was a convenient backdrop.

17. Current campus maps of UC Berkeley omit Founders' Rock. Once the Cory Hall building was erected in 1950, it blocked Founders' Rock's sweeping view of the San Francisco Bay and the Golden Gate. Reverend Samuel Hopkins Willey, a chaplain for California's first Constitutional Convention 1849, later recounted the meeting at Founders' Rock, but he didn't mention a tribute to George Berkeley or Berkeley's "Verses on the Prospect of Planting Arts and Learning in America."

18. When the first University of California Regents were appointed in 1868, none were College of California founders. Evoking George Berkeley's name was a clear reference to the triumph of Christianity, so the Regents may have shied away from the name Berkeley at first. The University of California was set up as public

trust, and the charter made clear that it must be "independent of all political or sectarian influence and kept free therefrom in the appointment of its regents and in the administration of its affairs."

Bear Territory

1. The National Park Service provides a well-researched account of the events that occurred during the Bear Flag Revolt in June, 1846 at nps.gov/goga/learn/historyculture/bear-flag-revolt.htm.
2. Journalist Rodrigo Pérez Ortega combines historical records and new research published in *Proceedings of the Royal Society B* to examine California grizzlies in the article "California grizzlies weren't as giant and threatening as people once thought: New paleontological data indicate the iconic predator was smaller and ate more plants," published in Science on January 9, 2024 at science.org/content/article/california-grizzlies-werent-giant-and-threatening-people-once-thought.
3. Monarch the Grizzly Bear collection at the California Academy of Sciences examines the series of articles about Monarch that William Randolph Hearst tag lined "Monarch of the Dailies" and work by Joseph Grinnell, director and cofounder (with Annie Montague Alexander) of the University of California's Museum of Vertebrate Zoology, who studied Monarch when he was alive and acquired Monarch's remains after he died. More is available at calacademy.org/explore-science/monarch-the-grizzly-bear. If the names Annie and Grinnell sound familiar it's because these are the names of the original breeding pair of falcons that nested at the top of the Campanile Bell Tower.
4. The University of California Rally Committee (founded in 1901) is regarded as the "official guardians of all campus traditions" and, together with the University of California Marching Band (founded in 1891), carries on Cal's century-old practices including card stunts (started in 1910) and on-field formations. The

most famous on-field formation combines alumni and current band members who line up to spell out a football-field length "California" in front of the fans at Memorial Stadium. Further historical information is available at calband.berkeley.edu.
5. UC Berkeley's News Archive published Oski's history in an article by Public Affairs official Kathleen Maclay in 1999 at newsarchive.berkeley.edu.
6. Each of the Oakland Zoo's grizzlies have distinct personalities. Rubicon is "large and in charge." The zookeepers call his brother Kenai "water boy" because he spends a lot of time in the pool. Tulare is the goofy "clown bear." Truckee is "the peace keeper" for breaking up fights and "supervising" so his brother and the other brothers when they start to get too rowdy. A live webcam is available online at oaklandzoo.org.
7. *Some Bears Kill* by Larry Kanuit is a compilation of dangerous encounters with bears. In Alaska, residents live alongside black bears and grizzly bears. In "To Shoot or Not to Shoot" Alaskan geologist Marti Miller describes a harrowing bear encounter. Miller contends that bears have different personalities, and what to do in a bear encounter depends on the bear and its behavior. Montana's Wind River Bear Institute is studying the success of Karelian Bear Dogs, originally from Finland, as a non-lethal solution to keep both humans and bears protected from dangerous encounters.

The Almond Cookie Revolutionaries

1. Pete Seeger's father Charles Seeger and his young family lived in the Berkeley Hills in the "Hidden Maybeck" on Buena Vista Way, where he built a round music studio for acoustical recording. The elder Seeger was a professor of music at UC Berkeley from 1912 to 1919, when he was fired for his public opposition to World War I. Pete Seeger was born in New York just after his father was fired.

2. Esther Gulick, Catherine Kerr, and Sylvia McLaughlin recounted the origins of their Save The Bay campaign in "Saving San Francisco Bay: Past Present, and Future" speech at UC Berkeley on April 14, 1988.
3. David Brower was born in Berkeley in 1912. Brower joined the Sierra Club in 1933, then served as Sierra Club's Executive Director, and afterward joined the board. He founded Friends of the Earth, the Earth Island Institute, the John Muir Institute for Environmental Studies, and other organizations.
4. The historic development of the San Francisco Bay and its shoreline in the anthropocene is detailed in *Down By The Bay: San Francisco's History Between The Tides* by Matthew Morse Booker, published by UC Press in 2013.
5. Updates on the Berkeley Waterfront projects and City of Berkeley politics can be found on the *Berkeleyside* online news site and the City of Berkeley's Capital Projects web pages at berkeleyca.gov.
6. *From Trash to Treasure: The Splendors of Berkeley's Cesar Chavez Park* by Martin Nicolau published in 2014 by Duplex Press is a compilation of photos showing the Berkeley shoreline's views and the park's animals, plants, and people.
7. *Bay Nature*, a quarterly magazine founded in 2001, provides in-depth coverage of the San Francisco Bay environment and wildlife with detailed maps, illustrations and photography. Each year *Bay Nature* honors four or five conservation leaders with the Bay Nature Local Hero Award.
8. The Metropolitan Transportation Commission, responsible for shoreline projects in the nine counties that surround the San Francisco Bay, offers 25 maps of hiking trails that can be downloaded from mtc.ca.gov.

Lois The Pie Queen

1. Lois The Pie Queen opens for breakfast at 8 a.m. every day and closes at 2 p.m. on weekdays, 3 p.m. on Saturdays, and 4 p.m. on Sundays. Order in advance to take home a whole pie.
2. The *Green Book* was published annually from 1936 to 1967 by New York City mailman Victor Hugo Green. The movie called "The Green Book" is based on the true story of African-American jazz pianist Don Shirley, who used the Green Book as a guide to find safe places to stay in the segregated South of the 1960s.
3. A "treasure trove" is often how the African American Museum and Library at Oakland (AAMLO) at 659 14th Street in Oakland is described by locals and visitors. The AAMLO features rotating exhibits, live music performances, featured speakers, and an extensive archival collection of letters, diaries, photos, and historical artifacts that preserve the local and historical culture of African Americans.
4. Letters from Mary Tanner Byrne that describe life in Berkeley starting 1859 and are part of the Bancroft Library's extensive special collections. The Bancroft collection includes letters, papers, documents, photographs, art, architectural blueprints, illustrations, newspapers, and oral histories. It's among the largest special collections in the world, and holds documents from historical figures, including literary manuscripts from Ina Coolbrith, California's first poet laureate, from Coolbrith's protege Jack London, and from Joan Didion, who received her bachelor's degree in English from UC Berkeley in 1956. Didion won her first writing job at Vogue for her essay on Berkeley architecture professor William Wurster. Wurster is the namesake of UC Berkeley's architecture department building. Students sometimes joke that there isn't a building "worster" than Wurster—perhaps especially for architecture students who feel obliged to do all-nighters in the building to complete their conceptual and working architecture design model assignments.

5. California's pro-slavery pro-Confederacy Southern Democrats, called "Chivalry" Democrats, were a strong political force in early California state politics. Their belief in the racial inferiority of non-white people shaped California's first labor, real estate, and immigration laws (e.g. the 1882 Chinese Exclusion Act). They joined the Southern California cattle barons to call for the secession of Southern California from Northern California according to the Oakland Museum's project *Picture This: California Perspectives on American History*.

6. Dorothea Lange lived on Virginia Street in Berkeley with her husband UC Berkeley professor Paul Taylor, an economics professor focused on Mexican-American labor in California. The apartment below the house served as her darkroom. Lange's documentary photography features a range of subjects, including WWII shipyard laborers, migrant workers, and the Japanese Internment. The Oakland Museum of California holds the Dorothea Lange Collection, a gift to the museum containing 25,000 negatives and hundreds of prints from 1919 to 1965 that were donated by Paul Taylor after Dorothea's death in 1965. The collection is available at oac.cdlib.org. Paul Taylor and Dorothea Lange were politically well-connected, and may have helped steer Work Progress Administration funds to create the Berkeley Rose Garden, completed in 1937, and a short walk from their home on Virginia Street. The Berkeley Rose Garden has 1,500 rose bushes and 250 varieties of roses.

7. *Sign My Name to Freedom: The Unheard Songs of Betty Reid Soskin,* the musical dedicated to the life of Betty Reid Soskin opened on March 29, 2024 at Z Space in San Francisco. The musical weaves material from Soskin's books and her blog cbreaux.blogspot.com. Here's the playbill's synopsis: How do you chronicle 102 years of life? Flood survivor, racial integrator, World War II defense worker, business owner, activist, revolutionary, songwriter, and... park ranger? Bay Area icon Betty Reid Soskin has survived it all. In this World Premiere musical based

on her life, acclaimed playwright Michael Gene Sullivan weaves Soskin's original music in and out of dialogue between The Four Bettys—Little Betty, Married Betty, Revolutionary Betty, and Ranger Betty as they take us through a century of the Negro, Colored, Black, and African-American experiences of this amazing woman. Conceived by Jamie Zimmer, the production boasts choreography direction by Laura Elaine Ellis, aerial choreography by Joanna Haigood, and direction by Elizabeth Carter. Based upon the life, music, and writing of Betty Reid Soskin. Book by Michael Gene Sullivan. Directed by Elizabeth Carter. Concept by Jamie Zimmer.

8. A 1977 interview with Frances Mary Albrier is available from UC Berkeley's Regional Oral History Office on Calisphere.org. The interview includes references to Albrier's work with Oakland/Berkeley NAACP Chairman Walter Gordon. Walter Gordon's life is documented in the PBS special *All-American—The Walter Gordon Story* from director and producer Doug Harris, a Berkeley native and former Golden State Warrior basketball player. Gordon broke a number of barriers at UC Berkeley: In 1916 he was Cal's first Black football player, and in 1919 he became Cal's first Black law school graduate and first Black football (assistant) coach. He also became the City of Berkeley's first Black police officer in 1919. President Dwight D. Eisenhower appointed Gordon as governor of the U.S. Virgin Islands in 1955. After his term ended Gordon became a Federal Judge of the District Court in the U.S. Virgin Islands.

9. The PBS Special "The Black Church: This Is Our Story; This Is Our Song" from Henry Louis Gates, Jr. covers the 400-year history of black church. pbs.org/show/black-church.

10. Footage of the Black Panthers attending Bobby Hutton's funeral service at the Ephesian Church of God in Christ on nearby Alcatraz Avenue Black Panthers can be found posted on YouTube at the 2:00 minute mark after Marlon Brando's speech available at youtu.be/QRdCf0joJXo and posted by @DannyiLL.

Berkelium, Californium and the Red Enemy

1. For more about the quixotic and well-loved Moe Moskovitz, read *A Life of Moe Moskowitz* published in 2016 by daughter Doris Jo Moskovitz, and *On The Finest Shore: Poems and Reminiscences of Moe* published by Moe's Books in 1997.
2. *The Loneliness of the Electric Menorah* by Aaron Cometbus and published in 2008 is an insider's look at the life and times of Moe Moskovitz steeped in the same acerbic playfulness that Moe was known for.
3. Berkeley Free Clinic is one of Berkeley's most iconic and enduring collectives. Here's the description from berkeleyfreeclinic.org:

    The Berkeley Free Clinic (BFC) is a radical volunteer health collective that has been providing dental and medical care, peer counseling, and community referrals since 1969, when we formed a street medic collective to care for protesters injured by UC Berkeley police during the People's Park Riots. Our clinic has stood in solidarity with Black Panther clinics in the 1970s, with lay health workers in the Global South, with queer folks who were rejected by mainstream medicine, and with police brutality victims who feared seeking medical care. It has become an icon in the area, and has served countless thousands in a variety of ways during its 50-year history.

    Fees have never been charged for any services, materials, medications or supplies provided at the Berkeley Free Clinic. Income has been generated solely via individual or organizational donations and government programs.

    We believe that healthcare is a fundamental human right, that power and knowledge should be shared collectively, and that everyone has the right to basic knowledge about their bodies. Unlike most clinics, we are almost exclusively non-professionals

– medical services are provided by ordinary people whom we train to provide specific medical/social services. All of us are volunteers and we share decision making power equally.

At the Berkeley Free Clinic, we treat each client with respect and dignity and view their needs within the larger context of their unique circumstances and access to resources. Treatments, referrals and guidance are provided in a client-centered context, and are appropriate to their lifestyle, culture, language and financial situation. We attempt to include clients as thoroughly as possible in their health care process. **HEALTHCARE FOR PEOPLE. NOT PROFIT.**

4. Ernest O. Lawrence describes the capabilities and design of the new RAD Lab facilities located at 37°52′N on the hill crest overlooking the UC Berkeley campus in the The National Farm and Home Hour, a 1942 radio news broadcast for rural Americans. The audio with photos from UC Berkeley Physics Department Archives can be seen here: https://youtu.be/8tJrJ9dSLFg?si=jo-BsbHkuXcjYeJav.

5. LeConte Hall, now the Physics South Hall, was named after brothers John LeConte and Joseph LeConte, and was unnamed in 2020. The LeConte brothers contributed their expertise in chemistry and physics for bomb making for the Confederates during the Civil War. The two relocated to Berkeley from South Carolina because they were unhappy with the newly-won rights of Black citizens. Joseph LeConte stated in his autobiography that the "sudden enfranchisement of the negro without qualification was the greatest political crime ever perpetrated by any people."

6. Lawrence and his idea for an atomic particle-splitting "proton merry-go-round" is described in Michael Hiltzik's 2015 book *Big Science: Ernest Lawrence at the Invention that Launched the Military Industrial Complex.*

7. Katherine A. S. Sibley in *Red Spies in America: Stolen Secrets and the Dawn of the Cold War* explains the web of Soviet spies and their connections to UC Berkeley. According to the 1940 United States Federal Census, Soviet Spy Bernadette Doyle lived on Berkeley Way, across the street from where the Trader Joe's market is located now. Her entry identifies her as a 30 year-old single, college-educated woman who does housework for a living, with a salary of $600/year.
8. The 2023 film *Oppenheimer* is based on the book *American Prometheus: The Triumph and Tragedy of J. Robert Oppenheimer* by Kai Bird and Martin J. Sherwin. *Brotherhood of the Bomb: The Tangled Lives and Loyalties of Robert Oppenheimer, Ernest Lawrence, and Edward Teller* by Smithsonian historian Gregg Herken provides detail of Berkeley's communist cell of professors and Haakon Chevalier's writings which tie Oppenheimer to them. Ray Monk's biography *Robert Oppenheimer: A Life Inside the Center* is rated "Compelling" by *The New Yorker*.
9. Robert S. McNamara admits his mistakes in the Vietnam War in his 1995 memoir *In Retrospect: The Tragedy and Lessons of Vietnam*, co-written with Brian VanDeMark. The videotaped interview with McNamara during his UC Berkeley teaching stint is available at https://iis.berkeley.edu/file/449.
10. "EXCLUSIVE LOOK: The Superman Strips that freaked out the U.S. Government" is available on 13thdimension.com. Darren Bleuel's comics can be found at nukees.com.

The Free Speech Movement

1. SLATE was a leftist student political party on the UC Berkeley campus from 1958 to 1966. UC Berkeley's Oral History Center conducted a series of interviews about SLATE. Two oral history interviews, from former student activists Julianne Morris (ucblib.link/OHC-Morris) and Susan Griffin (ucblib.link/OHC-Griffin), give background on the connections between SLATE,

the Associated Students of the University of California (ASUC), McCarthyism, and the Free Speech Movement.
2. The *Time Magazine* cover article "Education: Master Planner," featuring the career of Clark Kerr, was published on October 17, 1960 and is available at content.time.com/time/subscriber/article/0,33009,895026,00.html.
3. Clark Kerr's 2.1 pound, 585 page memoir *The Blue and the Gold: A Personal Memoir of the University of California, 1949 - 1967: Volume 1, Academic Triumphs,* and its companion *The Blue and the Gold: A Personal Memoir of the University of California, 1949 - 1967: Volume 2, Political Turmoil,* a more diminutive 458 pages, cover Kerr's experience at UC Berkeley, first as a faculty member, then as chancellor from 1952 to 1958, and then as president of the University of California. The San Francisco Chronicle named *Volume 2* of Kerr's work one of the "Best Books of 2003" with a glowing review: "For those seeking the real man behind the warring reputations, the late Clark Kerr completed a memoir that recalls not just the view from the UC president's office of the biggest upheavals in the university's history...but also the personal anguish, philosophy and dreams of this Quaker pacifist and son of a Pennsylvania farmer who found himself at the famous university's helm during its greatest trials. Kerr is by turn self-critical and free of false modesty in describing his accomplishments and accolades, while he settles old scores and forgives old enemies."
4. For an in-depth understanding of UC Berkeley's $3 billion budget, the Office of the Chief Financial offers an overview, called "Budget 101" that is available at https://cfo.berkeley.edu/budget-101.
5. "Which American presidents have visited UC Berkeley" written by Tor Haugan and published on February 19, 2018 is available on the UC Berkeley Library news site at lib.berkeley.edu/about/news/which-american-presidents-have-visited-uc-berkeley.

6. The Free Speech Archive at fsm-a.org provides hundreds of pages on documents, photos, and eyewitness accounts of the history of the Free Speech Movement.
7. "Songs and Speech of the Free Speech Movement" is available at fsm-a.org/CDA and includes mp3 audio recordings, song lyrics, and eyewitness accounts that explain historical context of the songs and speeches given during the Free Speech Movement.
8. *Berkeley in the Sixties* is a two hour documentary that covers the origins of the Free Speech Movement from the House Un-American Activities Committee (HUAC) hearings in May, 1960, through the political events of the 1960s in Berkeley, and ending with the creation of People's Park on university property in 1969.
9. Steve Wozniak and Steve Jobs started Apple in the Cal Residence Halls by selling "Blue Boxes"—mini-computers that disguised phone calls so students could avoid paying their phone bills. Steve Wozniak's user name was "Berkeley Blue"—the first online user name in history! Students in the Cal Residence Halls make life-long friends and spark each other's creativity and passion for finding ways to build a better society. Wozniak's 2017 autobiography, co-authored with Gina Smith, is called *iWoz: Computer Geek to Cult Icon: How I Invented the Personal Computer, Co-Founded Apple, and Had Fun Doing It.*

People's Park

1. "A People's History of Telegraph Avenue" Mural is located on Haste Street near the intersection of Haste Street and Telegraph Avenue. Osha Newmann painted the original mural in 1976 with O'Brien Thiele, Janet Kranzberg, Daniel Galvez and others. The City of Berkeley Landmark describes the scene as follows: "Images, from left to right, include Mario Savio speaking at the October 1, 1964 sit-in on Sproul Plaza that sparked the Free Speech movement; Vietnam War protesters; Black Panthers; the street scene on Telegraph Avenue in the Sixties; the creation of

People's Park; the corner of Telegraph Avenue and Haste Street on 'Bloody Thursday," May 15, 1969, when the streets in the neighborhood exploded in violent confrontation between police and demonstrators protesting the University of California's seizure of People's Park; the shooting, by Alameda County Sheriff's deputies, of James Rector who was watching the demonstration from a rooftop on Telegraph Avenue. He died four days later."

2. Osha Neumann's 2008 book, *Up Against the Wall Motherfuckers: A Memoir of the 1960s, With Notes for Next Time* illuminates the grittier battle for free expression in an era of rampant police brutality.

3. *The Battle for People's Park, Berkeley 1969* by Tom Dalzell, published by Heyday Press in 2019, coinciding with the Park's 50th anniversary, provides eyewitness accounts of the people who were there. The unfolding events are documented by a trove of previously unpublished photos, along with quotes, documents, news articles, and testimonies from the students, politicians, police, bystanders, family members, and administrators whose lives were upended by the tumultuous events surrounding the People's Park standoff between protestors and police.

4. *People's Park: Nick Alexander*, a short film by UC Berkeley Master of Journalism students Jennifer Wiley and Laura Garber, stars Nick Alexander, People's Park activist and purveyor of the People's Park "Meat Kitchen." Available at youtu.be/mf0GLybi-CuI?si=DeSI_jDpftjQ3K4o.

5. UC Berkeley's *People's Park Housing* at peoplesparkhousing.berkeley.edu, is dedicated to "Student housing, housing for the unhoused, revitalized public park space, and commemoration of the site's history." The site explains the reasons for developing the People's Park site for student housing.

6. Since the 1956 Long Range Development Plan (LRDP), UC Berkeley has published long range development plans that set out campus development projects for the following 15 year-long period. The 1962 Long Range Development Plan was a revision

of the 1956 Plan. Next was the 1978 Campus Historic Resource Survey, and then the 1990 Long Range Development Plan. The latest is the 2021 Long Range Development Plan, now a state-mandated blueprint, is available on the capitalstrategies.berkeley.edu website. Links to previous Long Range Development Plans are on the same site available under "Retried/Historical Planning Documents." Sasaki, the architecture firm that developed the 2021 Long Range Development Plan has some impressive futuristic AI-style images of what campus will look like in the coming years at sasaki.com. The next Long Range Development Plan is scheduled to be released 2036.

7. The UC Board of Regents approved the 2021 Long Range Development Plan (LRDP) growth plan, an expansion that predicts a population increase of about 22 percent, from 55,130 people to 67,200. The Plan's central idea is to make campus car-free, safe, and enjoyable for pedestrians and cyclists.

8. "As a matter of Reagan's honest convictions but also as a matter of politics, Reagan launched an assault on the university," said UC Berkeley professor of sociology Neil Smelser, recalling Ronald Reagan's turbulent relationship with the university from the start of his political career. Smelser is interviewed in a 2004 UC Berkeley News story titled "Ronald Reagan launched political career using the Berkeley campus as a target" by Jeffrey Kahn archived at newsarchive.berkeley.edu/news/media/releases/2004/06/08_reagan.shtml.

9. Ronald Reagan blamed the actions of "beatniks, radicals and filthy speech advocates" for anarchy and rioting in Berkeley, and blamed UC Berkeley faculty for "a leadership gap and a morality and decency gap" in a 1966 campaign speech In San Francisco. Source: Ronald Reagan, "The Morality Gap at Berkeley," speech at Cow Palace, May 12, 1966, in *The Creative Society*, 125–129.

10. *People's Park: Resources from The Bancroft Library* at https://guides.lib.berkeley.edu/peoplespark provides resource

materials, including photos and historic documents, about the history of People's Park.
11. *Berkeleyside* reported extensively on People's Park. "It's not just People's Park that will see housing. UC Berkeley chancellor vows to build 7,500 beds in 10 years," wrote Frances Dinkelspiel on May 11, 2018. The article gives an overview of the plans to convert People's Park into a new student housing complex.
12. Janine Wiedel's 2019 photobook, *People's Park Berkeley Riots*, contains 33 photos that deftly show the unfolding human drama and passion surrounding People's Park in 1969. Available at Moe's Books.
13. In 2017 Ari Neulight signed on to be the university's full-time social worker and outreach coordinator for the homeless population in People's Park. Neulight partnered with City of Berkeley social worker Eve Ahmed to connect those in need with housing, health, and other community services. A profile of Neulight called "Tough job, light touch: Campus social worker assists area's homeless" by Gretcgen Kell was published on news.berkeley.edu on February 23, 2022.
14. Julia Vinograd is profiled in "Julia Vinograd," Contemporary Authors, Gale Research, volume 26, 1997, pages 293-310. Her poetry was published by Zeitgeist Press and appeared in a number of anthologies, including *Berkeley! A Literary Tribute* edited by Danielle La France in 1997 for Heyday Books.
15. Walter Hood's award-winning designs, including for the International African American Museum in Charleston, SC can be viewed at hooddesignstudio.com. Hood's biography for his position as Chair and Professor of Landscape Architecture & Environmental Planning and Urban Design is at ced.berkeley.edu/people/walter-hood.

Black Panther Party and the Third World Front

1. Kamala Harris spoke about her experience growing up in Berkeley at her presidential campaign kickoff speech in Oakland, California, on January 27, 2019. In the June 26-27 Democratic primary debates hosted by NBC News, MSNBC, and Telemundo, in a retort to candidate Joe Biden, Harris said she'd experienced desegregation busing when she attended the Thousand Oaks Elementary School in Berkeley.

2. A concise history of UC Berkeley's Loyalty Oath is summarized in an article published on update.lib.berkeley.edu, UC Berkeley's Library news site, called, "I take this obligation freely: Recalling UC Berkeley's Loyalty Oath controversy," posted on March 21, 2022 by Jill Schlessinger, and authored by Shannon Write with research from Adam Hagan.

3. The text of the Loyalty Oath that all UC Berkeley faculty and staff were required to sign or face dismissal is as follows: "I do solemnly swear (or affirm) that I will support the Constitution of the United States and the Constitution of the State of California, and that I will faithfully discharge the duties of my office according to the best of my ability; that I do not believe in, and I am not a member of, nor do I support any party or organization that believes in, advocates, or teaches the overthrow of the United States Government, by force or by any illegal or unconstitutional means, that I am not a member of the Communist Party or under any oath or a party to any agreement or under any commitment that is in conflict with my obligations under this oath."

4. The Online Archive of California, available at oac.cdlib.org, offers insight on why UC Berkeley's Academic Senate holds so much political sway in comparison to other campus faculties in its documentation of "The University of California: In Memory of Benjamin Ide Wheeler" published by University of California Press in 1928.

5. The regents were also temporarily tamed by tempestuous President (1899-1919) Benjamin Ide Wheeler, a white-mustached

autocrat who wore cavalry boots and galloped about campus on a white charger. Wheeler unintentionally created another freedom. His highhanded ways provoked a faculty revolt in 1919 that established the strong Academic Senate.

6. Two sources on the founding of the Black Panthers are: Jeffries, Judson. L. 2002 *Huey P. Newton: The Radical Theorist.* Jackson: University Press of Mississippi. Seale, Bobby. 1970. *Seize the Time: The Story of the Black Panther Party and Huey P. Newton.* New York: Random House.

7. *Black Power Black Panthers 1969,* by Janine Wiedel is a 2017 photo book that provides an up close view of Black Panther gatherings in the San Francisco Bay Area in 1969. Available at Moe's Books.

8. PBS and the African Heritage Network debuted *A Huey P. Newton Story* in 2002. The film is based on the 1996 stage play by Roger Guenveur Smith and produced by Luna Ray Films with the original production by BLACK STARZ! The film is available at pbs.org/hueypnewton.

9. The National Museum of African American History and Culture Exhibit "The Black Panther Party: Challenging Police and Promoting Social Change" is available at nmaahc.si.edu.

10. *Crip Camp: A Disability Revolution,* a 2020 documentary by Nicole Newnham and James LeBrecht, describes how a summer camp inspired hope and political change for the American disabled community. The documentary includes scenes of the Black Panthers bringing meals to disabled activists camping out at the San Francisco federal building during the 1977 sit-in to enact Section 504, a watershed victory for civil rights in American history.

11. *A Disability History of the United States* (2012) by Kim E. Nielsen details the historical discrimination and harm to Americans with disabilities, and summarizes the political struggle for disability rights in recent decades.

12. *Power if the People Won't Stop: Legacy of the TWLF at UC Berkeley* is a collection of writings edited by researchers Harvey Dong and Janie Chen and published in 2019 that provides an in-depth look at student organizing, actions and legacies of the Third World Liberation Front.
13. More information about Mexican-American Student Confederation (MASC), its successful grape boycott at UC Berkeley, and the fight for farm workers' civil rights and protections is detailed in: Araiza, Lauren. *To March for Others: The Black Freedom Struggle and the United Farm Workers.* First ed. Politics and Culture in Modern America. Philadelphia: University of Pennsylvania Press, 2014.
14. The Asian American Political Alliance (AAPA), or "aa-pa" as it's affectionately known, was founded in the living room of Emma Gee and Yuji Ichioka at 2005 Hearst Avenue. They were joined by Vicci Wong, Floyd Huen, Richard Aoki, Victor Ichioka and together they originated and popularized the term "Asian American" to politically solidify American civil rights activists with roots in China, Korea, Japan and the Philippines. In addition to joining the Third World Liberation Front student coalition, AAPA educated the public about the incarceration of Japanese Americans during WWII and organized to repeal the 1950 McCarran Internal Security Act, which established a Subversive Activities Control Board, with broad powers to investigate political activists. AAPA also organized support for the Native American Occupation of Alcatraz in 1969, and advocated for social services for Californians living in Chinatown and Filipinotown.
15. According to FBI files, in one of their "strangest" cases, Patty Hearst was kidnapped from her apartment at 2603 Benvenue Street on February 4, 1974 by the Symbionese Liberation Army (SLA), an extremist domestic and terrorism group that sought to incite guerilla warfare against the U.S. government. The SLA's use of "Liberation" for their nefarious cause, plus the later discreditation of the label "Third World" as a pejorative term, may

have contributed to the fade of Third World Liberation Front's name recognition over time.
16. Berkeley's Lorin District hosts Berkeley's annual Juneteenth celebration, and is the historic center for generations of Black families in Berkeley. Lorin, originally an unincorporated neighborhood with its own cable car stop, was also home to Japanese families until the Japanese Internment began in 1942. Some Japanese families were able to return to their Lorin homes in 1945, after President Roosevelt rescinded the exclusion orders. The origin of the name "Lorin" is a mystery. According a Berkeley Historical Society document, a clerk named Mrs. Elizabeth S. Whitney appears to have crossed out the name Garfield and wrote in Lorin on an 1862 Post Office Department form.
17. *Welcome to the Neighborhood*, Pam Uzzell's 26 minute 2018 documentary about South Berkeley hero Mable Howard and her daughter Mildred Howard, shows how two women activists from Berkeley worked with local politicians to save their neighborhood.
18. The description of projects and research sponsored by Black Lives at Cal is available at the website blac.berkeley.edu. The site also provides information on how to take a self-guided tour of Berkeley's Black history.
19. Tupac Shakur's free flowing audio interview with Entertainment Weekly was turned into an animated film called *Tupac Shakur on Life and Death by Blank on Blank* available at youtu.be/6x2FqX2YZws?si=5fOqroBR80DEx-Oc.
20. Tupac Shakur's poetry anthology is called *The Rose That Grew From Concrete* published in 2009 by MTV Books.

Fires and Faults

1. In 1989 geophysicist James J. Lienkaemper wrote, "Field Trip Guide to the Hayward Fault: USGS Open File Report," a public

guide to the attributes and visible evidence of activity along the Hayward Fault.
2. The City Museum of San Francisco keeps an extensive online archive called The Great 1906 Earthquake and Fire at sfmuseum.org/1906.
3. *Earthquake Exodus, 1906: Berkeley Responds to the San Francisco Refugees* by Richard Schwarz (2005) features photos and first hand accounts of survivors after the 1906 earthquake, when Berkeley's population exploded from twenty-six thousand residents to thirty-eight thousand residents.
4. The East Bay Vivarium, the largest and oldest reptile store in the U.S., houses an incredible selection of pythons, scorpions, tarantulas and other exotic animals. In the 1989 Loma Prieta Earthquake, when liquefaction caused the buildings to wobble and car alarms to blast loudly throughout West Berkeley, some of the East Bay Vivarium critters got loose, and their progeny may still live in the neighborhood.
5. *The 1923 Berkeley Fire: Memoirs and Mementos* is a monograph written in 1992 by the Berkeley Architectural Heritage Association's Susan Cerny and Anthony Bruce. First hand accounts and photos—including overhead photos taken from an airplane—depict the destruction and aftermath of the fire.
6. *Fire in the Hills: A Collective Remembrance* edited by Patricia Alder is a compilation of dozens of essays from survivors of the Oakland Firestorm of 1991.
7. John Vaillant's award winning book *Fire Weather: A True Story From A Hotter World* explains the science behind the increasing danger of firestorms.

Bleeding Blue and Gold

1. Cal attracts top athletes from all over the world. In 2024, Cal athletes won 23 medals at the Paris Olympics. This raised Cal's total Olympic medal count to 246, including 126 gold medals. Cal's

top sports are swimming, water polo, and rowing, and swimmers Nathalie Coughlin and Matt Biondi won multiple gold medals while at Cal. Information on these athletes and their awards is available at calbears.com.

2. Helen Wills is arguably Cal's most successful athlete. Wills won 31 Grand Slam tournament titles, and had a 180-match winning streak the lasted from 1927 until 1933. She shares her visit with Queen of England in her autobiography *Fifteen-Thirty: The Story of a Tennis Player*. Wills enjoyed playing tennis into her 80s. She died in 1998 and bequeathed $10 million to UC Berkeley to establish a neuroscience institute, now called the Helen Wills Neuroscience Institute.

3. Berkeley has been a center for gay activism since the 1960s. The now-closed Mama Bears Coffeehouse and Bookstore on Telegraph Avenue in Berkeley was an anchor of the Bay Area lesbian community. According to judygrahn.org, poets Judy Grahn and Paula Gunn Allen held regular Sunday and holiday gatherings for lesbians there. Nearby, the White Horse Inn is oldest operating gay bar in the U.S. The history podcast *The Memory Palace* released the episode "A White Horse" in April, 2016 that delves into the history and activism that originated on Telegraph Avenue at these openly gay businesses.

4. The story of All-American Cal football star Walter A. Gordon, the first Black scholar to earn a Doctor of Jurisprudence from the Berkeley School of Law, is featured in campus tours supported by Black Lives at Cal (BLAC). Gordon, who also represented Cal in boxing and wrestling, played both offense and defense in football. Black Lives at Cal (BLAC) at urapprojects.berkeley.edu is a research and archival initiative that began in 2021. More on Walter A. Gordon is at alumni.berkeley.edu/the-walter-gordon-story.

5. Amazing photos of UC Berkeley's tree sitter protest are available at treespiritproject.com/portfolio/law-of-attraction. An excellent photo essay is at sgphotos.com/photostories/treesitters.

How Berkeley Can You Be?

1. Local news is well-covered Berkeley. The *Daily Californian*, established in 1871, is an independent, student run newspaper. It's one of the oldest news sources on the West Coast, and one of the best quality student run newspapers in the country. For local color, *Berkeleyside* is indispensable. *Berkeleyside* was probably my most used source for this book. *The East Bay Times, Bay Nature, Diablo Magazine, Berkeley News, Californian Magazine* are all also excellent sources of local news. A good source of ideas and public policies to support local news is available at newsrebuild-localnews.org.
2. Podcast listeners can keep up with Berkeley's innovations by subscribing to *Berkeley Talks, Berkeley Voices,* both produced by *Berkeley News,* and *One Bold Idea, a* podcast produced by the University of California and Berkeley Advanced Media Institute.
3. During the anti-apartheid protests in the 1980s, UC Berkeley administrators removed the door handles for California Hall. Doing so prevented protestors from chaining themselves to the doors, which was an effective way to lock in top administrators so they couldn't leave while the protestors demanded that UC Regents divest from the apartheid government of South Africa. Later an escape elevator was installed so administrators could easily leave the building without protestors getting in the way.
4. Richard Bolles sold ten million copies of *What Color is Your Parachute*, putting Berkeley publisher Ten Speed Press on the map.
5. Vimeo and Youtube have a few videos of the How Berkeley Can You Be Parade.
6. Stanford Institute for Economic Policy Research at siepr.stanford.edu published "Homelessness in California: Causes and Policy Considerations" in 2022.

Appendix

UC Berkeley's Principles of Community

- We place honesty and integrity in our teaching, learning, research and administration at the highest level.
- We recognize the intrinsic relationship between diversity and excellence in all our endeavors.
- We affirm the dignity of all individuals and strive to uphold a just community in which discrimination and hate are not tolerated.
- We are committed to ensuring freedom of expression and dialogue that elicits the full spectrum of views held by our varied communities.
- We respect the differences as well as the commonalities that bring us together and call for civility and respect in our personal interactions.
- We believe that active participation and leadership in addressing the most pressing issues facing our local and global communities are central to our educational mission.
- We embrace open and equitable access to opportunities for learning and development as our obligation and goal.

UC Berkeley's "Principles of Community" statement was developed collaboratively by students, faculty, staff, and alumni, and issued by the Chancellor. Its intent is to serve as an affirmation of the intrinsic and unique value of each member of the UC Berkeley community and as a guide for our personal and collective behavior, both on campus and as we serve society.

UC Berkeley's Long Range Development Plan

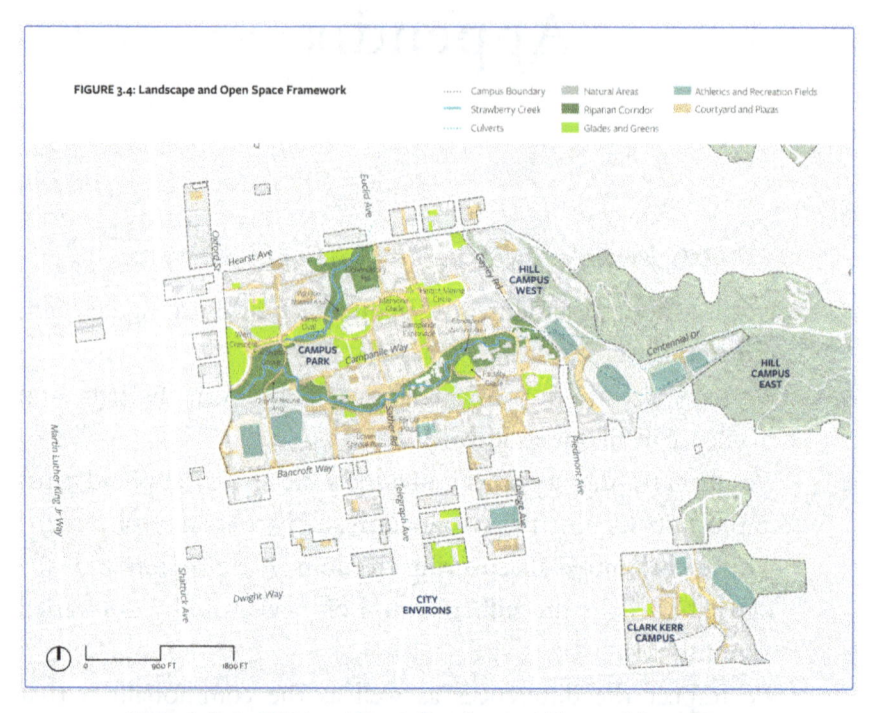

UC Berkeley's 2021 Long Range Development Plan envisions dozens of new buildings while increasing the amount of open recreational space. The plan includes 2.5 million net new gross square feet of academic and campus life space, 4 million gross square feet of renovated space, up to 11,730 net new beds of housing, and significant open space, mobility, and infrastructure improvements expected to be completed by 2037.
Courtesy of UC Regents.

Author Pamela Gleason enjoying a Berkeley sunset.
Courtesy of Helen Christensen.

Pamela Gleason works in the Master of Computational Social Science program, UC Berkeley's newest graduate program. She marvels at the brilliance of the students, loves Berkeley weather and its restaurants, and is amazed by the every day adventure of walking anywhere in Berkeley.